THE COMMANDER X FILES
- UPDATED -

IDENTIFYING THE REAL "COMMANDER X" ALIEN HUNTER!

BY COMMANDER X — AS TOLD TO JIM KEITH

THE COMMANDER X FILES - UPDATED

IDENTIFYING THE REAL "COMMANDER X" - ALIEN HUNTER

By Commander X
As Told To Jim Keith

INNER LIGHT - GLOBAL COMMUNICATIONS

THE COMMANDER X FILES - UPDATED
IDENTIFYING THE REAL "COMMANDER X" - ALIEN HUNTER
By Commander X As Told To Jim Keith

Copyright © 2017 - Timothy Green Beckley DBA Inner Light/ Global Communications

All Rights Reserved

Nonfiction - Printed in the United States of America

No part of this book may be reproduced, stored in retrieval system or transmitted in any form or by any means, electronic, mechanical, photocopying, recording, without express permission of the publisher.

Timothy Green Beckley: Editorial Director
Carol Rodriguez: Publishers Assistant
Editor and Layout: Tim R. Swartz
Sean Casteel: Associate Editor
William Kern: Editorial Assistant

Email: mrufo8@hotmail.com

For free catalog write:
Global Communications
P.O. Box 753
New Brunswick, NJ 08903

Free Subscription to Conspiracy Journal E-Mail Newsletter: www.conspiracyjournal.com

Mr. UFOs Secret Files on Youtube
https://www.youtube.com/user/MRUFO1100

CONTENTS

Will The Real Commander X Please Stand Up 7
1. Escape To Abduction 11
2. An Alien Overview 17
3. Aliens and Nazis 25
4. Alien Collaboration 30
5. Alien Demands 36
6. Other Projects 41
7. The Secret War 49
8. Aliens Underground 55
9. Secret Projects 65
10. No Alternatives 69
11. Time Bomb 77
12. The Return 82
13. Implants 90
14. Abduction Recall 97
15. Into The Matrix 103
16. Working Against Time 112
17. Allies 117
18. Adversaries 125
19. Alien Control 133
20. Overthrowing Control 138

SPECIAL SECTION

Weather Control Operations 154
Technology Used For Guiding The Underground Bases 163
Brain Transmittors And How They Are Used 178
The Mental And Spiritual Influences of UFOs 205

WILL THE REAL COMMANDER X PLEASE STAND UP
By Timothy Green Beckley

I am going to tell you something that I have never revealed to anyone else before.

Some of the books by Commander X were not written in their entirety by him.

He had help.

Some think that Commander X has been involved in a disinformation program, but I can tell you as far as I know this is not the case. Though he has gone into seclusion I have always found him to be above board in his dealings with this publisher. True I have never met him in the flesh, but in the "old days" we did exchange correspondence and a couple of telephone calls. I think if you have been an avid reader of the Commander X books you will agree that he has made some striking revelations.

He says he worked at Area 51.

That he knows about the underground base at Dulce.

Was involved in the government's teleportation program.

But the truth of the matter is that he didn't write some of the books under his name by himself. He did have help.

It seems that the Commander – a retired military intelligence operative – lived pretty much out of a suitcase. He was on the "run" from his tormenters, be they part of an international cabal or the aliens themselves. Often he would submit a few pages at a time, ramble on a bit and not complete a project he had started on in all earnest.

Even as a small publisher we had to adhere to some sort of schedule for the release of a new title. This was not because we were competing with the Park Avenue publishing conglomerates, but because our printer at the time found it necessary to set aside necessary time slots to run the presses, so all his other publishers could also get their books on time."

In order for us to fit into a specific time slot, we had to get the good Commander a bit of literary "help." We had to find someone who could polish up a manuscript and fill in some of the missing blanks, nothing drastic mind you, but still you can't put out a book that is full of incomplete thoughts and not rendered in a professional manner.

We had to find someone who knew the subject and would not just shoot from the hip.

At the time, we were on friendly terms with a writer who was quickly establishing himself as a conspiracy theorist. He was putting out two or three books a year but like most freelancers could always use a bit of extra cash to supplement those far and few between royalty checks. So we turned to a west coast writer, by the name of Jim Keith, for help in "tidying up" some of Commander X's scripts that contained a lot of good material but lacked some degree of "literary arrangement."

Truth is if you have ever been into alternative topics such as black ops, UFOs and mind control, you probably have a number of Jim's books close at hand. Keith was a damn good writer – he knew his subject matter inside and out – and I know I have read through a couple of his books more than once making sure I didn't miss something of relevance that had passed me by initially. His most important works include **Saucers of the Illuminati**, **Mind Control, World Control, Casebook of the Men In Black, Black Helicopters Over America**, and **OK-Bomb!**

Unfortunately, tragedy struck at an early age, when Jim Keith passed away suddenly – some say under mysterious circumstances.

At this point, we call upon friend and colleague Peter Robbins to draw upon the facts surrounding the passing of Keith. Robbins, who is the co-author of **Left at East Gate**, which deals with the Bentwaters UFO incident, wrote a chapter on the controversial deaths of certain conspiracy and UFO researchers. His chapter was in the book: **UFOs – Wicked This Way Comes: The Dark Side of the Ultra-Terrestrials**.

Says Robbins: "Jim was truly a consparicist's consparicist. He spoke at numerous conferences about numerous conspiracies and contributed many articles to journals and magazines. Keith did not subscribe to the extraterrestrial theory of UFOs and viewed the phenomena as human in origin. He felt that the craft involved were entirely the product of highly classified governmental programs, employing advanced technology, and maintained that, those responsible were involved in an ongoing, concerted effort to advance the extraterrestrial hypothesis as a form of cover story for their nefarious activities.

"In September 1999, Jim took some time off to attend 'Burning Man,' a huge, weeklong arts festival held annually in Black Rock, Nevada. An accidental fall from the stage there resulted in a painful broken knee, and he was taken from the venue to Washoe Hospital in Reno (where he resided) for emergency surgery. During the operation, it's understood that a blood clot was released and entered his lung, which was the official cause of his death. It's particularly tempting to yell murder when someone so dedicated to conspiratorial thinking, and to bringing government abuses and cover-ups to the attention of the public, dies under such freaky circumstances, and I don't think any of us have any problem wondering why. But if the cause of death was as reported, a blood clot that had traveled to the lung, it is a legitimate one that, while tragic, is not unknown in many types of surgical procedures. If this was not the cause of his death, as some still maintain, I doubt if we will ever learn what in fact it was."

Kenn Thomas (long time publisher of *Steamshovel Press*) who had worked with Jim Keith on a book about the long tentacles of an international faction of despots known as *The Octopus*, went on the record shortly after Keith's death with these remarks:

"Jim was a dear friend of mine and an important person to the world. The loss is immeasurable. He was not just the co-author of **The Octopus**, but a dharma combatant who demonstrated time and again that the world is far more multi-dimensional, far more interesting, than the pabulum that usually passes for news, information and normal discourse. Unfortunately it is also far more dangerous.

"Rumor has it that Jim may have been killed because he mentioned the name of the physician who declared Diana was pregnant at the time of her death. I have long noted the connections between Diana's death and the Octopus. Diana was the subject of Jim's last column for *Nitro News*, which has been linked at *Steamshovel's* 'Link Tank' for the past couple of weeks. As you know, *Nitro News* has not been accessible since Jim's death, although I reached it just before receiving word of his passing.

"This rumor may be nonsense. Danny Casolaro may have committed suicide. It is the way of the Octopus. It exists but it doesn't exist. These are blood clots or suicides or non-suspicious homicides or real accidents. They just happen to cluster coincidentally around a certain set of facts or a certain perception of an organized conspiracy."

Interestingly enough, at about the same time as Keith's passing – whatever the cause might have been – a "wild rumor" started to circulate. It was being said that Keith was in reality the mysterious Commander X. These rumors were denied by Jim himself and "verified" by at least one "close friend" who thought that Jim had taken him into his confidence. And actually, Jim was not lying or covering up for Commander X or for that matter our publishing company. He was NOT Commander X! There was – and still is somewhere out there – an actual Commander X!

Most authors don't want it to be known that their books were even partially "ghost written." And furthermore, I don't think Jim wanted people to know that he had latched himself to someone else's coattails and was masquerading as some farfetched intelligence operative with a reputation of relating some pretty far flung stories.

To my way of thinking it really doesn't matter. The proof, as they say, is in the pudding. The Commander X books are in a class by themselves. They are hopefully both well written enough to be "entertaining," while at the same time being educational to those desiring to be among the inner circle of recipients to previously "classified" and "Top Secret" revelations.

The Commander X Files tells an intriguing story of alien intervention in our planet.

We don't have a "guilty conscious" that the fabulous Jim Keith took pen to hand and helped our author out. In fact, if anything, we are honored and present Commander X's story in its entirety in the pages that follow.

Timothy Green Beckley

CHAPTER ONE

ESCAPE TO ABDUCTION

It began with my worst nightmare, and then became worse still. I was reading some foreign intelligence agency-originated documents in my study on the afternoon of August 7, 1995, when the phone rang. I picked up the receiver and said, "Lawson Business Associates,*" the fake business name that I had been using for just over two years.

"Erik?" came the answer from the person on the end of the line, and that was when I knew the game was up. I recognized the voice as that of one of my oldest friends, a veteran American intelligence operative who works within a little nest of spooks even the director of the Secret Government doesn't know the name of.

*Name changed for the purpose of this text.

I'll call the man "G." I have known G. for over twenty years, and I know him well enough to realize that he would never have used my real name under any circumstances (not even my first name) if it wasn't now common knowledge among certain parties, parties who were, shall we say, "unfriendly" to me.

After a long silence, I finally spoke, but all I said was, "Yes."

"Thank God I was able to get hold of you, Erik. Your cover is blown and you don't have much time to get out of there. Unless you want to do a replay of the Alamo with you as Davy Crockett, then you'd better run like hell. There's probably a wet assignment team coming to visit you right now."

'Wet work' was one of the colorful terms applied in the spy business to mean assassination. G. needn't have even said that much, since we both knew there could be only one reason for him to call me at home, and only one reason why he would have used my real name.

I muttered an expletive I won't repeat, and then another one, and then I got a grip on myself. "Thanks. I owe you one... I mean, another one." I said.

I slammed the receiver down in its cradle and grabbed the locked metal briefcase I kept by my side at all times. By the time I reached the driveway and my gassed-up pickup truck I had broken into a run. I was leaving almost everything I possessed behind: the books, the papers, the photos, the notes, the maps, the interview tapes. At least I had never put names on anything that would implicate my sources, and I had even carefully excised names from letters and documents that people had sent to me telling about their own knowledge and encounters. All I possessed now were the clothes I had on my back, a briefcase full of the most sensitive papers in my possession, enough money to last me for a few months, and a camper full of survival rations and supplies.

A second before I slipped the key into the truck's ignition I checked my hand and felt a chill go through me. In my hurry to escape, I had forgotten the ritual that had been drilled into me, a ritual that had saved my life more than once. I got out of the truck and then slipped underneath it, carefully looking for a bomb that would have put a quick end to my escape. Yeah, a bomb would have been the way for them to go if they had wanted to spare themselves the trouble of meeting me face-to-face. It would have put a quick end to "Commander X," and an end to my writing about the threat of the Secret Government and their Grey alien pals. I found nothing underneath the truck. I slipped out from underneath the truck again, and then climbed back into the cab.

My eyes were glued to the rear view mirror of the truck, watching to see if anyone was following me, as I sped through the small town I had called home for two years, then turned on to a main thoroughfare and headed toward the state highway.

So much for my life as Terry Lawson, I thought, a business consultant who never seemed to do much consultation, and so much for an almost-normal life in a small town in Northern California. Hell, against my better judgement I'd even begun dating a local girl who I had met, but that was over now. She would never see me again, never even hear from me. It wouldn't be safe to contact her again, not even to explain why I had disappeared.

My anonymity had given me a breather for a short while, but now the breather was over. Now there was nothing to do but run and dodge and try to find a place to hide, when what I knew was that there was nowhere to hide for long.

I drove for something over 12 hours straight, stopping only for gasoline and for a couple of burgers at a drive-through joint at a small town on the coast. My mind was working overtime while I drove:

How long had they known about my whereabouts? Long enough to place a bug on my truck and then zero in on me when I had pulled over to sleep? Probably not: If they were going to place something, it would more likely have been the bomb.

Had they been surveilling me for long? No. They would have dealt with me as soon as possible.

Did they know who I had made friends with? Possibly not, since they would certainly have terminated me already if they had known where I was.

Was I under satellite surveillance at this moment? It all depended on how soon G. had been able to warn me. Probably not. They most likely would have taken me in the daylight if there was a satellite fix on me.

Finally I decided that it didn't matter whether they knew where I was or not. I had given it my best shot, and that was all I could do. I had done my best to warn the people of the world about the Secret Government and the Grey aliens and their plans, and if I didn't last another day, it would have all been worth it.

The problem was, I thought, was that there was still so much work to do. I had to understand more about the alien takeover plan, and what could be done about it. Resistance had to be in place when the tentacles of the conspiracy tightened, as they inevitably would, and at this point we hardly even had a plan of resistance. We couldn't just let them have the world so easily without putting up a struggle. It wouldn't be right for mankind to go that easy, without even a fight. I just kept my foot pressed to the accelerator.

It was still light when I pulled off the highway into a stand of shaded evergreens that would conceal the truck from the eyes of passer-bys — at least, hopefully. I stepped into the cool night air, then pulled together and tied enough tree branches to conceal the truck from detection. Then I walked to the back of the truck and unlocked the camper. I took out my sleeping bag, my briefcase, and some other supplies, then locked up the truck again.

If anyone came across the truck they would assume I had concealed it so that it wouldn't be ticketed in an illegal parking area; that is, unless they were specifically searching for me.

I hiked along what looked like a little-used path through the shadowy, dense woods, alert to the sights and sounds around me, and then emerged near a grassy overlook above the lapping green waves of the Pacific Ocean. It was so peaceful that it felt like I was on vacation, not running from hired murderers who had been hunting me for years, ever since my defection.

I hiked downward through sand dunes, getting my boots filled with sand, and then came out on a beach strewn with driftwood. Then I headed north for rocky cliffs in the distance. When I reached the cliffs, I climbed upward to finally perch on a jagged outcropping that gave me a 200-yard or so vantage on the beach.

The scraped knee I'd gotten on my way up the cliff face was more than worth it. I thought that at least I wouldn't be taken by surprise in this position. It would take nothing sort of a bazooka to dislodge me from my sheltered ledge overlooking the beach. Little did I know that the Glock pistol that I was carrying in my shoulder holster wouldn't be of any use when "they" finally found me. And that the "they" who found me wouldn't be who I was expecting at all.

I don't know for certain since I didn't look at my watch, but it was probably shortly after midnight when I heard something that startled me and brought me to attention from my half-sleep. I had been propped behind a jutting boulder, with the whole long stretch of beach brightly lit from the moon. No one could have sneaked up on me from that position.

I'm not sure if I heard the sound or simply felt their presence, but I sat up and looked out over the moonlight-illuminated beach. First I saw the shadows of the two craft flitting above the breakers and then down the beach, then I saw the two blobs of blackness as they approached me.

I pulled the gun out of my shoulder holster, knowing that it would do no good against the firepower of what confronted me. Hovering directly in front of me, as black as pitch and about 400 feet apart, were two helicopters — two black unmarked Apache choppers armed with both rockets and machine cannons. Those weapons were trained directly on me and I assumed that at any second they were going to open fire on me. The rotors of the choppers were on "whisper mode," and I could barely hear them, but I could feel the cool wind from the chopping blades.

I thought it was all over, but still I waited to see what the ominous black choppers were going to do. Little did I know that they were only an escort for something even more horrifying.

The vivid white light of the Moon had somehow gotten brighter... The light only kept getting brighter the longer I looked at it.

And then I saw the other craft as it moved toward the cliff I knelt on. It started out as a coin-sized glinting disk skipping across the ocean toward me, and grew larger and larger, heading straight toward me until I recoiled and lurched back on the cliff face, thinking the thing was going to crash right into me.

At first I couldn't think, and didn't even relate what I was seeing to the research I'd done on UFOs for so many years. But finally it dawned on me what I was looking at: that huge alien craft hovering and positioned directly between the two armed black helicopters. Now I wasn't even thinking about the black choppers.

The saucer was composed of a pearlescent silvery metal that seemed like it was illuminated from within. The disk was huge — perhaps 200 feet in diameter. The craft, for I was certain it was a craft, kept moving toward me until it silently loomed over the cliff face where I huddled, more awestricken than afraid.

If they were planning on killing me, they could have blown me off of the cliff face with the armaments on those black helicopters... They didn't even need to dispatch the chopper to me. So, what exactly did they have planned for me?

The alien craft was truly beautiful in a purely artistic way, but there was something about it that was utterly unhuman, unlike anything ever manufactured on earth. There was no sound as it hovered directly above me at about 150 feet in altitude, only the slapping and crashing of the waves at the base of the cliffs and the whooshing of the chopper blades. I was totally transfixed by the incredible sight that I was witnessing, not even blinking at the gigantic craft I watched hovering above me, hovering between those two malevolent choppers.

And then, without warning, without time to think, I was blasted, blasted by a cool white beam that thrust out from a module on the bottom of the saucer and engulfed me with what seemed like a shaft of pure white electricity. And that beam of energy grabbed me and took hold of every fiber of my body, invading me, sucking me in, and injecting me... injecting me with the most intense and distilled fear I have ever felt.

It's hard to explain, but I think that's what happened. I think that fear was injected directly into my body through that beam of energy, and that fear spread through my veins until it took over my body and brain, and then I knew nothing but that electric fear. I screamed out with every fiber of my being, but no scream came out of my mouth, and then I was lifted upward bodily toward an opening iris-like door in the belly of the saucer. I was about to say that that was when I blacked out, but the term isn't appropriate. I whited out. I knew no more.

CHAPTER TWO

AN ALIEN OVERVIEW

The most horrifying truth that ever confronts a researcher into UFOs and aliens is the realization that at a certain point, forces within the U.S. government capitulated to and, at least to a certain degree, joined forces with the aliens in their goal to dominate the earth. If you have read my earlier works, particularly The Ultimate Deception ($15, available from Inner Light Publications, Box 753, New Brunswick, NJ 08903) then you know that the history of the collaboration of the reptilian Gray aliens, which apparently hail from Zeta Reticuli 1 and 2, Orion, and other stellar locations, and the Secret Government dates as far back as 1933, although information on this early period is somewhat scanty.

Why do the Grey aliens seem to be reptilian in form? What dictated this form of evolution which is so different than humankind, the highest form of intelligence which is indigenous to this planet? We can only speculate on this matter, but the well-known UFO and paranormal researcher Brad Steiger has commented,

"In the late 1960's I presented my hypothesis that the reason why the most frequently reported UFOnauts resemble reptilian or amphibian humanoids may be because that is exactly what they are, highly evolved members of a serpentine or semi-aquatic species. A provocative theory is that the dinosaurs didn't really vanish, they 'evolved' into a humanoid creature that

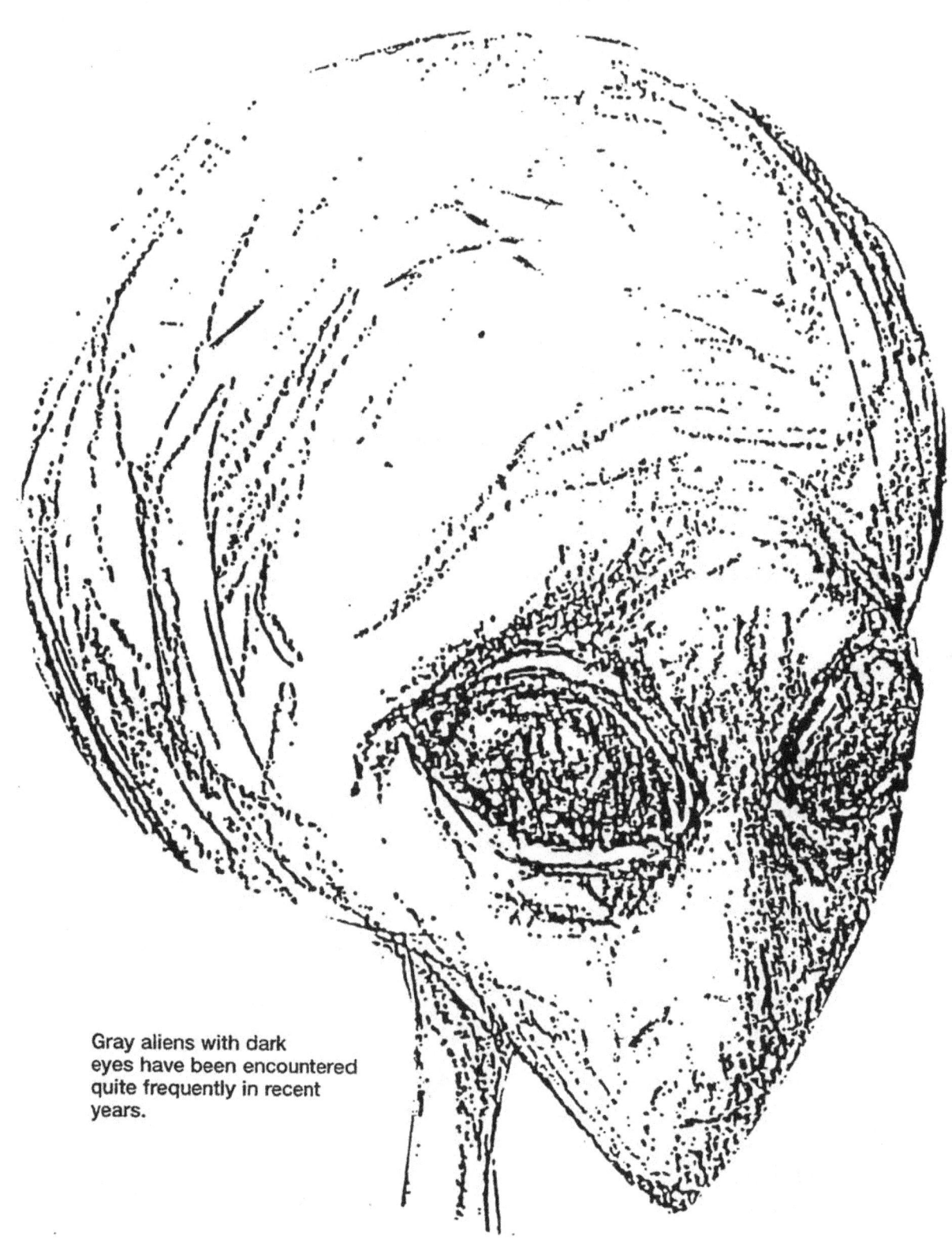

Gray aliens with dark eyes have been encountered quite frequently in recent years.

eventually ran its course, or was destroyed in an Atlantis-type catastrophe..."

Steiger also says, "I had developed this hypothesis considerably... so I was delighted when I received word that Dale Russell and Ron Sequen of Canada's National Museum of Natural Sciences of Ottawa, had fashioned a model of a humanoid dinosaur using Stenautcosaurus and Equallus as their inspiration. Stenautcosaurus, according to Russell, had a rather large brain and eyes with overlapping visual fields. The 90 pound dinosaur also walked on two legs, and it appears to have had a particularly opposable thumb on its three-clawed hand. The result of such scientific speculation was an astonishingly humanlike creature that Russell terms a 'Dinosauroid.' The creature stands four-and-a-half feet tall, has a large, domed head, green skin, and yellow reptilian eyes. It should probably have had ears, Russell conceded, but the effect would have made it appear too human. As it is, the dinosaur on display at Canada's National Museum of Natural Sciences almost exactly fits the descriptions of UFOnauts provided by thousands of men and women throughout the planet who have reported close encounters..."

In all probability, the reptilian and Grey races have been residents on earth for many centuries, and some of these beings may in fact be native to earth. It is not outside the realm of possibility that the Greys are the original inhabitants of earth, and we humans are descendents of space-wandering Nordic extraterrestrials. But that is information to delve into some other time.

The insightful researcher who conceals his identity with the nom-de-plume "Branton" has done a good deal of investigation into the historical nature of the reptilians and their early contact with the human race on earth, and has detailed it in his research paper titled "The Cult of the Serpent". Remember that the Grey aliens commonly described in UFO abduction cases are one race classified within the "reptilians" which Branton describes:

The possibility that an ancient reptilian-saurian race may exist below the surface of this planet is not an idea which is relatively new. This infernal yet physical race has been referred to in spiritual and historical records which date back to the beginning of time. Ancient Hebrew history, for instance, records that our human ancestors were not the only intelligent, free will beings who inhabited the ancient world. Genesis chapter 3 refers to the "Serpent", which according to many ancient Hebrew scholars was identified with a hominid or biped reptilian being. The ancient Hebrew word for "Serpent" is "Nachash" (which according to Strong's Comprehensive and other Biblical concordances contained in itself the meanings: Reptile, Enchantment, Hissing, Whisper, Diligently Observe, Learn by Experience, Incantation, Snake, etc. all of which may be descriptive of the serpent-sauroid race which we have been referring to). The original "Nachash" was not actually a "snake" as most people believe, but actually an extremely intelligent, cunning creature possessed with the ability to speak and reason. It also stood upright as we've said, as did many of its descendants, the small "saurian" predators which ambled about on two legs. Many of these reptilian creatures retained their bi-pedal form while others mutated via natural selection, adaptation and atrophication into the other "saurian" species...

These infernally-empowered beings, who once roamed the surface of the planet and preyed on humanity, were later forced to go underground and make their abode in the subterranean networks which honeycomb the sub-crust of the earth. From these nether regions they have for thousands of years been carrying out their ancient and secret warfare against God and the souls of men, whom they hate intensely.

Some years ago a lady by the name of Robin Collyns wrote an article referring to this serpent race and its influence upon the human race throughout history. Collyns was of the opinion that (as these creatures alleged) the serpent race "created" man and planted him on this planet. All indications however strongly point to the fact that this is just one of many propagandist lies which this infernal race propagates. If these alien deceivers can convince man that "they" created us and therefore they are our "creator-gods" so to speak, then we will be all the more likely to bow down and submit to these vermin in worshipful adoration. Such "revelations" and propaganda often come through "trance mediums" who claim to channel these alien beings. On a few occasions these alien creatures have spewed forth such propaganda directly to "abductees" during UFO encounters.

Since their race has long since lost any concept of righteousness or moral integrity, they will not think twice about using deception or whatever means at their disposal in order to advance their overall CONTROL of all things. Deception is and has been for thousands of years second nature to them, and therefore any statement made by them should be considered in light of this fact.

Although the alien physiognomy has been treated of extensively in my work and in that of other researchers, some readers might appreciate a comprehensive rundown on the subject. John H. Andrews in The Extraterrestrials and Their Reality provides a good thumbnail estimation of the Grey aliens:

The occupants of the UFOs, which we call flying saucers, are sometimes called EBEs, for 'Extraterrestrial Biological Entitites.' They are normally three to five feet tall. Their slender bodies, extra-large heads, long arms, claw-like hands, and big eyes give them the appearance of being an oversized human fetus... These little people are usually seen wearing tight-fitting, metallic, one piece suits to keep their body temperature from over-heating. Each suit is completely one color, but different colored suits have been observed. Sometimes these suits are equipped with a breathing and/or air-conditioning apparatus. One abductee estimated the temperature of these beings' hands to be 115 degrees F. These little people are quick moving and of light weight like birds, yet are quite strong. This suggests that they have a very high metabolic rate and perhaps a limited life span of 15 years or less.

Autopsy reports of some of these alien beings revealed some very frightening information. Their feet, genitalia, breasts, digestive tracts, lymphatic systems, vocal chords, earlobes, noses, mouths, teeth, lips, and eyelids all appear to be atrophied and partially or completely absent because of either evolutionary degeneration or because of gene damage suffered as a result of some sort of nuclear holocaust or a gene splicing experiment which went wrong. Their eyes appear to have no pupils or irises. Their hands most often have only four fingers with the little finger missing. Some hands are webbed. They have a smooth, reptilian skin which has been observed to have various colors from tan, yellowish green, pinkish green to gray, but never plain green. They have a heart and a single lung. Their bodies hold a transparant liquid containing no red blood cells which could carry oxygen.

Witnesses who claim they have been in one of the underground UFO bases describe having seen large containers with an amber liquid containing the body parts of human beings and cattle which had been mutilated. Some evidence suggests that the victims of these mutilations had their blood drained and body parts removed while they were still alive. This may have been done to preserve the effectiveness of the antibodies in the blood to protect the ETs from earthly microorganisms and viruses because their immune systems had long ago ceased to function. The body parts and blood from the victims in these containers were apparently being processed with hydrogen peroxide to produce a liquid food for the alien beings. To eat, they either soak their bodies in this liquid or rub it on their hands. The nutrients are absorbed through their skin and their waste products are expelled through their skin also...

These little people seem to communicate with one another and with some unseen intelligence by mental telepathy. However, certain electronic devices have been seen on these poeple which could enhance this process. A pencil-like device which can emit light is often seen held by the beings to temporarily paralyze humans when it is turned on them.

Whenever a group of the little saucer people are seen together, it has been noted that their heads and faces are identical, suggesting they might be clones. Sometimes their bodies have different proportions, conceivably by design, so that some of them would be better adapted for the particular jobs they will perform.

Their brain is possibly 40% larger than that of humans. It contains an extra segment in the front of their heads in the location where mystics tell us our 'third eye' is located. There are several functions which most humans cannot do which the ETs have been seen to do. These functions could be attributed to the workings of this extra segment of their brains. They can levitate themselves and other objects. They are able to partially dematerialize themselves and other beings and objects so they can float through solid walls. Reports indicate that this power may be limited. Some ETs have been held captive within deep underground installations. Electromagnetic shielding around these cells could also have helped contain these people. They can bend light rays around themselves with their minds so as to render themselves invisible. The only thing in nature we can think of which can noticeably bend light rays is a giant mass like our sun, and even it doesn't do nearly as good a job as do the ETs. They can also send a light beam to some finite point in space and then retract it or extend it at will. This special beam could be made for capturing and transporting abductees, both animals and people. They can also illuminate the inside of a totally enclosed structure through the solid walls.

These small ET people only have a small aura around themselves when compared to the auras of human beings. This fact generates some interest, awe, and even respect in the ET community for human beings. In dealing with the ETs, we should exploit this fact as much as possible. Their minimal auras strongly suggests that they are only manufactured biological robots who have a soul and/or spirit more like that of a lizard or other small animal. No wonder most of them have little compassion for humans. Only a very few of these creatures show any signs of having any great degree of intelligence over and above that required for accomplishing their assigned tasks. Many of them seem mean and irritable. Others are just plain malevolent and could be quite dangerous to humans.

ARTIST CONCEPTIONS OF NAZI-MADE UFOs.

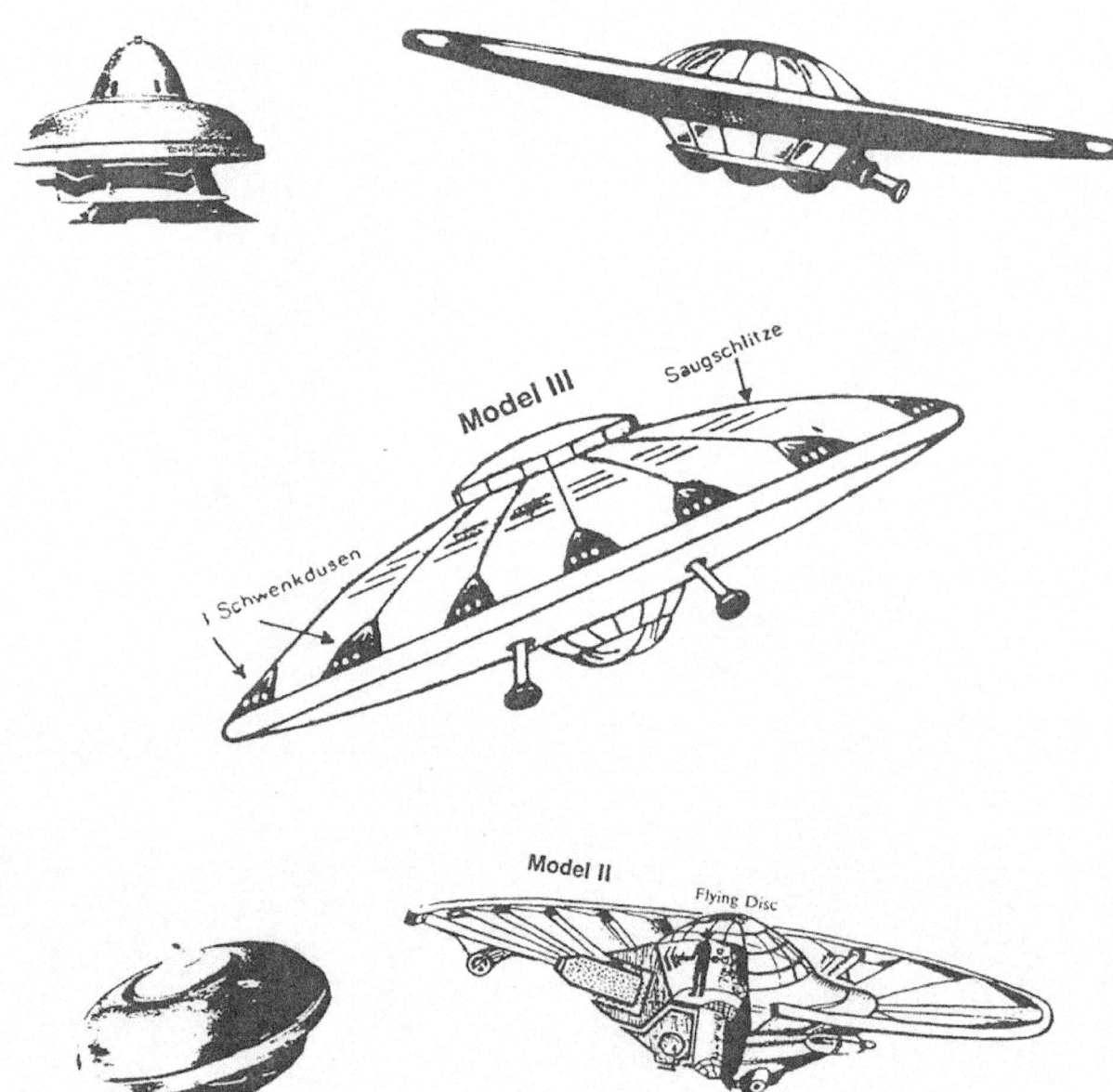

CHAPTER THREE

ALIENS AND NAZIS

One of the areas of greatest cover-up in the entire field of UFO investigation is the Nazi-alien collaboration, which began many years ago and seems to have continued until today, as far-fetched as that may seem. Sometimes, and quite often I am afraid to say, the truth is stranger than fiction.

Prior to World War II, the occult inner circle of the Third Reich (who were in contact with rogue occult secret orders planet-wide, and who drew their philosophy from these groups) contacted alien Greys from Rigel via ritual magic channelling methods, and later were able to make physical contact. The original contact between these occultists and Grey aliens may have been accomplished by the famous occultist Aleister Crowley during the early part of this century when he channelled a disembodied entity named "Aiwass." Aiwass dictated "The Book of the Law" to Crowley, a document which is considered a bible to many occult societies to this day, and which speaks of a New Aeon in human existence which may well be the advent of the aliens. My guess is that the original contact between the Greys and these magical secret societies took place at a much earlier date than Crowley's famous cosmic channelling, but again, that is a matter for the historians to debate.

Regardless of the original date of contact with the aliens, an exchange for their advanced technology was the reason that the Nazis were able to make tremendous strides in aviation and advanced weaponry before and during World War II, and it is this same technology which was the basis for much of the advanced weaponry and space systems developed by the U.S. in the intervening period. Later this technology became part of the secret arsenal of the U.S. and Soviet governments, with the most advanced technologies and craft being reserved for projects in the control of the Secret Government — which forms a control "umbrella" existing above the apparent control hierarchy of planetary governments.

Although the Nazis were pursuing researches into atomic fission on their own, we may be thankful that this was one bit of technology which the aliens did not offer them. The United States, independently doing research into the atomic bomb, was the first country to accomplish atomic fission.

The reclusive UFO expert who goes by the name "TAL" has summarized the early collaboration between humans and aliens in a privately-circulated research paper called "Alien Deceptions":

As many of you know, the Nazis were experimenting with flying saucers and exotic weapons systems. For more data on this, read "German Secret Weapons of the Second World War," by R. Luser (Spearman, 1959); "Intercept But Don't Shoot" by Renato Vesco (Zebra, 1974); "Genesis" by W. Harbinson (Dell, 1982); and "UFOs — Nazi Secret Weapon?" by Mattern-Friedrich.

Also keep in mind that they were doing genetic and mind control experiments. These projects were directed by a black uniformed militia, the Schutzstaffel (Elite Guard), later better known simply as the S.S.

Research centers were put below ground, by adapting already existent caves or excavating underground facilities. Also, back in 1937-38, Hitler, anxious for a foothold in the Antarctic, sent an expedition. From that time on men and equipment were shipped for slave labor, to the Antarctic. Also, a lot of valuable equipment, scientists and components for a flying saucer construction! By 1944, they had a saucer with a highly advanced jet propulsion system. They also had other fantastic inventions developed by the Technische Akademie der Luftwaffe experimental centers.

At the end of the war the U.S.A. snatched Werner von Braun and a large group of V-2 experts. The Russians got piles of documents on secret weapons. But the S.S. had already moved the saucer scientists and they were bound for the Antarctic. British and American intelligence picked up information on their escape. They did not want to frighten the public, because the saucers were very powerful. They knew they couldn't keep it secret — so when something leaked out, they just twisted it, confused the issues, wrapped it in myth and ridiculed it. Deliberate deceit dictated by circumstances!

In early 1947, the government launched "Operation Highjump." It was a military mission disguised as an exploratory expedition and its true purpose was to find out where the Germans were.

Flying saucers buzzed the expedition. Four planes went down when their ignition systems malfunctioned. The expedition was cut short because of this. Admiral Byrd returned to America, made some indiscreet announcements, then was told to shut up. From that time on we secretly were trying to catch up with the saucer technology and advanced weaponry. We suspected the Nazis had formed an alliance with a hidden subterranean culture and were being aided by beings now known as "Greys" or EBEs (Extraterrestrial Biological Entities). In the Southwest U.S. our high energy radar tests were able to disrupt some saucer craft and cause them to crash. This is when it was discovered the EBEs were humanoid, but descendents of reptilian species. That explains the secrecy about UFOs and also explains why the Russians and Americans have been cooperating with each other, to keep information from the public. The saucer technology was so far advanced, it constituted an unprecedented threat to the world. And now even more than ever!

The Alien/Nazi Fascists started a program to infiltrate all the governments of the planet. The early 1950's were a time for Fascist secret society groups and UFO cults. The early contactees had connections with Fascist leader William Dudley Pelly (leader of the Nazi "Silver Shirts"). The Nazi saucers (with three balls on the bottom) and the Aryan "Blonds" claiming to be from Venus, made contact with George Adamski, George Hunt Williamson (Michel d'Obrenovic), George Van Tassel, Howard Menger, and the list goes on and on.

Also, contactees like Reinhold Schmidt who spoke "German" with people claiming to be from Saturn. So, where are these Aryan aliens? It has been over 30 years. They have redesigned the saucers (now some with five balls on the bottom) and they speak "German" to Billy Meier and claim to be from the Pleiades! Wake up and smell the coffee... These are Fascists. The so-called New Age (UFO cult) movement, is the Fourth Reich!

Among other unfortunate effects for mankind of the early contact between the Nazis and the Grey aliens is that, after the war, Nazis were transferred into the midst of the American spy and space agencies, and the AIDs virus, according to information I obtained from an occult lodge connected with the Fort Detrick, Maryland research center, was engineered by these same forces as part of the Alternative 3 population reduction plans, which I shall talk about in detail later in this present work. As mentioned above, the Nazis were also involved in much super-secret genetic experimentation, including research into cloning of human beings. These researches have been continued with, among other effects, the accomplishment of human cloning taking place a few years ago. The use of human clones as replacements for assassinated politicians deserves a book of its own.

Will our planet someday soon be "invaded" from within by a secret "super race" living amongst us even now?

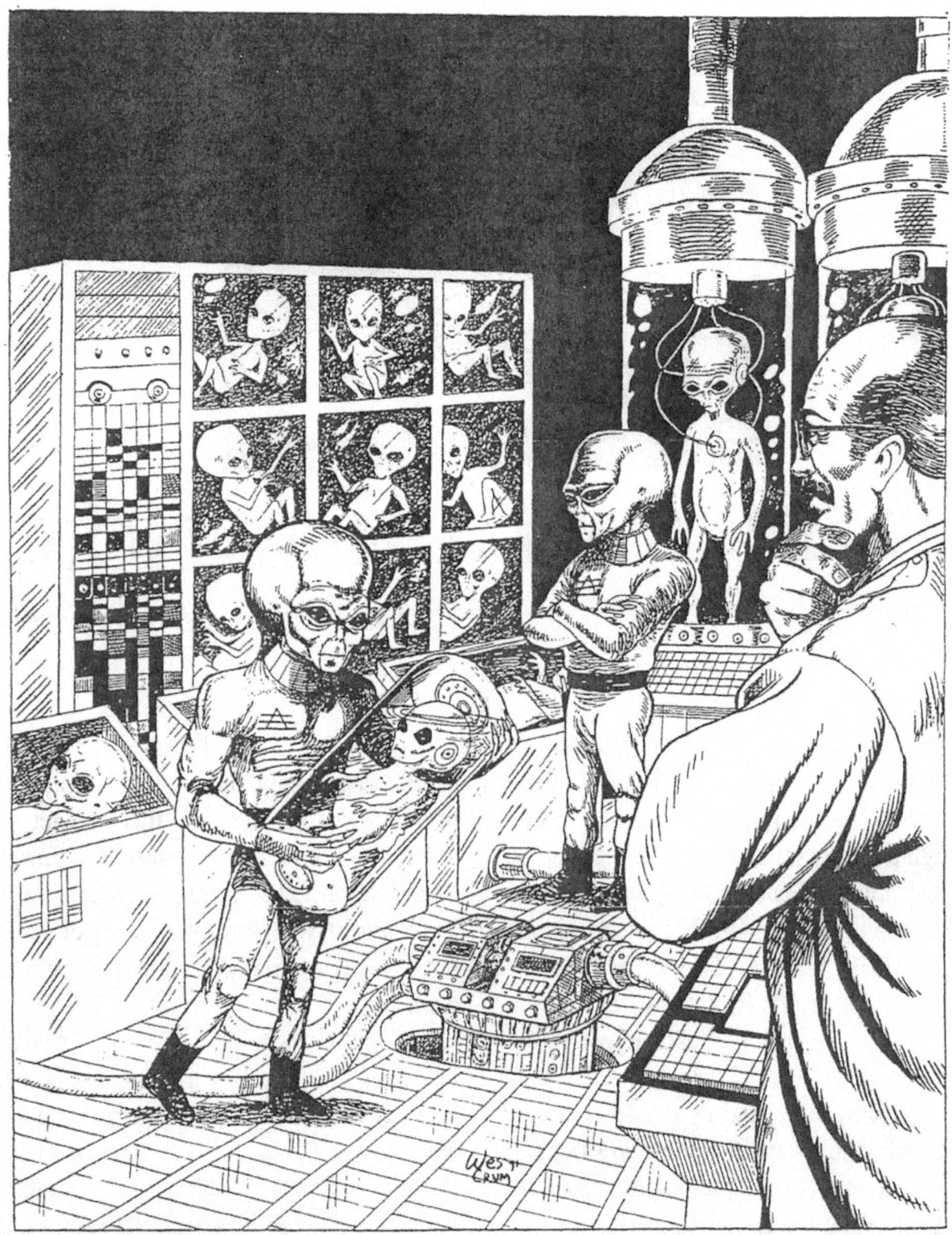
Some of the aliens sighted today may be half-human, half alien; a sort of high-bred race that has been "created" in a laboratory somewhere far beneath the Earth in underground bases.

CHAPTER FOUR

ALIEN COLLABORATION

A quick assessment of the attitude of the U.S. military toward the alien presence in the early 1950's can be gained through a report submitted to the Air Force Chief of Staff, General Hoyt S. Vandenberg, on August 5, 1948. The report, titled TOP SECRET ESTIMATE OF THE SITUATION, and written by the Air Technical Intelligence Command, makes it perfectly clear that the military had no doubt that the UFOs which were plaguing the nation at the time, and which were becoming so troublesome in terms of public relations, since at that point they could hardly be denied to exist, were examples of Grey alien technology and posed a potential threat to the populace. We know, in fact, from both documentation and from the reports of "insiders" who were there that the U.S. government had had varying contact with alien races for over 50 years, and that this contact and collaboration continues until the present. This is a dark secret that members of the government will not even whisper about, but which is finally coming out into the open.

The fact was that U.S. military and intelligence agencies were, essentially, over a barrel when it came to the aliens and their advanced aerial craft. The aliens had vastly superior technology which the U.S. military knew it had no defense against, even though they had gleaned certain scraps of the technology from the Nazis. The only choice was to pretend that we were willing participants in the subsequent human/alien collaboration, with the tacit understanding that the purposes of humans and the extraterrestrial aliens (especially those of the reptilian types) would always be in opposition.

Although much exists in terms of rumor and hearsay from a much earlier time, credible documentation on the pact between the aliens and humans exists beginning in 1954, when a secret meeting was arranged between President Eisenhower and the "large-nose Grey" species of extraterrestrials at Muroc Air Force Base (now Edwards AFB). The aliens had paved their way with a previous landing at Holloman Air Force Base in New Mexico. Five different craft, three saucers and two cigar-shaped craft, landed at the Air Force base, and President Eisenhower met with the inhabitants of the craft in front of a group of amazed military brass.

The aliens, using a high-tech electronic translator which enabled communications to take place in a fairly smooth manner, attempted to convince Eisenhower that the time was ripe for the information to be released that contact had been made between cosmic worlds. As always they presented their purposes as being strictly of a benevolent nature, and that all they were doing was to try and help humanity along with their knowledge and technology. Eisenhower, a wily negotiator himself who had honed his skills during wartime, refused to go along with their wishes for a public announcement of their existence, although he did not sever communications with the Greys, stating that extensive consultations with his staff were necessary before a final decision could be reached.

Eisenhower didn't believe that the public was ready for information which would challenge their worldview of centuries. Beyond his concerns about the public reaction to the news, I think that he was also rightfully suspicious of the intentions of the Grey aliens, who historically have always been duplicitous and to have had no respect whatsoever for any lifeform other than their own. As events progressed, it was proved that Eisenhower had every right to be suspicious.

These were times of high drama in terms of earth and extraterrestrial contact, times that were pivotal in terms of the future of the human race. Eisenhower had had previous contact with a group known as the "Benevolent Ones," human in appearance, who had attempted to engineer their own treaty with the U.S. government at an earlier date. They warned Eisenhower about the deceptiveness of the Greys who they stated would eventually attempt to overcome U.S. forces, and who had also had the planet earth under close observation from their orbiting spacecraft for several years. Eisenhower, it turns out, was even suspicious of this group of extraterrestrials, even though their body configuration was essentially identical to that of humans of earth.

I am also in possession of information that suggests that American presidents including Truman and Eisenhower were in at least sporadic contact with members of the repulsive alien Draco race, from Alpha Draconis, and that these aliens were closely connected to the leadership of earth's occult lodges whose lust for power has always forced them into collaborations detrimental to human life.

We do know for certain, however, that Eisenhower rejected the overtures of both the Benevolent Ones and the Grey aliens, although maintaining diplomatic relations as a substitute for severing communications or initiating a conflict between races. There were others in Eisenhower's administration who reflected the president's suspicious attitude toward the aliens and the portions of the government who were trying to downplay the potential menace from the stars.

Vice Admiral Roscoe Hillenkoetter, the Commander of Military Intelligence in the Pacific, and later, the director of the CIA, was one of those who were privy to high level intelligence reports about the extraterrestrials and their potential menace, and who was firmly in Eisenhower's camp when it came to doubts about the benign intentions of the aliens.

My own suppositions about Eisenhower's suspicions about the alien motives are borne out by a conversation I had with a man who had been a member of the Eisenhower cabinet, and who was also a close friend of the president's family during and after his administration. Although I was cautioned by him again and again not to reveal his name nor the circumstances of the interview, a request which I will respect, in an interview which I conducted with the elderly gentleman during the early 1970s the man said that after the meeting with the Grey aliens, Eisenhower had arranged a meeting with his highest level military and intelligence personnel and with members of the MJ-12 group, and had ordered them in no uncertain terms to immediately implement defense plans for an alien invasion.

An interesting side note on international scheming, is that a representative of the Secret Government was also present at the negotiations, and that this group communicated that they were adamant in wanting an alliance immediately struck with the aliens. At one point, according to Eisenhower's friend, the representative of the Secret Government handed the President a written note reminding him "just who had put him in office in the first place." Eisenhower, in the face of a possible removal from office or worse (for instance, the kind of fate that John F. Kennedy met with because of reputed threats to reveal the Secret Government/Grey alien collaboration), still resisted these Secret Government-sponsored urgings and went along with what he thought was best for the people of earth.

Either Eisenhower's plans for bolstering our defenses against the aliens were not entirely heeded, or there was a treasonous individual or group within the military establishment connected to the Secret Government who was actively working to circumvent Eisenhower's plan, for they were never carried out to any extent. Instead, these same orders were forwarded to several "planning committees," which was about the same thing as tabling the plans, and after Eisenhower left office, his intentions to counter the alien menace were simply pushed aside.

It was only much later that the evil intentions of the Grey aliens became abundantly apparent and the military became involved in researches into advanced weaponry which could be used against these strange adversaries — the genesis of the Strategic Defense Initiative or Star Wars program, as well as other less well-known tactical contingencies like the HAARP plan, which I shall discuss later in these pages.

FREEHAND SKETCHES BY COMMANDER X ON SOME MATRIX ACCESS VISUALIZATIONS.

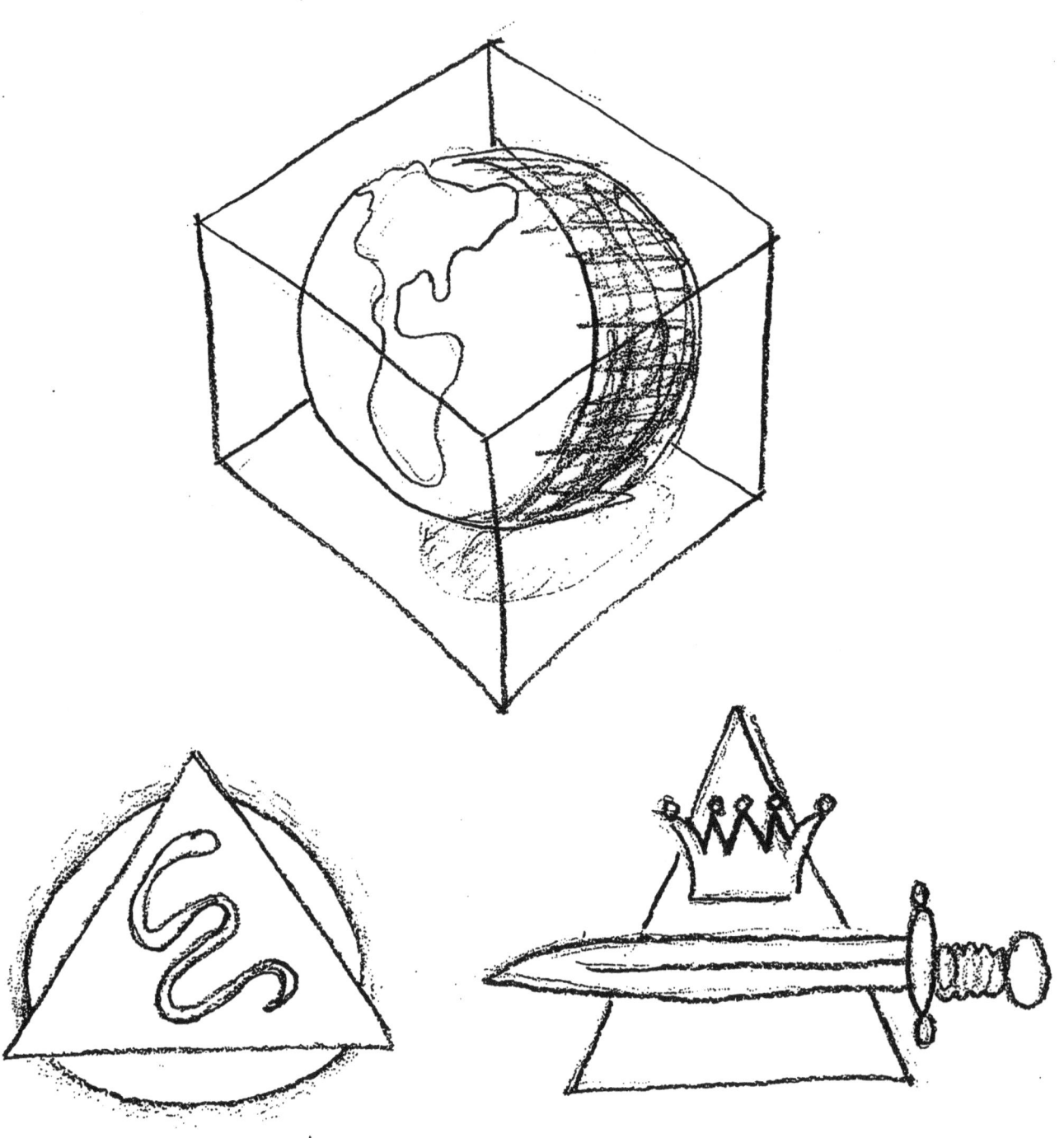

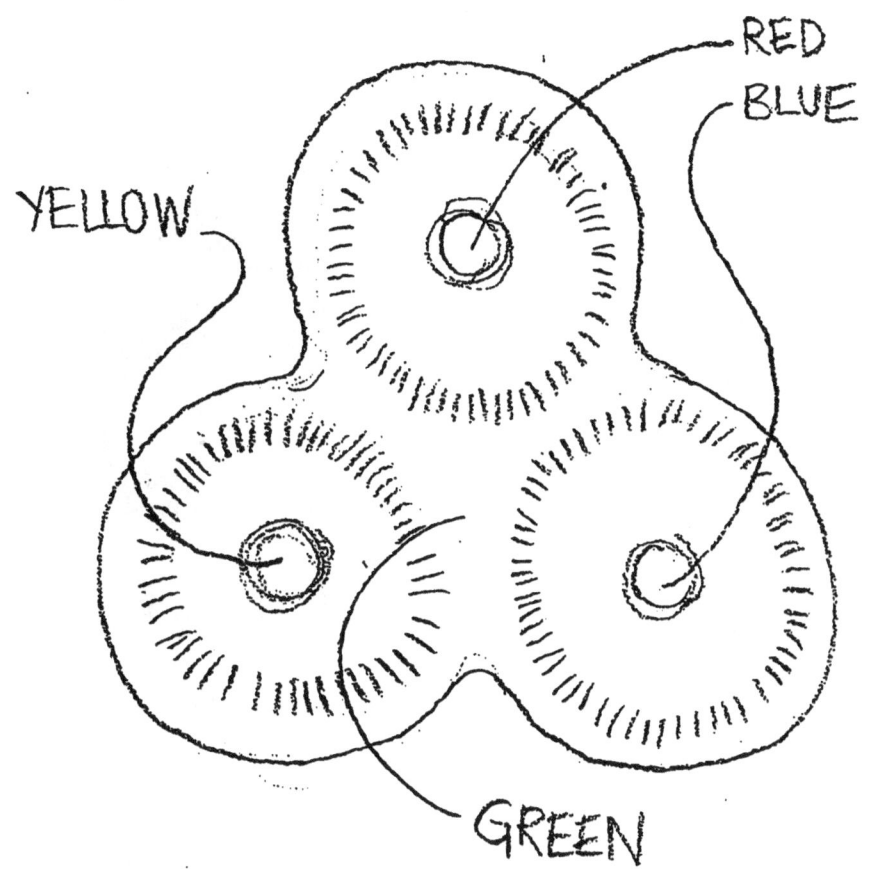

CHAPTER FIVE

ALIEN DEMANDS

Although negotiations with the alien forces continued between the U.S. government and the Grey aliens over the next decade after the 1950s, actual collaboration takes place somewhat later than the Eisenhower encounter. This outrageous "deal with the Devil" dates to April 30, 1964, when three saucers landed at Holloman Air Force Base in New Mexico, and the inhabitants of the craft met with American government intelligence officials, again communicating through sophisticated electronic translation devices which were provided by the aliens.

These meetings between agents of the U.S. government and the Grey aliens continued on a regular basis throughout the 1960s and early 70s, and involved an exchange of information and the offering of a highly attractive carrot: several varieties of advanced technology by the Greys. This continued until a deal was struck between the extraterrestials and the MJ-12 group. I am reminded of the explorers in the New World, who offered cheap trinkets to the Native Americans who met them, only later to show their true colors by confining them to reservations. Unless this warning is heeded, mankind will almost undoubtedly end up in the same condition or worse!

MJ-12, as you may know if you have read my books, is a super-secret governmental group empowered to investigate and negotiate with the aliens; at least this is the cover story. It is important to note that some researchers have pointed out numerous Secret Government connections to some of the members of this group. These so-called representatives of the U.S. (so-called because I don't think they represent our national or species interests at all, in most cases) agreed to ignore the rampant abductions, brain implantations, mind control programming, genetic experiments, and other terrible manipulation which the aliens were performing on U.S. citizenry on a routine basis, and which were gradually becoming common knowledge to the more well-informed populace. This was an outrageous criminal act, in itself, and judging from information which I obtained and which shall be described later in this book, apparently a "side-deal" was cut in which certain negotiators were bribed with alien technology and promises of power to sell out the interests of the human race. Again, this may have been merely a clause in a long-term collaboration between the Secret Government and the Grey aliens.

High treason is not all that was involved in the deal between the government and the Grey aliens, however. My belief is that honest representatives of the American government were blackmailed by the Secret Government into the collaboration with the Greys, and after initially resisting the deal, there was no choice but to go along with the alien demands and the pressuring of treasonous human forces, if only to buy time for the patriotic forces within the government to consolidate its position. Part of this blackmail took the form of a "demonstration" which was offered during a NATO exercise in Europe, which is described by R. Perry Collins in UFO Universe magazine, January 1990:

This incident, reported by a Belgian Army Officer, involved the overt display of a specific type of weapon used by a UFO to destroy antiaircraft missiles in flight. The NATO exercise involved the firing of numbers of such missiles on several pre-selected coordinates. For reasons at first unknown to the operators involved, all the missiles fired on one particular set of coordinates failed and exploded prematurely.

Upon examination of high resolution films made of the exercise, it was discovered that a circular, domed UFO, hovering near the path of those missiles, was emitting some type of intense beam which repeatedly destroyed the missiles in flight. The films were examined extensively by both Belgian and American military analysts. The point to be seen here is that the UFO was apparently deliberately demonstrating a beam weapon of significant capability in full view of military observers. It repeated the demonstration several times. The destruction of the missiles was not an act of self-defense —the missiles were not attempting to intercept the UFO but were moving along repeatedly identical and preset flight paths.

Now it dawned upon the U.S. Government's patriotic negotiators that they had no bargaining chips left whatsoever when it came to safeguarding the earth; all they could do was to take whatever deal the aliens offered, and this included allowing them to freely continue with cattle mutilations and other grotesque human experimentation and widespread murders. I have viewed some of the Secret Government documentation which talks about these programs, and it would be laughable the way that these activities are justified by these mealy-mouthed elitist controllers if the matter wasn't so terribly grim. Apparently the members of the Secret Government feel that they are going to be granted privileged positions in the cosmic government after the aliens have taken over. My bet is that they end up like the rest of us if we fail.

For a sense of the scope of abductions by humans which have been taking place in the United States, approximately 20,000 persons disappear during any given year, never to be found. From my research, it is probable that at least one-third of these disappearances can be attributed to the alien presence, and still the newspapers and electronic media generally do not speak out about the scandal, for fear of terrifying the public. But the public has every reason to be terrified! And every reason to demand that the government and the major media come forward with the truth of what is going on!

Tiny brain computer modifies behavior

Though the Orwellian implications for people control are horrifying, it is being hailed as a stroke of genius. A tiny computer which can fit inside your brain has been invented by Britain's "Whitehall Scientific Institute for the Betterment of Humanity." (1984)

Reports indicate the computer is smaller than a copper penny, and can be used as an information storing library on any specific topic or can be used to modify behavior. (Violent criminals are most often cited as the likely subjects of this behavior control.)

The device fits snugly at the base of the brain, and attaches to the brain's electrical system so that it works perfectly as part of the body.

The new invention was the brainchild of Dr. Sigmund Gieriech, a bioelectric wizard, probably the best in the world, according to his colleagues.

Prison officials at Birmingham's maximum security Rehabilitation Center for the criminally insane have already gone ahead and placed three devices into prisoners to see if their behavior patterns can be fixed.

The little computer monitors brainwaves. Whenever a thought passes through which has a criminal intent, it sends out a quick jolt of electricity to remind the person that they must not do whatever it is they are thinking about.

Prison superintendent Maxwell Primm notes, "So far we are extremely pleased with the results. The three volunteers for this were some of our worst prisoners. With the device installed, they have not been able to break a single prison rule."

The scientific community also is happy with the new device, called an Electro Computer Brain Enhancer (ECBE). A civilian volunteer now carries one in his brain.

Says the scientist, Dr. Ormond Shell, "I don't even know that it's in my head. It stores a list of mathematical formulas for me about the anti-gravity project I am currently working on. It certainly has made my work easier. I think soon there will be models out that anyone can use. It really is something that everyone should have."

Dr. Gieriech is perhaps the most pleased about his success. He comments, "The most difficult part was developing the coating that would make the computer biologically acceptable once implanted. It acts just like an extension of the brain."

IMPLANT COMMUNICATION

Since the implants in my body seem to be "locked on" to the electrical system and are pulsing electrical currents, the thought occurred to me that a manipulation of body meridian energy flows might be taking place.If the communication is along those lines, then it is only logical to try and reverse the process for the purpose of message transfer back to the intelligence behind the phenomenon.I have therefore decided to purchase a Chinese acupuncture machine (electrical), so that I may insert a needle into the implant area and and pulse a current of varying frequency and intensity of my own choosing.I will first see if I can begin an implant response by external electro - stimulation.Then I will see if I can establish some form of bio - energetic alphabet or symbol coding system.I will record all experimentation and responses as I progress in time.It is quite obvious to me that the "intelligence" wishes me to be fully consciously aware of the pulsations and the fact that they are activated by either an internal source or external mechanism (depending on which implant,the location on the body and correlative information : ie - my own internal body health and nerves or other people's energy systems).As I said before, one particular type of pulsation indicates to me the presence of UFO'S, which I call an "alternating pulse" - in this case I assume that the external switch is being activated by a biological entity inside the craft.It is this type of pulse that I wish to focus my attention upon and reverse. Because I am unable to afford expensive scanning analysis for confirmation and proof, and have already tried X-rays and ultrasound, it would seem sensible to attempt a different form of evidence gathering.A predictable pattern of pulsed communications which are demonstratable to laboratory scientists would be an initial goal.So far as of the above date, information via the implants is being portioned out to me without any imput on my part except to react and respond by free will choice to the directives and indicators.Perhaps this is some sort of experiment or test.Maybe there is an initiation period before metamorphasis.Possibly I am being led like a fish to a worm to a destiny I cannot see for the moment.Conceivably, I am just a very small player in a cosmic plan of human evolutionary development.WE SHALL SEE.

ULTRASOUND SCANNING RESULTS / NOV.29TH/91 : NEGATIVE SURFACE TISSUE FIND.
RECORDS : PTU151476 / VIDEO TAPED. AREAS SCANNED : LEFT,RIGHT THIGHS & LOWER LEFT BACK.
I.15 P.M. - 16 HZ. - GAIN = I DB, PRW = ODB / 50DB   1/2/0 - DEPT.40 /SPH.
$143.00 CASH, NOT COVERED BY MEDICAL PLAN.X - RAY ALSO PROVED NEGATIVE.MORE SOPHISTICATED MRI OR CAT SCAN WOULD BE COST PROHIBITIVE.NOT AN EASY THING TO PROVE.I AM GOING TO HAVE TO RELY ON MY NEWLY DEVELOPING SENSING & HEALING ABILITIES AS DEMONSTRATIVE PROOF UNTIL SUCH TIME AS I CAN OBTAIN VERIFIABLE SCIENTIFIC OR MEDICAL EVIDENCE.

CHAPTER SIX

OTHER PROJECTS

During the latter part of the 1960s, the U.S. military at Area 51 and other secret locations engaged in a variety of scientific projects with varying degrees of alien collaboration, ranging from access and research into purely theoretical scientific information (I have information which says that there was an alien liason team to the Hubble telescope project, for instance), to aliens and government workers and scientists working elbow to elbow in top secret underground laboratories.

At first it seemed ideal, with the Grey aliens seemingly collaborating freely and totally for the benefit of the earthlings. The situation, however, would not always remain quite so cordial, and difficulties between two such unlike species were bound to develop over the course of time.

Area 51 in Nevada, as I have mentioned in my other works, is part of the complex where America's most advanced weaponry systems are believed to be under development, at least some of these weapons systems intended to be used against the Grey alien forces. Dreamland as well as the nearby Papoose Lake are those portions of the vast desert facility where the U.S. government is now examining UFOs that have either crash-landed or have been captured by elite units of the military which are dispatched to every reported crash.

I have spoken to a member of one of this elite unit, and he expressed to me that these crashes are far more common that the public might imagine. These spacecraft, and in some cases their occupants, are now said to be undergoing examination by top specialists in the medical, anthropological, metallurgical, propulsion, and other scientific fields, for the purpose of understanding and utilizing their technology.

The entire Dreamland complex is constructed mainly underground to prevent any unauthorized observation from satellites, overflights, or individuals hiking in the surrounding mountains, and so what is known of the area has mainly surfaced through word-of-mouth from workers employed there. It should be mentioned that this facility is guarded by a small army of current military and intelligence services personnel, as well as a reputed hand-picked force of ex-servicemen who served in the Navy Seals, Army Airborne or Special Forces, and the Air Force's Air Commandos. It is obvious that these men have been fed a cover story telling them that what they are doing is in the interest of national security, because if they had not been then more of them would have come forward with accounts of what they have seen above and underground.

It is known that these guards have at their disposal armored vehicles, helicopters, mobile radar units, highly sensitive detectors on the ground, and more. There is also a strong working relationship with the local county sheriff's department, for any kind of assistance when called. Unfortunately the people who work at Area 51 do not fully understand the sinister nature of the Grey alien/human collaboration which they are participating in, and so are perfectly willing to work against their own and humanity's best interests by keeping the true story of the base secret.

All U.S. government vehicles that are authorized to enter the restricted Area 51 have on their front license place a "CSC" tag. It has been speculated that "CSC" stands for "Central Space Center," but nobody who knows is confirming what the logo means.

Area 51 was first coded "Operation Snowbird" and it is believed that at that time its main mission was to test fly captured UFOs. Hangar 18 was a movie about a captured UFO that the U.S. government was holding in "Hangar 18." When the film was first shown to the public it caused a lot of concern at the alleged home of Hangar 18, Wright-Patterson Air Force Base in Ohio. Supposedly a decision was made to find a new location for the recovered saucers at "Wright-Pat." In 1972 the most favorable site for selection was found in Nevada due to its remoteness from the general public, and was named Area 51. This was an ideal location because of two concealing mountain ranges in the dry lake bed area, Groom Lake, and the only road into the area was soon up-graded to a two-lane one suitable for heavy-duty trucks.

A thumbnail listing of some of the projects which the U.S. Government, the Secret Government, and the Grey aliens have been involved in at Area 51 (and other similar, primarily underground locations around the world) include the following major catagories:

— The "Reverse-engineering" of alien spacecraft that the government has in their possession, and the design and construction of spacecraft with the same functional capabilities as those of the alien disk craft. The Grey aliens, while providing information and technology, have often been seen to sabotage this research in various ways (including in the most extreme cases, murder of human technicians working on these programs), and this is quite understandable from their point of view, since they would hardly want earth technology to achieve technical equality with their own, regardless of the manner in which they might have represented themselves to the scientists and political bigwigs.

— The construction of extensive underground bases and connective tunnels throughout the United States and the world, a partial list of which will follow in this book. It is my belief that this is one of the most dangerous aspects of the collaboration, as many of these underground facilities are unknown to humans, and can be used for launching offensives if the aliens deem this necessary in the future. It is rumored that large spaceports and inter-dimensional ports have also been constructed underground, for the free flow of alien craft and supplies from other star systems.

— The creation of electromagnetic detection webs providing security for secret alien/government installations. This technology has also been used in the construction of mind control electromagnetic networks which are currently being employed upon humanity around the globe, and also in monitoring and surveillance systems for the tracking of humans. The HAARP project, which I discuss later, is one example of electronics research with multiple intentions, both good and ill, for mankind.

— The securing of vortex and other anomalous electromagnetic zones as entry and exit areas for both alien and U.S. government spacecraft. Although the physical laws which govern these strange natural areas are well beyond my own novice's scientific understanding, my researches have shown that these natural electromagnetic vortex areas do exist on the planet, have long been utilized as interstellar jump-off and entry points, and are planned to be used in the event of massive invasion by alien forces.

Vortex areas are also under research by several patriotic resistance groups working covertly within the U.S. government, as possible means of access to interstellar alien bases: a possible Achilles heel of the aliens, although this research is of too secretive a nature to provide further details without compromising my sources for this information.

— Facilities for the Secret Government's Alternative 3 contingency program, including joint human and alien bases on the Moon and Mars, and extensive transference facilities for slave labor in the Alternative 3 programs. Alternative 3 is one of the most sinister programs which has been undertaken to the detriment of mankind, according to my knowledge, in collaboration between the Secret Government and the hostile Grey aliens. Further details will be included later in this book.

Other activities which have taken place at these secret installations also include:

— Development of advanced weapons systems.

— Development of extensive mind control, social control, and social programming systems, undertaken partially under the auspices of "the Foundation" in England. Several writers have pinpointed "the Foundation" as being the origin of some of these kind of human control systems (in collaboration with the Secret Government on earth), without digging deeper and noting that not all of their instructions come from earth-based politicians. It should be noted that this group has also been heavily involved in setting the agenda for the entertainment industry as well as the educational establishment in America and worldwide.

— Cloning experimentation and production, of both human and alien bodies. This experimentation has paid off richly for the alien Greys and the traitorous human factions allied with them, as several human leaders in both the political and religious spheres have been kidnapped and replaced by subservient clones under the control of the Grey aliens. This provides the control necessary over these organizations, as well as a means to funnel off the monies which these groups raise.

— Breeding production using abducted human females and males. One purpose of this program is in the breeding of slave populations to be utilized in the Alternative 3 program, as well as for labor once the Grey alien overthrow of human control of the earth is totally accomplished. Some of these experiments have been of the most grotesque varieties, and tales are told of half-human, half-alien creatures, as well as even more horrible genetic concoctions housed in vats and holding facilities in underground compounds.

There have been other, even more bizarre experiments conducted by the aliens that the mainstream media is almost totally unwilling to touch for fear that the cover-up will crack wide open. These experiments include the stealing of sperm from men and the artificial impregnation of human women by the aliens, creating alien/human half-breeds, some of whom are reported to walk among humans at this time. The cloning of these grotesque, human-alien hybrids is also said to have taken place, and some researchers have said that some of the famed Men in Black are actually these sorts of hybrids.

Although there has been plenty of speculation about these kinds of experiments, sometimes the true horror of the situation is not fully presented to the public in the controlled media. The best thing to do for understanding how it feels to be abused by the aliens in one of their ghastly experiments is go to the source, namely someone who has had the experience.

Bruce A. Smith is an abductee who has spoken out about the alien programs in eloquent fashion (in Leading Edge magazine, among other places), urging abductees not to succumb to the kind of programming that says that abduction is a good thing and intended for the "enlightenment" or "evolution" of mankind. This is precisely the sort of propaganda which the aliens have been promoting and which, unfortunately, some members of the "New Age" brand of philosophy have been going along with. Listen to what Bruce Smith has to say, from the standpoint of one who has been there:

Are all the messages that excite and soothe us, such as the suggestion that the alien crossbreeding program is for the evolution of Homo Sapiens too, besides the alien species, just a lie to maintain us as willing partners in their program?

If the crossbreeding program is so critical to the advancement of Homo Sapiens consciousness, why are they doing it in such a secretive, clandestine, criminal and traumatic manner? We are being snatched, raped, and experience the loss of body parts and energy. This is a good thing? This is for our illumination? For our advanced consciousness? Give me a break!

Confucius said that wisdom begins by calling things by their proper names. Abductions for crossbreeding purposes is rape. Pure and simple. And making the victims feel good about it and even longing for continued relations, is the action of the most manipulative of minds.

So I call it rape. Let's look at the crossbreeding experience in a step-by-step manner. First the rapist paralyzes you so you can't physically resist, even if you wanted to. Then the rapist hypnotizes you into enjoying the rape and actually longing for more contact, both sexually and emotionally.

Then the rapist takes your sperm or ova. Then the rapist takes your sexual energy and your parental emotions, depleting you to the point that you become sexually dysfunctional in your earthly relationships. Then the rapist puts an implant in you so that he can find you whenever he wants, wherever you are. There is no place you can go and feel 100% safe. This rapist can ravage you repeatedly, throughout your life. The rapist can have you at any age. He can even steal your virginity, even begin to suck you dry as a child.

The rapist can listen to your thoughts and experience your feelings through the implant. The rapist knows who you love and why. He knows when you pray. Perhaps he is even responsible for putting the ideas of God and religion into your mind. Perhaps he is even responsible for shaping your sexual desires in your earthly relationships, so that your lovers and you are actually acting out a drama whose script was written by your rapist.

Then the rapist programs all your friends and colleagues so that they think your rape is a sacred and special event. So, even when you break through the programming and begin to call the abduction what it is, all your friends in your UFO group tell you, "You're being too negative." Even your associates in your abductee self-help group tell you that you're wrong, that you're missing the positive aspect of your experience. Perhaps your hypnotist even suggests that you lighten up on the negativity, that maybe the body parts they remove might actually be a surgical procedure that could be helpful.

Where do you turn? I turn inside. I listen for my own voice. I meditate. I walk in the woods. I listen to the birds. I talk to the trees. Nature, I feel, doesn't lie. When I can wade through the barrage of alien programming and mind control from our own rotten, polluted civilization, and I can hear my own voice, I know what to do.

INSIDE AREA 51 AT DREAMLAND

There is now impressive evidence that the military is constructing its own UFOs based on information derived from alien sources.

How to get to Area 51. While in Rachel, Nevada, stop in at the Little A'Le Inn.

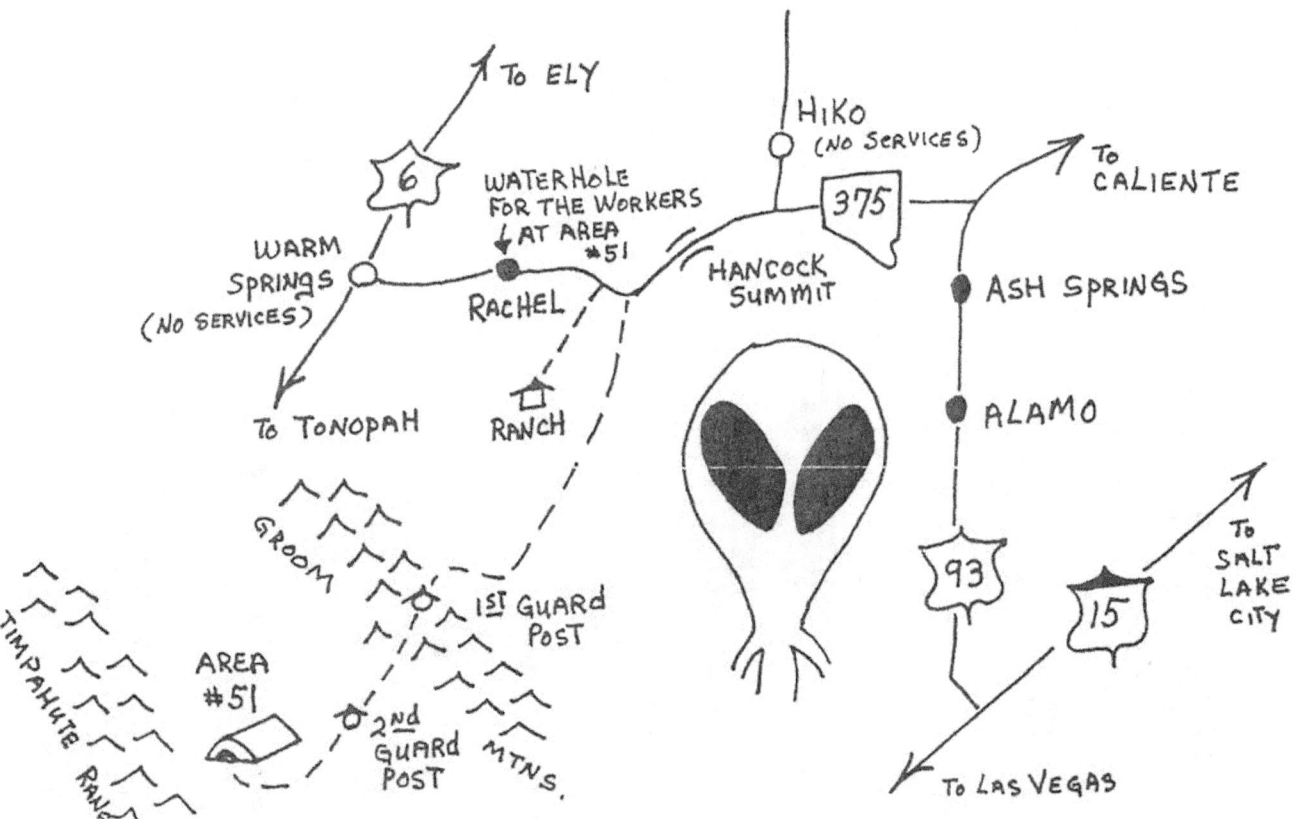

CHAPTER SEVEN

THE SECRET WAR

One little-discussed aspect of the Dreamland/Area 51 area is a super-secret and bloody internal "war" which has been going on there over control of alien technology and human/alien facilities. The conflicting forces include the patriotic U.S. government COM-12 intelligence group, who are allied with the extraterrestrial human Nordic Federation (who are an off-world group intent on putting Grey alien forces in check on this planet) and the treasonous Secret Government or Illuminati forces: these are the Aquarius forces who are allied with the destructive alien Greys, and particularly the Draco Empire, which I will discuss in detail later.

The Greys, acting covertly, were able to take over many of the deeper levels of the Dreamland facilities over the years, while the COM-12 group inhabited and controlled the above ground and upper levels of the complex, only occasionally making secret tactical and surveillance forays into the areas controlled by the Greys.

Although activity has been phased down in the Groom Lake area in the above-ground portions in recent years, due to the large amount of attention from the public and the media, there is still tentative alien Grey/government collaboration and exclusively alien Grey activity taking place there, although the greatest care is now being taken to insure that the installations involved in this kind of business are secure from possible interlopers.

One recent interloper was an amateur UFOlogist, Charles B. of Hawthorne, California, who explained to his friends that he was going to sneak onto the Area 51 compound and take films of the aliens which he was certain was there. B.'s bright idea was that he would sell the films to the television networks and make millions of dollars by revealing the truth about the Grey alien presence to mankind. Unfortunately, according to friends who contacted me, when B. sneaked into Area 51 in June of 1995, he did not return. What happened to him? Those who know are not saying, and repeated attempts to bring this story out in newspapers and on television has met a dead end. So much for the impartiality of the media in the United States.

The alien/human collaboration continues to take place in the underground sections of the Area 51 base, and occasionally a UFO (particularly of the small, robotoid "Spy-bee" type which are primarily used for surveillance and weapons applications) can be seen being flown in the airspace above the area. The Spy-bees are high-tech anti-gravity drones which come in a variety of types, including ones that can monitor thought patterns and send electromagnetic messages directly to the human brain. Although most of the traffic in UFO-style craft in this area has been terminated, the patient researcher is sometimes rewarded by seeing disk craft and even sometimes a large interstellar tanker going in or out of electronic "cloaking mode."

If you would like to investigate Area 51 personally, although I am not recommending and in fact am discouraging it:

From Las Vegas, Nevada, travel in a northeasterly direction on Interstate 1-15 (heading for Salt Lake City, Utah), for a distance of about 22 miles, then turn left onto U.S. Highway 93 for about 85 miles, then turn left again onto Nevada State Highway 375 for about 14 miles, then left once more at the bottom of Hancock Summit onto a two-lane gravel road that is well-maintained for about 13 miles. Follow this until you reach the first guardpost that is located on top of the Groom Mountain area.

Remember, the U.S. government and the aliens do not want you inside Area 51. Exercise extreme caution, and do not go onto any government lands that are posted as being illegal. Remember the case of Charles B., since it should be ovvious that dead UFO researchers are not much use to anyone.

Above all, you must keep in mind that the Secret Government and the Grey aliens will do anything to keep their dirty little secrets from being exposed, and so, as with all kinds of research into the Grey alien/Secret Government collaboration, assume the worst of the motives of these persons.

One of my sources at Dreamland, shortly after it happened, informed me of an attempt by five men to fly out a helicopter full of secret documentation and photos proving the existence of the alien base at Dreamland in 1991; but the chopper didn't get very far, unfortunately. Although, as I understand it, the helicopter contained a wealth of top secret material which had been "liberated" from restricted portions of Area 51, that allegedly would have completely blown the lid off the alien cover-up, the craft was shot down by heat-seeking missiles before the men could deliver the documentation to the Las Vegas-based investigative reporter whom they had been in touch with, and to whom they had arranged to furnish the documents.

After the helicopter had crashed, investigators from five different federal agencies rushed to the site within an hour, and the surviving documentation was quickly carried away and presumably destroyed or perhaps just returned to the various files which had been pilfered. Naturally, the official story was that the helicopter had accidentally strayed off course and struck power lines (even though there are no power lines in the area of the crash) and there the story has remained, at least until now. But take the fate of the men in that helicopter as yet another warning to all investigators who wish to research Dreamland (or any other secret Grey alien/human base, for that matter). This is not a joke, and the investigation of the aliens and the Secret Government is not child's play to be undertaken out of casual interest or for misguided entertainment of the hobbyist mentality.

The use of good investigative research of the way in which factions of our government have sold us out on a cosmic scale, of course, still exists. If it wasn't for the willing acquiescence of government and the hidden Secret Government manipulators of the world, then it is probable that the aliens would have a much more difficult time in carrying out their incredible catalog of misdeeds, a list which is so long and indeed so incredible that it discourages belief through its sheer incredibleness.

For serious researchers, an excellent overview of the Grey alien/Secret Government collaboration has been provided by the investigator known as "TAL" in the form of a privately-printed document which has circulated amongst researchers, titled "The Majestic Connection":

The National Security Council controls and coordinates with all other intelligence agencies (CIA; NSA; DIA; FBI; BI&R; and others). NXC formed "Committee Groups" within itself. In 1954, Executive Order 54/12 formed a Black Budget for technology and teams of covert agents (Men in Black) to cover-up the cover-ups! The NSC called this group the 54-12 Committee which was given responsibility of approving all "Black" covert operations. This committee has undergone changes over the years, and has been variously called the Special Committee, the 303 Committee and currently the 40 Committee (XXXX = The Double-Double Cross). It has been described as the "Directorate" of the NSC. The 40 Committee was once headed by Dr. Henry Kissinger (who was called the Majestic Overseer).

It is currently reported that the 40 Group controls all planetary intelligence and that P.I.-40 keeps all "cleared" government officials briefed on UFO (now termed IFO) developments and our Inner/Outer space visitors.

Key figures in shadow government (the New World Order) belong to the Bilderberg Group (formed in 1952) which has been meeting every year since 1954. The elite of the world's wealthy and influential, which includes Henry Kissinger; David Rockefeller; the Rothschilds; Allen Dulles; etc. (are all members).

The worldwide "Invisible Government" commonly known as The Illuminati is said to have organization co-directorships linked to people in the Trilateral Commission; the United Nations; the Club of Rome; the Rand Corporation; General Electric; Hughes; the Council on Foreign Relations, etc...

There are those within the CFR/TC/UN who are trying to maneuver the U.S. into a position where acceptance of the New World Order is our only alternative.

The New World Order is, naturally, a long-term joint operation of the aliens and the Secret Government (with the original plans actually alleged to have been channelled through members of the Illuminati in the 1500s or even earlier), so think twice when the politicians casually discuss the intervention of the blue helmeted U.N. troops in greater and greater numbers in the global arena. These may not be the peace keeping missions which they are touted as being. It is conceived that, if necessary, these U.N. forces will be used to quell patriotic resistance to the surrendering of national sovereignty to the Greys.

Research

HUBBLE TELESCOPE BIG LIE

At a time when NASA public relations needs an outstanding success, they have been ordered to report the Hubble Telescope as virtually useless. There has to be a big reason for that, and indeed there is a VERY BIG REASON.

As you know, the purpose of this giant "Eye in the Sky" was to give us information on the universe we had never had before. It was designed to probe the universe, yeilding visual images enhanceded visual images of deep space phenomena, by a hundred times or more, than any telescope trying to penetrate the earth's atmosphere. And it does all that and more, even as NASA's Public Affairs department is busy explaining why it doesn't work and pointing the dread finger of blame here and there.

"Empty" space is not empty! To the limits of the universe, where space turns back on itself and beginning and end become the same, there are to be seen a variety of vessels in progress from one point to another. We must assume that these are inhabited, but by what? Even our own solar system is not without its share of USVs, Unidentified Space Vessels. They occasionally dip into our atmosphere causing great excitement, but a whole department of government has been set up to explain them away. Weather balloons, indeed!

In our history, whenever an inferior culture has been exposed to a superior culture, it has languished and faded away. This is supposed to be proof that our world cultures will suffer the same fate, if exposed to a vastly superior extraterrestrial alien culture. In the past, that may have been true of cultures in stasis, peoples who were satisfied with their way of life and didn't want to change it. Today, we are in a vastly different situation. We are moving forward into a New World Order at a breath-taking pace. There is more technological progress in a day now than there once was in a thousand years before. We are not now of a nature to bow humbly to alien entities as "Our Masters." Give us some credit!

At least, that is the firm conviction of Dr. Hans Markowitz and the "Secret College," of top scientists the world over. They don't accept the politically fictionized history of man, but instead see a man as capable of holding his own. And deserving of the truth!

The big picture, the reason for the big lie, is this: We may be facing the greatest war, an interstellar war, that the universe has known. Far out in space, in the general direction of Sirius, the "Dog Star," a monstrous cloud of vessels is moving through space. All information obtained to this point has been subjected to computer analysis. The indications are that this is a space flotilla that will intercept Earth in approximately twelve years. The word "approximate" must be used because, at their speed through the universe, they are subject to some degree of time compression. Never-the-less, there is every appearance that our green planet could be a target, or at least their destination.

These vessels, though huge, do not give the impression of enclosing vast amounts of useful space, as would be the case with freighters, or passenger craft. They are up to five hundred miles long, sleek, apparently all technological muscle, and are assumed to be military in nature, and therefore likely hostile. Such a conglomeration of power would not be put together to pay us a friendly visit! We must assume the worst!

In the meantime, the "Powers That Be" favor the approach, "business as usual," and such preparations as are to be made, made in secret.

How long have the governments of the world had some inkling of this? Since the first "saucer" sighting was validated? Could this be the secret behind the "cold war," the apparent hostilities between the nations of Earth, requiring a rapid progress in military technology and expansion as possible to ward off space aliens? Was it assumed that we would be less fearful if the enemy were recognized as our fellow man? Better the evil known than the evil unknown. Is that their belief?

Given these facts, we must begin a world-wide psychological preparation, and an all-out technological effort to prepare our defenses.

Has mankind perhaps faced a similar situation in the past? A very primitive tribe in Africa claims to have come from "Sirius," the Dog Star. They describe in astronomical detail and exactness of the twin-star system, the situation of the planets, and the physical make-up of their home planet. Yet they don't even have a written language!

It may be that we are outgunned. On the other hand, it may be that other entities have underestimated mankind's ability to rise to the occasion.

Infrasound Generator Truck

Used by Psychological Warfare and Army Special Forces Units

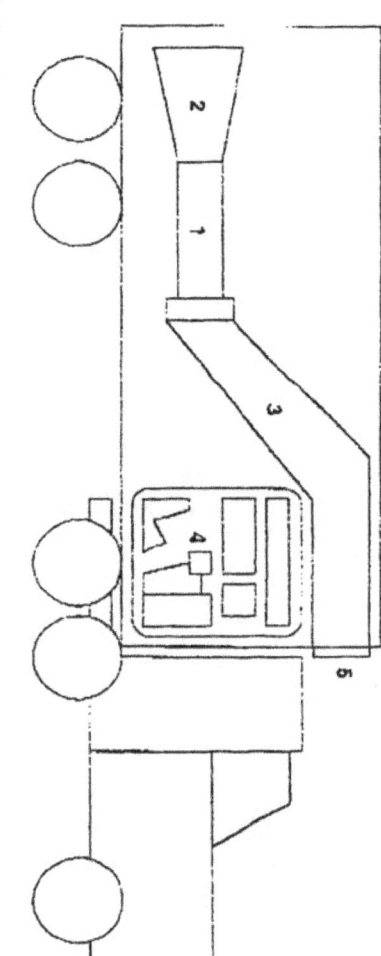

1. Jet engine from old T-33 aircraft.
2. Cone containing whistle shaped air chamber(s) to produce and direct infrasound.
3. Air intake channel.
4. Heavily insulated sound-proof crew compartment.
5. Grating over mouth of air intake (raised for emphasis).

NOTE: Location of fuel tank for jet engine unknown but probably in dead space beneath engine or under air duct.

DESCRIPTION: Outward appearance of ordinary semi truck and trailer. May be painted woodland camo or like a Safeway delivery truck or moving van. Weapon is lethal for several miles; far beyond audible sound of jet engine. Causes friction between internal organs and burst blood vessels in the brain ("strokes").

COUNTERMEASURES: The ONLY method of dealing with this weapon is to destroy it BEFORE the crew can start it up. When started, it will kill every living creature within range. There is NO protective defense.

CHAPTER EIGHT

ALIENS UNDERGROUND

As described, during the early 1970s (and later) the Grey aliens collaborated with military and intelligence agencies controlled by treasonous factions to build huge underground bases in a number of locations in America and around the world, including the most well known sites at Dulce, New Mexico, and at Groom Lake, Nevada. Soon, with Secret Government approval, humans began disappearing in these areas, and saucers were launched from these locales for "foraging expeditions," foraging for humans and cattle, that is.

This Secret Government/alien collaboration in underground bases, as I have noted elsewhere, quickly turned out to be somewhat of a Trojan Horse for the human race, and the greatest threat to human survival ever conceived. The military (at least those members who feel patriotism toward America and the human race) came to regret having surrendered the Grey aliens as much access to their bases and research labs and other underground facilities as they had, much as President Eisenhower had privately warned in the 1950s.

Almost as soon as the aliens had moved into these high tech, well-equipped, and well-fortified underground bases they began to expand them, to take over level after underground level that had been occupied by humans, and to build tunnels connecting their bases over great distances. Soon the entire country was riddled with underground tunnels. Now it can be considered that the Trojan Horse is placed well within the defensive walls of America, and the extraterrestrial forces hidden inside, I believe, are ready to strike.

Another aspect of the incredible treachery of the Grey aliens is the rampant theft of human technology of interest to them, of the surveillance of humans, and the termination of individuals (particularly many in the patriotic COM-12 group) who resisted their plans for infiltration. The power plays of the aliens led to inevitable conflict with the humans who inhabited the underground bases, and even a number of armed confrontations between the Grey aliens and patriotic factions of the U.S. military.

Judging from the statements of three men who were involved in an armed conflict which took place at Area 51, a deadly altercation arose over access into the alien areas by humans. When it was revealed that the aliens were conducting hideous experiments upon, implanting, and freely "terminating" human workers at the Dreamland complex, tensions were heightened even more. When a security guard was shot in an area controlled by the Greys (allegedly by laser) a fight broke out between the humans and the aliens, with the humans sustaining substantially greater casualties, and with the Grey aliens taking over large portions of the complex which they had previously not inhabited. They inhabit most of these areas to this day, although security has been tightened to the extent that very little information is currently leaking out about these underground areas.

Although it has remained under wraps, this was a period of alien/human relations which may be compared to the Cuban missile crisis during the 1960s: The Greys presented to the president of the United States outright warnings that if the in-fighting in the collaborative bases were not terminated, there might be war between them and the earth. Behind the scenes agents of the Secret Government worked to bring down patriotic members of the military and the government who were counselling that acquiescence to the aliens would be deadly.

The crack UFO researcher who goes only by the name "Branton" has done extensive study detailing the Grey alien/human collaboration and the reality of underground bases, sometimes at risk to his own life. In a privately-circulated research paper that I was able to obtain, he states,

Although it may sound unbelievable, several dozen sources claim that hundreds of people are being held captive in a 7th sub-level of a massive underground complex beneath the Archuleta Mesa west of Dulce, northwestern New Mexico. This enormous complex, much of which (especially the lowest levels) may be of very ancient origin, is allegedly being occupied (according to John Lear and many other sources) by the reptilians and, especially in the upper levels, several "controlled-manipulated" government-sponsored scientists. Some believe that this 'base' intersects with enormous cavern systems below.

The region beneath the four corners area of the southwestern U.S., according to some sources, is one of the major if not the major center of activity of these non-human beings in North America (although there are apparently other centers of activity beneath other continents — i.e. aside from Mount Archuleta in North America, there is Mount Illampu in South America; the Pine Gap plateau in Australia; the Himalayan Mountains of Asia; the island of Malta in Europe; and such activity also allegedly exists beneath Africa and Antarctica as well)...

In 1979, according to Lear's intelligence and CIA sources, a group of government scientists and workers managed to penetrate into the lower depths of this underground complex [at Dulce], and were horrified when they suddenly came across a huge chamber filled with the remains of untold numbers of human mutilation victims. Some of these remains were apparently those of children (Lear and his sources believe that many of these may be some of America's missing children!). This, and other indications suggest that there may be a hidden holocaust taking place deep underground which may make Hitler's 'final solution' appear insignificant by comparison.

The workers had no sooner discovered the 'Horrible Truth,' as some now refer to it, when they themselves were taken captive by the infernal creatures which controlled the deeper levels of this labyrinth; but not before these workers were able to warn other government workers (who were able to escape and warn their superiors) about what was really going on.

When MJ-12 and other deep-level government agencies learned of the situation, they decided to send in Special Forces units (Delta Forces and Blue Berets) based at Fort Collins, Colorado (N.R.O. or National Recon Organization headquarters) to attempt to seize the base and set free the people who had been captured. When the blood bath was over nearly 66 of the special forces were dead and the 'base' was not taken.

Aside from the large underground bases jointly occupied by the aliens and the military, the aliens have branched out, building additional tunnels and underground installations, and taken over pre-existing caverns to which humans not connected to the Secret Government have little access — except sometimes by accident. This has happened so often that it may be considered "S.O.P.", the standard operating procedure of the Grey alien forces. In the interests of a clear estimation of the alien situation, "Branton" segments the alien occupation into the various 'branches' located in the subterranean areas of the United States:

These 'branches' are basically as follows (i.e. areas of intense subterrain activity based on numerous accounts):

SOUTHERN BRANCH: Down along the border of Arizona-New Mexico and then into the Salt River Valley-Superstition Mountains, area of southeast Arizona and again spreading out towards Pie Town and Datil, Las Cruces, Dona Anna Mountains, Organ Mountains, Carlsbad, Guadalupe Mountains, New Mexico. From here reports of subterrain activity tend to reach south long the Guadalupes, toward the region of Dallas, and also the Big Bend region of Texas and on down into Mexico, Guatemala, and eventually South America;

NORTHERN BRANCH: North along the border of Colorado-Utah, stretching towards the Uncompagre Mountains, Creed, Colorado Springs, Pikes Peak, and then again up through eastern Utah and into southern Idaho and up towards the Mount Teton region of Wyoming;

WESTERN BRANCH: This tends to stretch along the Utah-Arizona border past Page, towards the Black Mountains area and then southern Nevada military complex, and on into southeast California through the general region encompassed by 29 Palms Marine Base, The Devil's Playground, Death Valley, Panamint Range, Fort Irwin, El Paso Mountains, etc., and on towards the San Francisco region and then upwards twoards Clear Lake, Mount Lassen, Mount Shasta, and then up through the region of Salem, Oregon, then up to Mount Rainier, etc.;

EASTERN BRANCH: Eastward through northern New Mexico, Los Alamos, San Cristobel, Taos, etc., and into northern Texas and then southern Oklahoma — Sulfur Springs, Bromide Springs, Binger, McCallister, etc., and then eastward through northern Arkansas — Cushman, Ozark Range, etc., and on into the Kentucky-Tennessee region — Sweetwater, Tennessee, Salem, Mammoth, Lexington, etc., KY., while a 'side branch' seems to run north towards Chicago and then into southern Minnesota. From Kentucky-Tennessee this area of activity tends to run through West Virginia — Helevita and Newville area and through northern Virginia and Maryland — Mount Weather/Blumont, Washington D.C. region, and again into southern Pennsylvania — Allegheny Mountains, Pittsburgh, Dixonville, etc., and then fanning out into western New York State — Salamanca, Syracuse, and again towards Hartford, Connecticut and Mount Moodus and then towards New York City and Boston, and the White Mountains of New Hampshire, and also into southeast Canada — Toronto, Lake Ontario, Schefferville on the Quebec-Newfoundland border, etc.

The sites just mentioned are all areas out of which reports have emerged describing one or more of the following:
1. excessively large cavern systems,
2. Ancient tunnels or artificial excavations of unknown origin,
3. Subterranean recesses in which non-human creatures have been encountered,
4. Subterranean recesses in which human beings have been encountered.

This dissection of the truth of alien-human interaction continues with a detailed account of "U.S. Conflict Scenarios":

The following areas are sites where conflict between the human and serpent races [or Grey and other aliens] have taken place...

DULCE, NEW MEXICO — Site of the 'Dulce Wars' which broke out within the subterranean mega-complex after the insidious nature of the aliens became apparent. Human government scientists working with "other" societies (Blonds, etc.) allegedly discovered remains of thousands of mutilated human victims in deep and remote levels of the complex. Reptoids, Chameleons, Dracos, and Greys are some of the reptilian-saurian mutations encountered in this underground facility.

NELLIS RANGE, NEVADA — (Covering S-4, Dreamland, Mercury, Nevada Test Site, etc.). MJ-12 and "Benevolents" working together against Grays concentrated at Deep Springs, California and several other areas. The subterranean mega-complexes are varied and highly compartmentalized. Upper levels of this mega-complex are in human control while lower levels (some of which reportedly descend OVER 30 LEVELS and intersect extensive cavern systems below) are controlled by the Reptilians — Reptoids, Chameleons, Grays and OTHER grotesque reptilian beings. "Controlled" humans who are kept in subjection by manipulation, intimidation and fear to the reptilians also work in the lower levels. Everything here is "way out of control" and the situation is such that when a "Test Site" worker learns "too much" about alien activity and infiltration of the lower levels they often end up dead or missing.

MOUNT SHASTA, CALIFORNIA — Originally an anteduluvian outpost and later re-inhabited by an early post-deluvian society of tall, blond humans. This society apparently came in contact with the ever-expanding reptilian empire and like so many other societies — like the U.S. government, for instance — they at first were led to believe the "benevolent" facade utilized by the reptilians... In time it became apparent that the humans and reptilians could never co-exist and that the reptilians intended to continue in their plan to completely conquer and subdue humanity.

According to Thomas C. [a man who was employed at the Dulce Base, and came into contact with the aliens — Commander X] the "original owners" (or rather those creatures that would have us to believe they are the original owners — the Grays and their infernal allies, the Deros or Demon-Robots animated-possessed by fallen supernatural entities are going to wage war on Terra [or earth].

SALT LAKE CITY, UTAH — According to various accounts, an ancient system of tunnels and caverns exists beneath this area. Once apparently under human occupation, this society was eventually infiltrated by reptilian influences. Certain "controlled" humans are now being used by the reptilians. Also, certain "resistance" groups that are opposed to the reptilians are involved as well. According to one Salt Lake police-security officer, one section of this large tunnel network which spreads out and intersects different parts of the city, was broken into during construction of the cinemas in the lowest level of the Crossroads mall-plaza in the downtown section. Numerous individuals who attempted to explore these tunnels were never seen again, and perhaps partly because of this the entrances were sealed and police alarms were set in place.

This act of sealing tunnels after the disappearance of would-be explorers has been carried out by the officials of several countries (Malta, Peru, Greece, etc.). One security guard who expressed an interest in exploring these tunnels was warned by another co-worker that it wouldn't be wise for him to attempt to enter them as there was a danger that he would encounter the "Lizard" beings and not return. Such creatures were said to have been encountered in these tunnels...

DIXONVILLE, PENNSYLVANIA — Sometime during the 1940's, 15 miners turned up dead or missing underground after breaking into an ancient tunnel of unknown origin. Claw-like marks were seen on some of the dead miners. One eyewitness (according to an article by Stoney Brakefield which appeared in the July 14, 1974 issue of the Pennsylvania newspaper NEWS EXTRA) reported seeing a humanoid but not human, grotesque creature which was totally "alien."

There are many, many accounts of contacts between aliens and humans which have been taking place in these caverns and mines and other underground access points, most of them not going well for the humans involved. Note that not all of these locales are areas of alien occupation in any substantial numbers. Many times alien groups are sent out on "expeditions", searching for animals or unwitting humans for experimentation or for re-stocking depleted food larders. For a complete account of these subterranean areas of conflict, read my book Underground Alien Bases, available from Inner Light, address listed above.

Before going any farther, I would again like to warn those of you who are curious who are thinking about undertaking excursions into underground locations in your area in order to gather intelligence. Unless you are a skilled "spelunker" or cave explorer, I would caution you not to do it. It is that simple. Don't do it unless you are trained. Not only is cave exploring a dangerous occupation for the untrained, you may actually encounter what you are searching for; and that can be the most dangerous encounter of all.

In 1979 another player entered upon the crowded chessboard of earth, one who had hitherto not been much involved. After startling setbacks for the human forces at Dulce, Dreamland, and other locations, the American government petitioned the Benevolent Ones, whose earlier contacts had been rejected by President Eisenhower. An electronic communicator was used which had been left behind with the humans for precisely this purpose.

According to a top secret informant who is known as "Yellow Fruit," but whom I have known personally for over ten years, the Benevolent Ones immediately re-contacted the humans and began a collaborative effort with MJ-12 designed to tilt the war with the aliens in favor of the humans. I am also told that, due to the dark allegience of certain members of MJ-12 (to the Secret Government), this new human-extraterrestrial collaboration was immediately broadcast to the hostile Grey factions.

For an example of the incredible treacherousness which has been displayed by the alien Greys on several occasions, I would like to print a transcript of an interview with a government worker who was employed as an executive secretary at what is known as the A.T.C. (the Alien Technology Center) at [deleted] Air Force Base, a secret sub-facility at this location which has been in operation since the 1960s. It had been believed until recently that this area of [deleted] was under the control of the human forces and engaged in researches positive to human aspirations, but subsequent events showed that this had been a ruse fostered by the Grey aliens.

I met this articulate and perfectly rational young woman, who is still employed at [deleted] and continues to work as an informant for me, at a UFO convention in 1988 (I often travel incognito to UFO conventions to chat with the attendees because, along with the gawkers, the debunkers, and the merely curious, one also sometimes meets individuals with a real knowledge of the planetary situation). Through my years of attending these conventions I have, in fact, become somewhat of a minor "celebrity," and you might be surprised to find out the identity which I have assumed (it is quite possible that you have even met Commander X idly chatting over the merits of some book or film at a bookseller's table).

It was apparent to me after speaking with "Miss N" for a brief while, and after having her pull me aside to see the array of government identification cards which she carried in her wallet, that she knew about what she spoke. While she was terrified and was looking for someone to ease her mind about what she had witnessed at [deleted], she also was privy to an otherwise unreported instance of alien betrayal that had been apparently been approved by the higher-ups in the military. The brief transcript which follows is of a private talk I had with Miss. N, transcribed from audio tape, and commencing approximately 20 minutes into our discussion:

X: You alluded to a "shut-down" and a "coverup" at the ATC portion of the base in 1991? I hadn't heard about that. Could you give me some additional details about that?

Miss N: Yes. [uneasily]

X: Could you...

Miss N: I'm surprised you didn't hear about it considering your connections in the military. There were a lot of people at the ATC who knew about what happened at the time, and the word got around fast, but we were all really scared. Maybe I'm the first one who has talked about it off the base. I won't pretend that I'm not scared telling you about all of this... They came in, came right into the lab area...

X: Who came in? Military intelligence?

Miss N: It was totally transparent what happened, my God, who do they think they are? The talk had been going round that the scientists in Section G, which supposedly dealt with anti-gravity research from what I heard, had made a big breakthrough. They were all excited about it, and the girlfriend of one of the technicians had said something that I guess got around. We thought that was supposed to be the purpose of the center, to actually make scientific discoveries, so I guess nobody was trying to hide what they heard, but I guess that wasn't it, at all. It was only supposed to look like that.

X: I'm not quite following you. What happened?

Miss N: Really, I can't believe that you didn't hear about this. I heard that it was an directive straight from the Greys that was issued to the brass at the ATC... an ultimatum, I guess. I heard that even though they didn't want to, they had no choice. They terminated the scientists in Section G, and they tried to cover it up by...

X: Terminated? Do you mean...

Miss N: You know as well as I do that I don't mean "fired from their job." I mean they killed them, they killed four scientists in the ATC, and they tried to cover it up by pretending it was radiation poisoning. They sent the hit team into the compound...

X: Humans?

Miss N: Yes, I'm sorry to say that it was humans who did the job. They came into the lab dressed in radiation suits, and the alarms were going off. They came through the hallway outside my office, so I didn't actually see them, but I heard the shots. I was in the annex off of Section G, and I heard the shots, even though they used silencers. I heard the shouts and the crashing of equipment. It didn't last long, maybe three minutes total. I talked to others who told me about the radiation suits and the blood in the lab. You don't get blood from a radiation leak. They were getting too close to breakthroughs in anti-gravity, and they were terminated because of it. Maybe this can serve as a warning to others.

X: What do you surmise about what happened, in terms of actual control of the base?

Miss N: I think you understand as well as I do what the situation is. The research is a total fraud, a cover-up, and they're keeping the scientists pretty much tethered, giving them little bits and pieces of information and technology. They know that if we know what they know, then we can fight them, maybe even win. God help me, I hope no one saw me talking to you here.

Miss N's story is not that unusual, but is one of the more dramatic first-hand accounts that I have come across. I agree with her assessment that the alien forces and the Secret Government will stop at nothing to keep humanity in the dark about advanced technology, while at the same time pretending to offer it to us.

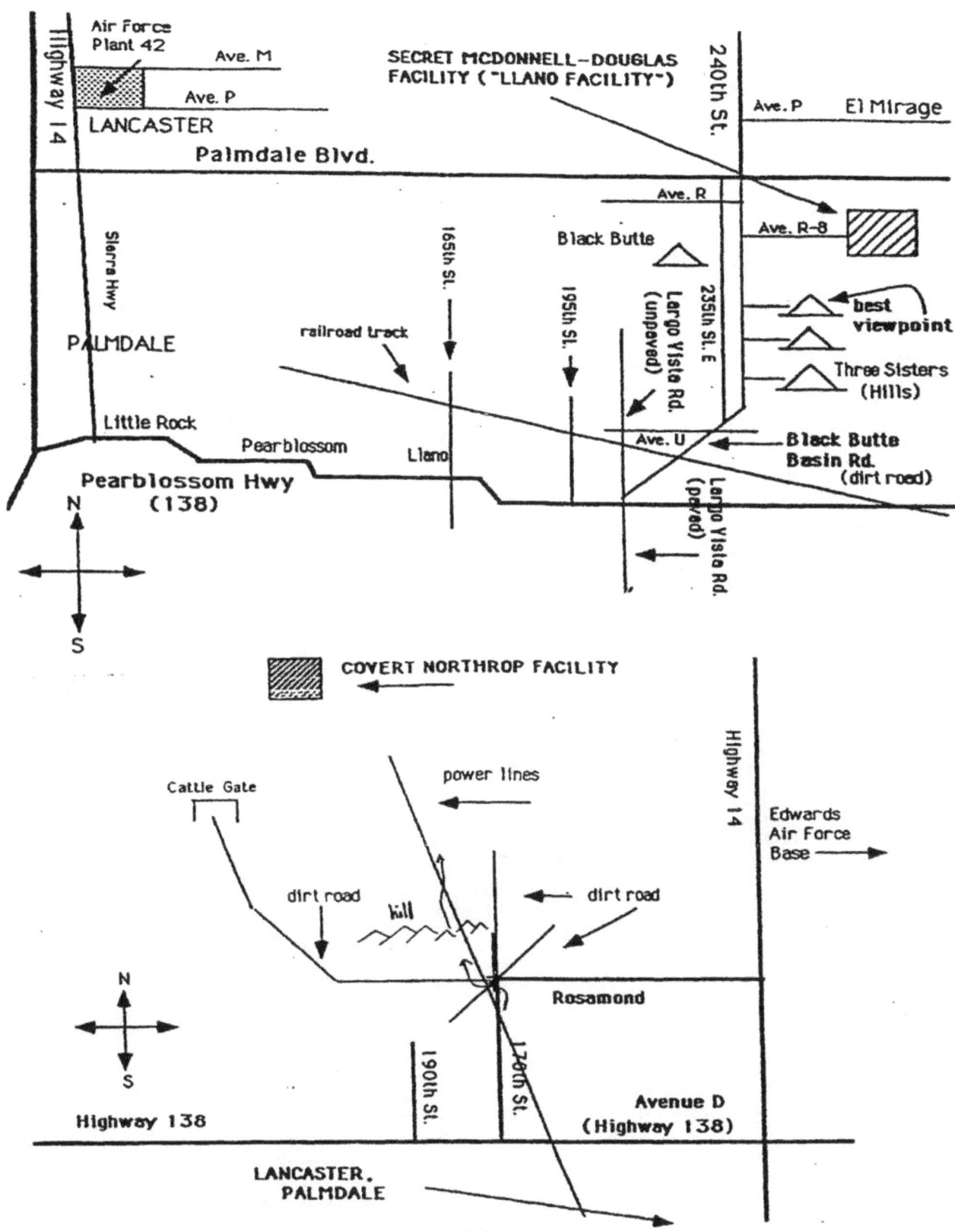

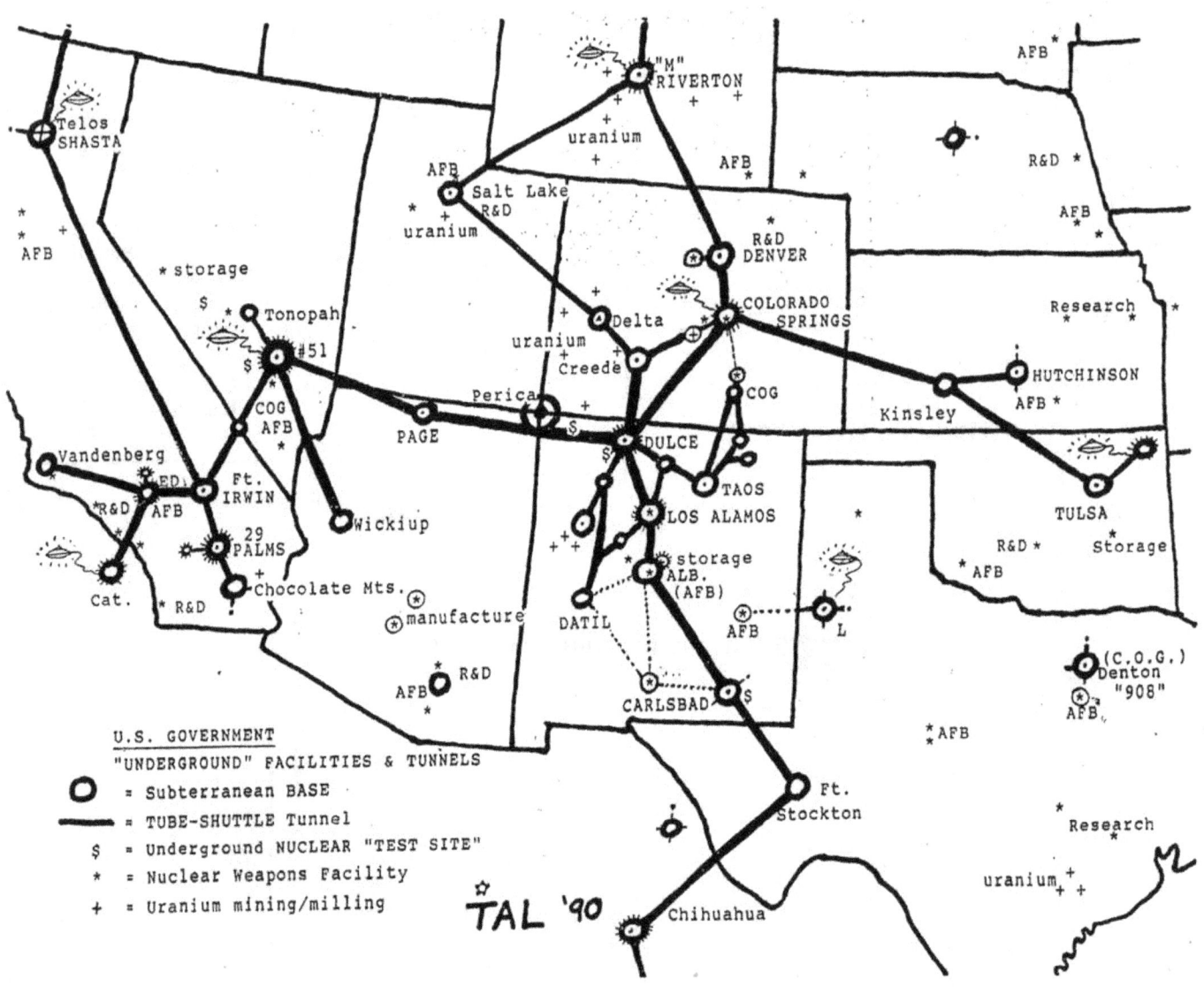

CHAPTER NINE

SECRET PROJECTS

In case I have given the impression that the locations of underground bases are limited to the United States, that is not the case. One base which is mentioned quite often in UFO literature, but about which very little in-depth information is offered, is the base at Pine Gap in Australia. Australian journalist Lucien H. Cometta has given a comprehensive run-down on this base, which was originally published in the third quarter of 1991 issue of Notes From the Hangar:

Soon after the start of the conflict in the Persian Gulf, the Australian media explained the missiles launched by Iraq were spotted by satellite, thanks to the heat they generated when launched. They said the satellite immediately sent the information to the US base of Pine Gap in Australia, that this information was instantly and automatically transmitted to Washington, D.C., and the allied H.Q. in the Near East. The signal sent by the satellite took only 3 or 4 seconds to rfeach the US High Command in the Gulf, although it transits via Australia.

Even in our times of knowledge and progress, this is a feat quite out of the ordinary, which requires electronic systems of very advanced technology.

But why, among all the bases Americans have all over the world, Pine Gap is the one to fulfill this task? What is Pine Gap base anyway? Why did the Americans install it in Australia? Many ask themselves those questions, but, for the time being, none have found any satisfactory answers.

Right from the start, during its building, this base was shrouded in the most absolute secrecy. No one knows exactly what it is, nor what the real purpose is. Members of the Federal Australian Government do not even know! Of course various and unexpected tales go around, probably mostly because it is built entirely underground. In fact, the little that is known about the base can be summer up as told in the following lines.

This top secret underground base is located west of Alice Spring, at the foothills of the southern slopes of the McDonnell Range. Only a few scattered buildings can be seen from the surface, and the secret entrances are practically invisible. It lies within 140 miles from the geographical center of Australia. Only a very small number of people have the knowledge of what is going on inside the earth around Pine Gap; the only information source available to the public are some vague statements made in a few US or Australian magazines, and anything strange or unusual the locals may notice.

It is said the deepest hole in Australia (5 miles deep) was drilled where the base stands, and that it could be used as an inground antenna, for the transmission of waves able to recharge batteries of submarines crusing in the Pacific or the Indian Ocean. It is also claimed a huge nuclear generator gives the necessary power to a new type of radio transceiver. It is possible a high-voltage plasma accelerator was installed by the Americans, in order to transmit electric current, or maybe to produce a "Death Ray." It might also simply be used to feed a plasma gun. Is it possible that the technology used in the base makes it possible to transmit an electric current powerful enough to recharge a submarine's high-voltage batteries? Some say that that is the reason why US submarines trail a wire antenna.

While the base was being built, people of the area saw big 30 foot discs bearing the Air Force emblem being unloaded from the USAF cargo planes. It is quite possible that they could be used in assembling some sort of flying saucers, since it is known one of the research projects done there concerns Electromagnetic Propulsion (EMP). The frequent and numerous UFO sightings in the area convinced the locals something of the kind was going on there. Another thing is even more surprising: an astronomical quantity of pieces of furniture of all kinds was delivered by plane from the States. The quality of that furniture would put a five-star hotel to shame! The locals also saw an astronomical amount of foodstuffs brought in from the USA, and presumably taken to a huge underground warehouse, in what could very well be a multi-level underground city.

The official name of the Pine Gap facility is: Joint Defense Space Research Facility. It is entirely financed by the Americans. It is known to be the most important center for the control of spy satellites orbiting around the earth, and that with its sister-base in Guam, it is also used for the control of photogaphic missions fulfilled by big American satellites. It is claimed the quality of the photos is such than a 7 1/2" object can be easily seen and identified on the pictures.

It is said that in this underground facility a very important number of computers with the latest technical updates can be found. They are reported to be connected to the main computer centers in the US and Australia, storing information not only on finance and modern technology, but also, it is claimed, on most ordinary citizens (like you and me). In addition, the computer network thus created, is connected to identical facilities in Guam, Krugersdorp in South Africa, and the underground US base of Amundsen-Scott in Antarctica.

The most disturbing rumor about Pine Gap, is that most of the people who work there have been brainwashed, and that some have even had intracranial implants put in their brains to ensure their unconditional obedience to the masters!

As you would have it, EBE (Extraterrestrial Biological Entities) are said to live in these underground installations. In that case, we would expect to hear reports of abductions and animal mutilations on a fairly big scale in Australia, and particularly in the Pine Gap region. Yet, no information could be had about the number of abductions or the ocurrence of animal mutilations in the area. Around 1986 the Australian police only mentioned a little over a hundred persons disappeared without leaving any trace during the two or three previous years.

One aspect of the secret war between humanity and the aliens has been the SDI or Strategic Defense Initiative, more popularly known to the public as the Star Wars program. This program was ostensibly presented as a space-based weaponry system to protect America from Russia and other potential nuclear missile threats, but was actually the government response to the messy situation at Dulce, Dreamland, and at other underground strategic locations. Under the cover of the military's Star Wars program, the above ground Los Alamos facilities and the Nevada Test Site worked on the development of the "Excalibur" nuclear strike capability, which is intended to penetrate deep into the earth and destroy alien underground bases. The Excalibur program was run, according to the information I have, by the famous nuclear physicist Edward Teller, also a member of MJ-12.

One of the most recent secret projects primarily intended to combat the alien menace is HAARP, the High Frequency Active Auroral Research Project, based in Gakona, Alaska. HAARP consists of 33 acres and 180 72-foot tall towers that look like giant clothes lines. These towering antennae are aimed straight up toward the sky, and have the ability to focus their microwave energy at specific targets in the upper atmosphere. HAARP, like so many projects fostered in the secret Grey alien-Secret Government collaboration, is a two-edged sword that can cut us deeply as well as defend us. It can be used both by the aliens against humans and by the patriotic factions of the government against the aliens.

The anti-alien aspects of the HAARP program provide the capability to disable and knock down incoming saucer craft, but also to chart the subterranean regions of the earth. HAARP is planned to be used to locate alien underground bases using its almost X-ray like capabilities, while the Grey alien program's purpose is to induce mind control in the human populace.

HAARP is our best technological hope so far in terms of defense against the Greys, but seeing as how the project is thoroughly infiltrated by alien influence at the uppermost levels, it looks to me like it may be another false hope for mankind.

Another betrayal by the aliens which created a crisis within American intelligence that was on the scale of the defection of the Soviet spy Kim Philby from British intelligence, was an alien "mole" or spy within military intelligence. This person was a human/reptilian halfbreed whose features had been altered through advanced cloning technology so that he was unrecognizable from those of a human. The "mole" was reportedly discovered when he lost a contact lens, and it was revealed that he had a vertical slit eye.

After the "mole" was captured and locked up his quarters were searched and found to be a virtual communications hub relaying SDI and other technology to the Grey aliens on a day-to-day basis. During his interrogation the human/reptilian died, although it is not known whether he simply willed his heart to cease or perhaps was terminated through some unknown technology controlled by his masters. He would have been too valuable an asset to the patriotic members of the American government for them to have done him in.

CHAPTER TEN

NO ALTERNATIVES

Another, and perhaps the most horrendous of the projects that were launched by the aliens in tandem with the Secret Government were the "Alternatives," with the primary program implemented being Alternative 3, which I have already mentioned earlier in these pages. This was a scheme for the members of the Secret Government of earth to escape the planet, after it was determined by scientists that pollution and global warming were going to render the earth unsuitable for habitation.

For informational purposes, Alternative 1 was a scheme to detonate nuclear bombs in the atmosphere in order to dissipate pollution, while Alternative 2 involved the construction of the underground bases, where the Secret Government would escape when planetary conditions became unlivable. Naturally this was only one reason for the construction of the underground bases.

Whether the Alternative 3 scheme is actually true or just a manufactured ruse to throw us off the track, I'm not sure. I do not that in many of the public statements of individuals connected to the Secret Government, they often champion theories and plans which seem to be in alignment to the Alternative 3 contingency.

According to Alternative 3 documentation, the labor required to build bases on the Moon and Mars was to be provided, according to informants and secret documents, by de-sexed and mind controlled humans abducted from earth. Perhaps those extraterrestrial bases were intended to be interim Paradises that would be inhabited by the members of the Secret Government; at least until the earth had healed sufficiently enough for a return to the planet.

Was the Alternative 3 plan ever implemented, or was it just a wild pipe dream? We do know, at least, that several Moon and Mars bases were built. I have photographs of them, and these installations cannot be mistaken for natural formations.

I have discussed the details of Alternative 3 elsewhere, and the topic has been treated by a number of knowledgeable researchers. Some have doubted the truth of Alternative 3, and I admit that there may be aspects of the story which has surfaced through these second hand sources which are disinformation. For my own part, there are certain telltale notes in the original book (Alternative 3, Avon Books, 1979) that suggest to me that the authors were intimately familiar with the world of spy agencies and covert operations; these are things that it is unlikely the authors would been aware of without an intimate knowledge of the activities of the clandestine services.

Whatever the truth of the matter, for the Doubting Thomases I would like to print the text of several Alternative 3 memos which I received a number of years ago through a reliable informant:

Here are the texts of the Alternative 3 memos:

POLICY COMMITTEE
Dept. 5
Attn: Dept 7
Re: Batch Consignment Components

April 6, 1972
National Chief Executive — Dept. 5
MEMO TO ALL DEPARTMENTS

Dept. 1,2, & 3 have reported that with the current interest in various forms of occultism and a movement away from the more traditional lifestyles of society, it should now be considered that we target occult-minded people who actively engage in de-socialization in their peer groups and mystical teachings. These persons are particularly susceptible to any sort of story which will be concocted by departments manufacturing propaganda, and should provide a rich source of components for projects.

POINTS OF CONSIDERATION

1. These people leave the establishment and thus their families and friends to find "peace and harmony." Point: If missing, it is thought of as simply a hippie notion to leave society behind. Whatever the case, they are less likely to be missed than productive members of society.

2. Because these people leave family and friends behind they are safe targets for batch consignment components and, after appropriate measures, can be provided for immediate shipping. Also, they are safe targets for batch consignment components. Also, they are susceptible to any occult type of brainwashing and conditioning so long as it is hedged in spiritual gobbledygook or attributed to some guru from India.

3. Dept. 4 has agreed and studied the matter, and will produce an array of appropriate electronic effects for further convincing the populace and, particulary, the mem-

bers of these occultist groups of the truth of their beliefs. This can be done starting on an individual basis using the same technology which has been utilized for this purpose in the past. Another means of convincing selected parties would be through the use of electronic broadcasts putting appropriate words and messages in their heads. Dept. 4 has also advised that Dept. 2 create a plan by which "extraterrestrials" have come to earth to save these people.

It is not even necessary that we utilize the survices of our real collaborators, as our special effects groups are perfectly able to simulate this kind of extraterrestrial contact. In previous experiments in this area, we find that people who are dissatisfied with society are ready to believe that beings from another world will save them, enlighten them, give them power, etc.

One way of encouraging these beliefs and paving the way for more grandiose contact is through the subsidizing of publishing efforts which will portray the aliens as benevolent providers of wisdom, and "Elder Brothers." This is certain to be an approach which will find eager believers in the occultist and New Age movements, and may even provide additional sources of funding.

As per policy, any monies accrued during these activities should be duly noted in agents' reports, but are allowed as rewards for a job well done. See Files EX-2hT88 and EX-99LjY.

4. It is further believed that Dept. 3 and Dept. 1 can help out in their expertise.

Under separate cover, please find the notations and minutes of this meeting dated March 5, 1972. Please note the psychological profiles and the experiments to prove the theories of Dept. 2., along with an appended list of occult organizations, UFO groups, book publishers, and New Age groups which may be contacted and whose leaders will be easily persuaded to assist us with these projects (or will be replaced with suitable persons).

POLICY COMMITTEE
OFFICE OF THE CHAIRMAN
SPECIAL REPORT
Re: Sept. 2, 1965
De-sexing October 1, 1971
De-sexing January 6, 1974
De-sexing TO ALL NATIONAL CHIEF EXECUTIVES

A somewhat unpleasant matter to consider, but necessary: The process of de-sexing, recuperation, and its attendent costs and labour have outweighed the benefits it has heretofore provided, and is not conducive to the purpose and aims of the A-3 project. The document of Oct. 1, 1971 outlines some of these concerns.

As of January 8, 1976 we have concluded that:

1 — Medical de-sexing is a detriment as it incurs depression and a low work rate.

2 — It is time and monetarily draining on our resources, when far less expensive procedures including drugs and selective implants are available to us.

3 — We do not have the medical personnel to keep up with our needs in this area, even given recent push for technicians

to be drafted into the program through the usual incentives.

4 — More importantly, there is evidence of medical tampering when a person is brought back to earth, and this could potentially result in a public relations disaster if any of these consignments were traced back to source.

We have concluded at the last board meeting of National Chief Executives that the alterations must be done, from now on, on a psychological level, not medical, using the wide variety of technologies which are at our disposal.

Dept. 3, with the help of Dept. 1 & 2 have established, on precedent of the Act of 1972, that those people who break from the socialization of earth society, have a tendency to "alternative thought and answers," and that this tendency can be utilized to the benefit of the program. In this case, our current line of defence in de-sexing is to create within the Wiccan, occult, UFO and New Age establishments a line of thought concerned with "alternative sexuality," which will make our recruitment techniques all that much more easy.

This was experimented with from 1968-1974 under jurisdiction of Tech JL399, with working groups in Dept.s 1, 2, & 3. Their conclusion is that certain people who wish to escape traditional society and even traditional mysticism and occultism, often turn to homosexuality and lesbianism. This provides a basis for de-sexing, on a psychological level, as well as supplies us with a social forum in which to collect batch consignment components. Also, many of these people who opt for an "alternative" sexuality and lifestyle leave their loved ones (families and friends), because of their lack of acceptance by same. There is abundant literature of a psychological nature suggesting this, and quotes should be obtained for spokesmen to use during interviews with media sources. The severing of these links is very important to us so as to not draw batch consignment components from tightly knit socially acceptable groups of people.

Thus, Depts. 1,2, & 3 are in the process of setting up Wiccan, Neo-Pagan, New Age, UFO, and occult-type groups who draw on these anti-social elements of society, and have initially been meeting with tremendous success — further reports on this to follow.

Is it not ironic that they use the word ALTERNATIVE to describe their lifestyles?

The Chairman
POLICY COMMITTEE SPECIAL NOTICE FROM THE CHAIRMAN
April 7, 1977
SPECIAL CLASSIFICATIONS

Note that as of the meeting on January 24 of this year, all departments are now to have a specialized classification. The reclassification is as follows, while all departments remain subsidiary to Dept. 7. Dept. 1 will be in charge of all surveillance programs and be responsible for the location and targeting of potential/non-suspicious batch consignments in quantities sufficient to our needs. They will target those who will not be missed by family or associates, and report on all those groups which tend to have social misfits as members. Dept. 2 will take charge of all planning and operations to secure access to said groups and people, as well as setting up said groups to attract these misfits. Payments will be made to the heads of some of these groups to provide us with opportunities for this kind of "recruitment" from their ranks, and when these persons are not amenable to such incentives, then they should be replaced or re-molded using the standard avenues. Most persons who have already been contacted have proved to be very amenable to reasoning, after their position has been clearly explained and the benevolent and humanitarian purposes of the Alternative 3 project have been described to them. Dept. 3 will concern itself with infiltration of these groups and developing standard procedures for same. Dept. 4 will be in charge of all electronic effects necessary, and if this falls in the purview of your department, contact Dept. 4. Costs should be sustained by the contracting department, of course. Dept. 5 will provide reports on all suitable occult and UFO- type groups and people who can be targeted as components. The members of these groups number in the hundreds of thousands, so there will be no shortage of able bodied types. Dept. 5 will also set up occult, New Age and similar-type groups to break down the resistance of members so they will be susceptible to our control. New Age centers should be set up entirely for the purpose of obtaining batch consignments, although care must be taken that this is not done in a noticeable manner. Dept. 6 will work with Dept. 5 and disseminate to target publics effective propaganda of such a character as to attract those who are extremely gullible. They will be in charge of Deception and Belief. We strongly recommend that they work the Wiccan and New Age circuits, especially in the U.S. Glossy brochures and other handouts based upon proven and surveyed public "buttons" will be generated by this department as necessary. Dept. 7 remains as is, and is in charge of batch consignment components and their transportation.

POLICY COMMITTEE
OFFICE OF THE CHAIRMAN
August 27, 1982
Attn: Nat'l Chief Executive Officers
Re: BATCH CONSIGNMENTS

Each designated mover will, it is estimated, require back up labour consisting of 8 able bodies. These bodies, which will be transported in cargo batch consignments, will be programmed to obey legitimate orders without question and their principal initial duties will be in construction.

Priority will naturally be given to the building of accomodation for the designated movers.

However, it is stressed that, in the interests of good husbandry, accomodation will also be provided for the human components of batch consignments — as well as for relocated animals — as a matter of urgency. The completion of this accomodation, which will be of a more basic and utilitarian nature than that allocated to designated movers, will in normal circumstances take precedence over the erection of laboratories, offices, or other places of work, and recreational centres.

All exceptions to this rule will require written authorization from the Chairman of the Committee in Residence.

It is estimated that the average working life-span of human batch-consignment components will be fifteen years, and in view of high transportation costs, every effort will be made to prolong that period of usefulness.

At the end of that life-span they are to be considered disposable units, for although this is recognized as regretable, there will be no place for low-grade passengers in the new territory. They would merely consume resources required to sustain the continuing influx of designated movers and would so undermine the success potential of the operation.

Preliminary work is now progressing to adapt batch-consignment components, mentally and physically, for their projected roles and the scope of this experimental work is to be widened. Further details will be provided, when appropriate, by Department 7.

Pre-transportation collection of batch-consignment components will be organized by National Chief Executive Officers who will be supplied with details of catagories and quantities required. No collection is to be arranged without specific instructions from Department 7.

The Chairman
Policy Committee Director
SbGGy/773-7-6

Although I am not ruling out that these memos have been faked for some disinformational purpose that I am unable to fathom at the moment, the imprints and expensive printing on the originals suggest that the documents are either real or an extremely elaborate hoax. My tendency is to suspect that they are factual, and the gobbledygook of their language suggests "bureaucrat-ese" at its best (or rather, its worst).

So there is a brief rundown on the alien and the government situation, specifically focusing in the United States and on the Alternative 3 project. Now you know what I knew prior to my abduction.

INNER LIGHT
THE VOICE OF THE NEW AGE

ISSUE #28 – INCLUDES UPDATED BOOK CATALOG

WORLDWIDE EXCLUSIVE: ALIEN IMPLANT REMOVED FROM WOMAN ABDUCTED BY UFOS

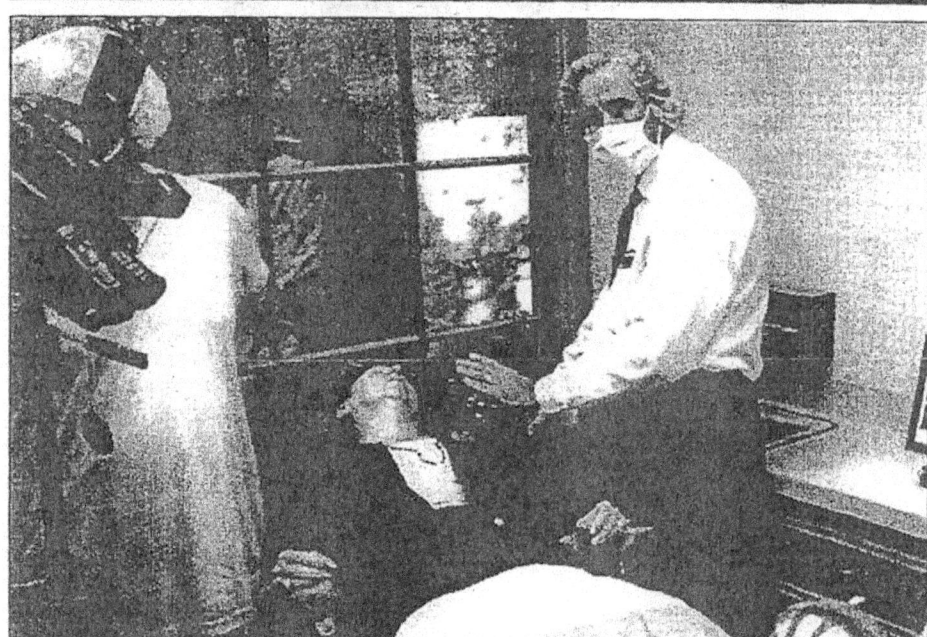

Those attending the Rocky Mountain UFO & New Age Expo will have the opportunity to hear Houston researcher Derrel Sims discuss his work in the operation room with doctors as they remove implant left in a woman by extraterrestrials.

Contacting Derrel Sims

If you have medical or physical evidence, including pictures, film, X-rays, substances, etc., that you believe may be somehow connected to the UFO phenomenon, please call Derrel Sims at 713-587-5455 or write to him at P.O. Box 60944, Houston, TX, 77205. His web page is at www.compass-net.com/~dwsims.

NASA SP-5094

IMPLANTABLE BIOTELEMETRY SYSTEMS

A REPORT

By
Thomas B. Fryer
Ames Research Center

Technology Utilization Division
OFFICE OF TECHNOLOGY UTILIZATION   1970
NATIONAL AERONAUTICS AND SPACE ADMINISTRATION
Washington, D.C.

This is the fourth transmitter in my head and it was inserted in connection with an appearance at Nacka Police station, just outside Stockholm, on 26th November 1975, ostensibly for interrogation. I was locked up in a cell, but after a short while I fall into a deep sleep from which I emerge to an entirely new life. It is during these hours when the transmitter is implanted, and when, I awake I have a seering highfrequency signal at about 100 dB in my skull. This was to plague me for about 16 hours a day for the past 8 years and completely transform my life. It depressed the functional capacity of my right cerebral hemisphere and altered my personality, behaviour and abilities as if they no longer were part of myself. This torture finally ceased during 1983.

REMOVED
This is the first transmitter implanted in my head: it was inserted during an operation at Söder Hosptial in 1967 under the authorisation of surgeon Curt Strand. A great many Swedish doctors, as well as the Swedish National Board of Health and Welfare (N.B.H.W) have refused the presence of the transmitter in radiographs, yet it was surgically removed at a private clinic in Athens in March 1978.

REMOVED
After having the 1967 transmitter surgically removed in Athens in March 1978, leaving it for analysis to New York University, I returned home in June only to find myself arrested for fraud. After one month of being detained, a fresh transmitter was suddenly activated; it had been placed som low down in my right nostril that it was possible to feel the top with the finger and visible to a doctor with the aid of a nasal specula, an instrument with which one can inspect the nasal passages. This transmitter was surgically removed in Athens, in 1982 but can be clearly identified on other x-ray pictures.

Professor P.A. Lindstrom wrote in one of his statements concerning this and other x-ray pictures; "I can only confirm that some foreign objects, most likely brain transmitters have been implanted at the base of your frontal brain and in the skull. In my opinion there is no excuse for such implantations. I fully agree with Lincoln Lawrence who in his book on page 27 wrote; "There are two particulary dreadful procedures which have been developed. Those working and playing with them secretly call them R.H.I.C. and E.D.O.M. - Radio-Hypnotic Intra-cerebral Control and Electronical Dissolution of Memory..."

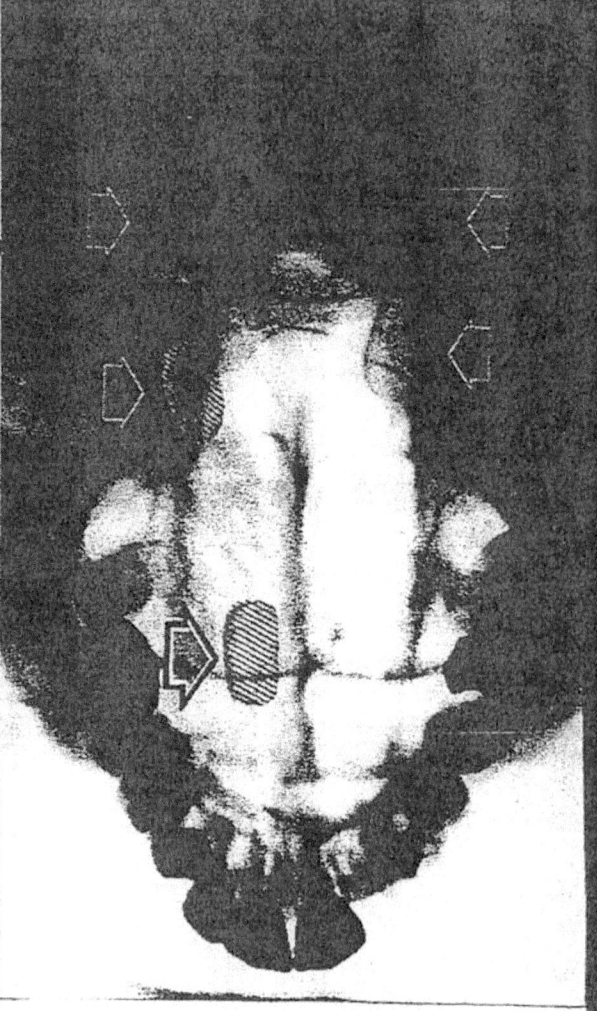

This is a detail on an x-ray photograph taken directly from above. In the centre are the nasal passages and the dark semi-circular area are the teeth in the upper jaw. The picture was taken at Karolinska Hospital where all radiographers deny that any foreign object can be identified in this picture. However, there are a number of overseas physicians who testify the obvious fact, that several transmitters can be seen quite clearly.

ROBERT NAESLUND

This is the third transmitter placed in my head and the first which was embedded in my brain. Without doubt it was implanted while being detained by the police in Stockholm 1973; this was my first period of custody and afterwards I underwent considerable personality modification, a process which had already begun in 1967 but accelerated rapidly towards criminality after the implantation of the second transmitter.

This is the second implanted transmitter; this device appeared under rather unusual circumstances on 10th March 1972 when I became tranquillised in the hotel where I was temporarily lodging. This implantation preceded a period of prolonged torture with personality-altering radio signals 10-20 hours a day and they started communicating directly with my brain. It was then I realised that they could dicern my thoughts and, indeed, experience my entire range of cognitive activity. The transmitter ceased functioning almost a decade later and with it the communication with my thoughts and the destructed signals.

CHAPTER ELEVEN

TIME BOMB

After I woke up from the abduction which took place August 7-8, 1995, I at first thought that I had dreamed the whole encounter, suffering from an imagination strained by the type of materials and people that I come in contact with over the past few years. Or perhaps I hoped that I had dreamed up the abduction, and that all I had to factually contend with were human intelligence agency forces who were searching for me.

As I have given it some consideration, I have come to the conclusion that I was probably subliminally programmed to believe that it had all been a dream; it would have served the aliens' purposes better if I had believed that and had written it all off as delusion. But I couldn't shake the terrible experience which I was subjected to that night, and it continued to trouble me even though my recall of the event was virtually nil.

Imagine: I speak to many researchers into the area of alien deception and control, as well as quite a few members of intelligence organizations both domestic and foreign, and I am often given interviews with people with knowledge of the Secret Government/alien collaboration, as well as sensitive documents of varying degrees of secrecy. My belief is that it would have been very valuable to the hostile aliens to monitor my day-to-day activities and my communications and contacts with qualified researchers, in fact it would have given them access into the areas of the most dedicated resistance to their efforts to control the world.

Could it have been that I had not only been tracked down by elements of American government intelligence, and possibly other intelligence agencies, but also that I had been monitored by the aliens all along? Because I knew that they (at least certain hostile alien factions) were the real enemy on this planet. Certainly the spy forces of the world had engaged in a great deal of evil and mayhem, but the acts of those men was nothing compared to the long term control program of earth that the aliens had mounted.

What had happened after I had gone unconscious, "whited out" as I put it earlier in the book? After that, my memory ended, and try as I might I could not summon up even a scrap of memory about what had taken place once I was inside the saucer.

Had I been programmed by whoever had been inside the disk craft?

Had I been implanted with an electronic control or monitoring device, the kind that so many of the people I had been in contact with or interviewed had?

Or had I perhaps been intercepted by a human intelligence force, and programmed to think that I had had an alien encounter, masking the real nature of the event?

In fact, it was quite possible that I could be a walking time bomb constructed by the Grey aliens or by some clandestine human agency: if I had been implanted, then I could lead them right into the heart of the resistance movement to their plans for world control.

Now I knew that I could not safely contact any of of my friends, anyone in the intelligence community who I knew, or any of my fellow researchers, even though I would have dearly loved to have been able to talk to someone about what had happened to me.

I knew that some of my regular contacts would fear the worst if I disappeared from sight, particularly that small group of dedicated individuals who have pretty much given up private life in the interests of freeing mankind from bondage to the Grey aliens.

Did you know that there are individuals actively working on a day-to-day basis to stop the alien plans to overthrow the human control of earth? In my earlier books I have mentioned a number of authors whose work reflects what I believe to be the truth, and they are still carrying on the essential work of discovering the truth and getting out that information to the public. What I have not mentioned except perhaps in hints here and there is that within the past few years several covert groups have been formed with the express purpose of resisting alien control.

You've heard of the "Men in Black"? Call this group the "Men in White," if you like, although none of them would choose to be so obvious as dressing in uniform fashion. Perhaps it has more to do with white light than it does dressing in any particular color.

The resistance of these patriots takes many forms, although the most sensitive and classified forms cannot be mentioned in these pages for fear of alerting the enemy to the projects which they are currently engaged in. Still, I can mention some things that the resistance movement is concerned with.

One vital effort consists of getting out factual information to the public and investigation and monitoring of UFO sightings and encounters, but this thrust also has involved the scouting of suspected areas of alien occupation (both above ground and subterranean locations). There is a technical corp affiliated with the resistance movement, also, whose chief projects have involved research into electronic weapons which may be used against the Grey and other hostile aliens and their craft, as well as another unit which has done extensive research into the electronic implants that the aliens use on unsuspecting abductees. That is pretty much all that I should say on that matter for the moment.

In the past few years I have been acting primarily as a research consultant to several of these associated groups, adding all of my notes and any significant written and photographic materials to their archives which exist at several locations on the planet, but I have also taken part in several missions which were not so theoretical in nature: reconnaissance missions.

At this time we have compiled information on a number of locations which conclusively prove the alien and human collaboration, but we are witholding these materials until certain intelligence sources would not be compromised, and until the time is right.

The humans involved in presenting a united resistance front to the aliens are a tough, dedicated group, and we owe them our respect and support.

UFO RADIO-RECORDER BEAM RECEIVER

©90 by Richard T. Woodmaster

How can anyone modify a standard or short wave radio and recorder pick-up special beamed signals from a craft out in space? The following instructions are an "attempt" to piece together available data and diagrams on a "stationary" directional beam set. To undertake this experimental project, will require basic electronic knowledge and skills to wire your receiver correctly and safely. I cannot guarantee the modified unit will operate for everyone, because the space people themselves make the final choice to open any communications via their power beams to operate this set! Due to the enormous quantity of information on this subject, and limited space within which to present it, only the most fundamental principles can be conveyed, as part of an overall concept. An open mind, able to consider and re-orient itself to understand any new or different concept and follow instructions persistently to advance and in turn assist others, makes the choice of two-way contact easier for them.

Concept, evidence indicates that UFOs possess a "multi-wave" power beam, that can be made to pulse, alternate, vibrate and directed to modulate up or down the spectrum. Any wave band, under certain conditions can be made to produce a polarity, charge and phase by the application of two or more band combinations heterodyning one by the other(s) vibrations to produce one or more conditions. The Magno-Solar Beam ionizes the air, making it a conductor and as these charged electrons move, magnetic fields are generated. As these wave particles jump, a vacuum, flash of visible or invisible light-photons, electromagnetic oscillations, gasses condense into a cloud vapor, audible, or inaudible, sound, and so on, can result. This omni-beam is the pivotal point or cause translated into a myriad of effects, which are but only different expressions of its utility. It has been given many names and words to define its functions or modes of operation, but is only proving that energy regardless of wave band, can be made to transfer through resonance either by a beam, standing wave or conductor, and for almost any use. The "type" wave and not the amount of power is important.

A beam radio transmission, with ultra short waves directed like a ray of light can pass readily through all ionized layers of the upper atmosphere and down to the earth's surface. Microwaves are effective between planets in the form of a beam, because they form their own conductor. Radio waves are not useable for outer space transmissions, because they require the atmosphere and ground as a conductor. The beam consists of two or more rapidly alternating or directed energy pulses, peaked resonantly on magnetic wavelengths to form ionized particles. These are modulated by compound resonant feedback on two or more bands, and synchronized or phase-tuned for tracking by an inverse proportion of amplitude and frequency modulation to resolve into one audio signal.

UFOs emit signals that can be "detected" because they interfere with conventional radio and electrical power transmissions. These signals sound like they carry several channels of information, similar to those used for telemetry data transmission from research instruments in satellites and balloons. This high speed pulse code is an almost unintelligible system of tones (or colors), in dots and dashes, more of which are used for each letter or number than used in Standard International Morse Code. The coded transmission may be received for tape recording and decoded later at slower speed, or to turn on power relay switches, tune oscillator circuits and slide through a given range of pretuned coil signals, for radio voice or TV picture messages.

The signal usually comes from a certain direction straight to the turned oscillator(s) of the receiver and not through any aerial antenna. When this portion of the radio is covered by your hands, the signal dims and static comes in. If the radio is off, a modulated electromagnetic beam aimed at the speaker coil or connecting wires can activate it. An audio speaker consists of an electromagnet which vibrates a cone of paper or plastic, and in turn the air to create sound waves. To pick up messages on voice coil by induction via a beam, requires a cold solder joint in the beat frequency oscillator (BFO) or audio circuit to act as a rectifier to the antenna.

The VHF and VLF bands for beam reception are seldom used to hear outer space messages, which is why these are chosen. For extra precaution, pulse signals are used, which sound similar to CW, and require the set be modified to remotely power and tune the receiver.

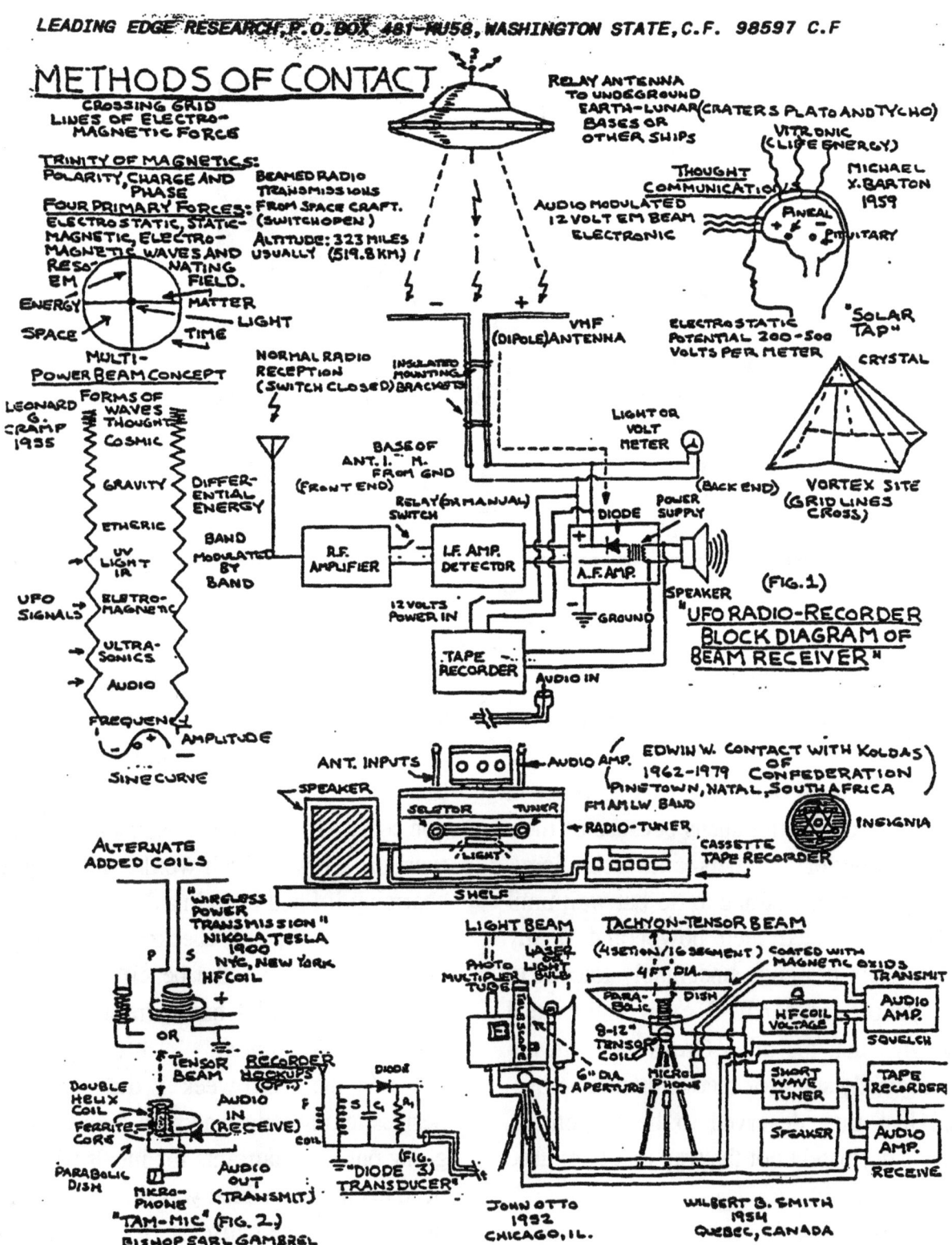

CHAPTER TWELVE

THE RETURN

After my abduction it seemed like I was existing in a hazy dream state. Without consciously choosing to have the thought, I knew that there was no point in trying to combat the aliens because of their vastly superior numbers and technology. Now there was nothing to do but wait until they consolidated their power and finally made their presence undeniably known to the people of earth. I even entertained thoughts that the alien Greys were an ancient, vastly superior race to human beings, and that they deserved to be in control. That's definately not the way that I am used to thinking!

Looking back, what was going on inside my mind should have been perfectly apparent to me, but given the programming I had received during my abduction, I remained in mystery and confusion.

After the abduction and return, I drove to a small community on the northern Oregon coast which sustains itself mostly off of tourism, a town which would have seemed charming if I had been in a different state of mind. Once there I checked into a small motel not far from the beach, deciding to cool my jets until I had formulated a plan about what to do next.

For the next week I did very little besides taking long walks on the beach and going out to restaurants for meals when the need to eat arose. That was the extent of my dedication to the cause of freeing the earth at that point. Frankly, I didn't even care if the men in the intelligence community found me in the condition that I was in, and I'm not sure if I would have even offered any resistance if they had wanted to "terminate me with extreme prejudice."

The truth was that I didn't care any longer after my abduction, not about humanity, not about Commander X, not about the Secret government, not about the aliens, be they Blond or Grey or Purple with little white spots. Although I didn't say it to myself in so many words, I knew that my life was essentially over for me and my compatriots, and that I had failed in my quest to help mankind.

I knew that resistance to the aliens was futile, that it was only a matter of time before they took complete control of the earth, and that all the work I had done was futile.

I don't know why, but at some point I took hold and tried to shake some sense into myself. I realized that I was probably programmed, and that the aliens (or perhaps some Secret Government intelligence operation) were probably the ones who were force-feeding the messages into my brain that my quest was useless. Down deep I, Commander X, knew that it was important to continue our battle against alien conquest even if it ended up in complete and ignominious defeat. And that was when I remembered an old friend, and thought about taking a desperate chance and contacting him.

I have long maintained a mail transferral point where I can send a letter and have it re-sent, in order to obscure the origin of my message. I had no idea if it was still functional, but I took a chance, taking another chance and including information in the letter about my whereabouts. The letter was forwarded to Professor C. in hopes that we could meet, and he could offer me his advice.

Professor C. is a brilliant psychologist and the author of a revolutionary research paper called "The Alien Mind" which, although remaining unpublished for security reasons, has circulated in photocopied editions among some of the leading figures in the UFO research community.

In his own way Professor C. has been struggling against the alien influence in the same way I have, but he reserves most of his efforts to a research project which provides therapy for those who have been traumatized by abductions and other kinds of encounters with the alien controllers. Professor C. has evolved a number of advanced techniques (both psychological as well as electronic) which he uses to counteract alien mind programming, and it seemed to me that that was exactly what I needed at the moment.

To give you an idea of the seriousness of Professor C.'s work, I am going to reprint, with his permission, a short segment from the beginning of his primary research paper. I am only reprinting the introduction because exact information of the techniques and knowledge that he has pioneered might endanger the future of his Starfire Project.

THE ALIEN MIND: Introduction
It began as a research project to investigate the sources of human fear and neuro-

sis and quickly took a turn that no one suspected. At this time, nearly six years after the initial investigations engaged in, and after the documentation of almost two hundred case studies, we believe that we have at least opened a window into understanding and future discovery.

Future work will, no doubt, provide new breakthroughs in the area of this research, as well as providing greater more effective therapies that obtain quicker and better results than those already accomplished. But for now we are at the threshold of a new and fantastic realm, delving into matters that have been kept secret for thousands of years. These are matters too important to the sanity and well-being of mankind to remain secret, and too important not to go forward.

Some of the subjects that are dealt with in this paper will surprise you. Some of it will test your ability for belief. Some of the information may scare you. But once this information has been revealed to you it will never be able to affect you and control you in the ways in which it has in the past.

The simple fact is that Mankind has been controlled by alien forces since ancient times. Throughout his history there has been an unseen stratum of control which few have even speculated about, and it is only by partial accident that we have been able to unlock the secrets that we have. All of the answers are not here, but at least we have accomplished a broad theoretical outline and some workable techniques providing roads which can be followed to greater discovery. It is my hope that qualified researchers will understand what I have outlined here and will work with the psychological, hypnotic, and electronic methods which I have provided in rudimentary fashion in this paper, to accomplish far more than I could alone.

The initial researches of this subject were undertaken in order to find out why people were not living up to their full capabilities in life. Why the vast majority of people who were consulted felt that, at least in some ways, they were suffering from unwanted anxieties, fears, and disabilities over which they had no control.

The initial researches led to the same kind of speculations that have been engaged in through the centuries as regards these matters. Using hypnotic and wide-awake regression therapy, the causes were sought for the various reasons that man seems to fail, in his government, in the street, in his home, and in his own self.

Preliminary researches led to various speculations, none of which, when applied, achieved the sorts of results that we were looking for in increasing the comprehension and abilities of people. We were looking for answers that, if applied one-for-one, could be counted on to provide results. It was at this point in the research that we realized that there must be unseen factors which we were not taking into consideration.

We had been regressing individuals in therapy back to times when they had experienced unwanted experiences in their lives, times, primarily in their childhoods, when they had felt loss, fear, pain, regret. Although getting the individuals in therapy to examine and to re-experience these incidents did, in many case, cause them to experience relief and in some cases actually cured them of some minor neuroses, habits, and other unwanted behaviors, it was extremely rare when this approach provided long term and lasting improvement.

And so another approach was tried. We had been concentrating on "real" events in the person's life, at least those events which we happened to believe were real. We had focused on happenings that could be verified by friends and family, and experiences that conformed to what we considered to be factual and not delusory events. And yet, applying ourselves to this kind of information, we found that we did not achieve the hoped-for results in terms of handling patients problems and disabilities. We decided to, shall we say, open up the floodgates of the mind, and to start to let the individuals recount their fantasies about events and to recount events that had happened to them which were "obviously" of a fictitious nature.

This was the approach that led to the data which began to resolve the question of human disability, and in addition opened wide the doors to a comprehensive theory of why man as a creature fails. This is the subject of THE ALIEN MIND. We present the results of these cases of investigation into the sources of human fear and insanity. If anything, we were more surprised when the seemingly impossible basis of these afflictions began to appear in case after case studied.

We found that the sources of human disability often did not stem from early childhood deprival or abuse, not from fears and confusions regarding Mother, Father, or The Opposite Sex. The source of the problems that beset the human mind stemmed from another unsuspected source: an Alien one.

As you read over the information that is compiled here, you will no doubt be shocked, shocked that the sources of mind behavior control have been successfully hidden for so long. If you are able to overcome those first initial fears you will be in a better position as a therapist or a research worker in this field to, not only conquer your fears, but also to consider the approaches that all Mankind must make to conquer the source of their fears, for that source is a singular one and, it seems, that the majority of human beings are subject to that source.

As earlier stated, our research training, in the beginning, consisted primarily of the standard approaches and techniques of mental therapy, and using those approaches we tended to devolve to the standard answers.

And the standard answers yielded only partial results.

We changed our techniques from the standard Freudian-pioneered approaches and, against our better judgement, began to research more "holistic" and traditional forms of therapy. This occupied a number of months in which dream recounting, free association, automatic writing and other less accepted methods of delving into the consciousness and subconsciousness were used.

These approaches, in fact, surrendered up much useful data. And then the thought occurred: perhaps the problem was not so much with the techniques which were used, the majority using standard memory, but perhaps the problem was with the researchers themselves.

Perhaps we were filtering out the very information that we were looking for, on the basis that it was illusory, fictitious, imaginary. This was the realization that ultimately led to results and to the improvement, and in many instances, the resolution of cases.

We stopped throwing out the fears, the dreams, the horrors and the mythologies of Mankind. We began to correlate and cross-check the content of dreams and of nightmares, the things that "couldn't possibly have happened". And that was the approach that finally netted results.

This manuscript is offered to you only because I am familiar with your work, and feel that the techniques which are here elucidated will be used by you. My belief is that the future of mankind depends on it.

In summation, we found that by throwing out "imaginary" incidents in the patients' lives, we were bypassing the very events which were actually causing them harm. This was the thinking that led us into researching alien abduction.

This has been a quote from Professor C.'s major written work. He goes on to detail a large variety of research and therapeutic approaches, most of which would be more appropriate to the trained researcher, rather than the casual reader. I offer this excerpt of Professor C.'s writing only to acquaint you with his thought processes.

And so, I took the chance (dangerous to both he and I) and contacted him. Within two days, Professor C. had put aside the important work that he was engaged in in his home state on the East Coast, and had flown to where I was living in Oregon.

The first thing that Professor C. did when he entered my motel room was to open up one of the two large briefcases that he had brought with him, extract a small hand-held electronic device, and begin a quick search for electronic bugs in the room. I quickly assured him that I had already done so, but he went ahead and completed his search with a negative result. Then we were relatively free to speak. If we were being monitored, then it was through a more sophisticated approach than an actual, physical electronic device.

After not much more than a quick greeting and the search for electronic bugs, Professor C. turned the television on. My first thought was that he was doing it to interfere with any other kind of electronic surveillance that might be going on, but in a moment I could see that wasn't the case. Professor C. carefully adjusted the television, turning the channel and working with the contrast knob until he had the picture just where he wanted it.

Later I talked to Professor C. about it, and he explained that he had developed a method for turning a television into a primitive kind of UFO detector! He said that he had learned the technique from another UFO investigator, and found that it worked with a good degree of accuracy, making it unnecessary to carry along the much more bulky instrument that he had formerly used for just that purpose. Although it wasn't perfect, the technique just possibly might afford us some warning of approaching alien craft.

According to Professor C.'s research, UFOs emit an electromagnetic field of great strength falling usually between 27 to 70 megacycles, although in certain instances the crafts emit electromagnetic waves which vary from this range. The television can access electromagnetic frequencies which partially fall within this range. Channel 2 detects signals from the 54-55 megacycle range.

He explained to me in detail the method that this kind of detector employed, and it may be of some use to other researchers, or to electronics buffs who may even be able to improve on the method:

The first step is to adjust the "contrast" on the television to maximum.

Next, turn to channel 13 with the channel selector.

After that, darken the television screen until it is just short of darkness, where there is still a bit of optical activity.

Now, turn to channel 2. If a UFO or other anomalous electromagnetic-emitting object is in the area, you will see white bands on the television screen. When the UFO is nearby or overhead the screen goes completely white. With an interior antenna you will be "reading" the electromagnetic spectrum for 5-10 miles. An outdoor antenna will read the electromagnetics of the area for up to 30 miles, and if you use a rotary antenna you can "follow" the UFO as it travels.

Throughout the day, as Professor C. and I talked and went over an assortment of documentation that he had brought with him, the television was on like a darkened, unseeing eye. Occasionally it would flicker, making us start and be silent for a moment, but then it would return to darkness.

Professor C. and I actually didn't engage in much small talk after his arrival, but confined ourselves to the nuts and bolts of the situation. Somehow we both sensed that time was short, and we both knew the reason that I had summoned him to my hiding place on the coast of Oregon.

After I had briefed Professor C. on what I knew about the encounter (which wasn't a great deal, to tell the truth) the Professor used a small sonic detector that he had brought with him to find out if I had been implanted with an electronic control device. The answer, he told me in short order, was an affirmative. I was stunned to realize that there was an alien device implanted in my head. Now there was no question of the abduction being a dream resulting from too much stress. Now I knew that I had been gotten to by the Greys.

U.S. Building Secret Prisons, Suit Charges

HOUSTON, Tex.—A suit now on file in U.S. District Court here alleges that the federal government has established secret concentration camps and mental hospitals for the purpose of jailing political dissidents for temporary confinement until they can be shipped elsewhere to undetermined fates.

The suit, filed by Houston businessman William R. Pabst, charges "that there exists at Livonia, Mich., ... an obscure military operation called the 300th Military Police, Prisoner of War Command."

This military camp, said Pabst, is used for the purposes of "detention (incommunicado and otherwise)" and as a "holding point for citizens of the U.S. for shipment elsewhere to undetermined fates. Said prisoners are classified as 'inventory.'"

Pabst said a massive computer program for quick access to government officials exists to give the names of "an indeterminate number of U.S. citizens" in order to arrest and control them.

A controversy erupted in 1969 over the 1950 Internal Security Act which authorized detention camps in the U.S. At that time rumors were rampant that the detention camps were being revitalized to jail political dissidents—left and right.

In 1969, Sen. Daniel K. Inouye (D-Ha.) introduced a bill to abolish the section of the act which dealt with detention camps and it was quickly passed into law. But despite the government's official policy, some believe the law has been violated.

"The geographical areas or centers to be used for such concentration and detention facilities include but are not limited to: Allenwood, Pa.; Millpoint, W.Va.; Greenville, S.C.; Montgomery, Ala.; El Reno, Okla.; Tule Lake, Calif.; Florence, Ariz.; Elmendorf, Alaska; Wickenberg, Ariz.; Avon Park, Fla.," Pabst charges.

U.S. BLACK SHIP DELTA. & CRASH EVALUATION

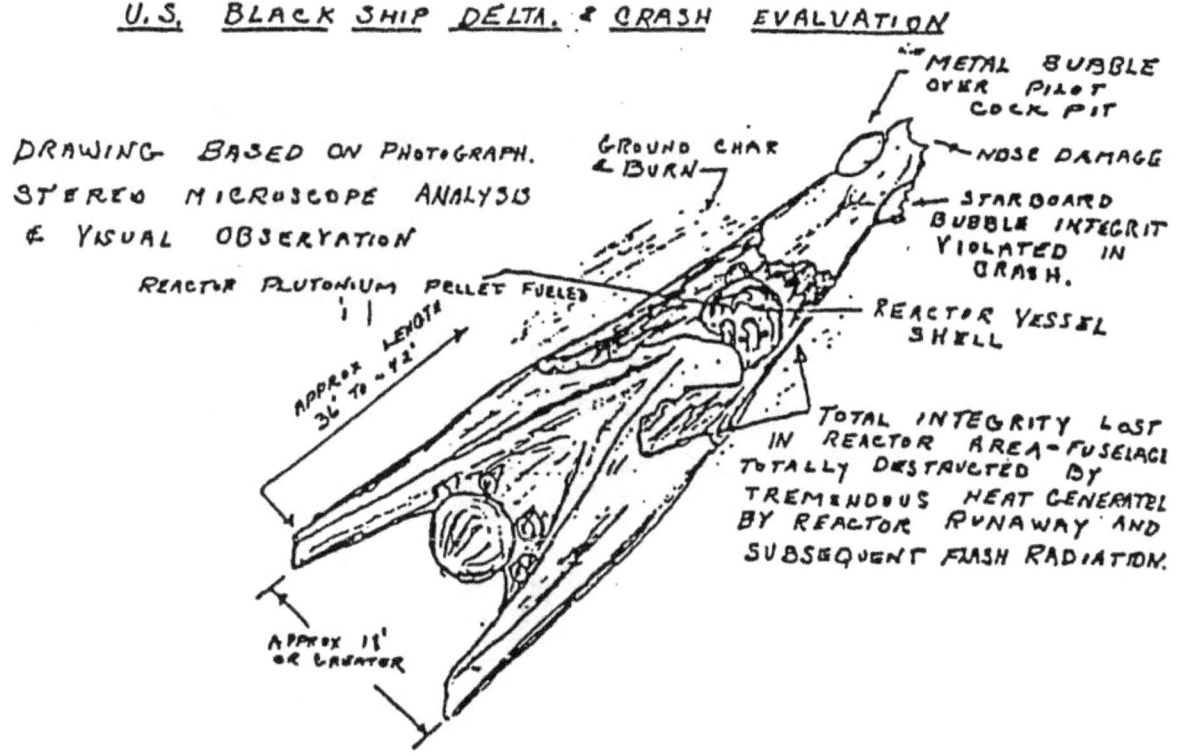

DRAWING BASED ON PHOTOGRAPH. STEREO MICROSCOPE ANALYSIS & VISUAL OBSERVATION

Labels on drawing:
- METAL BUBBLE OVER PILOT COCKPIT
- GROUND CHAR & BURN
- NOSE DAMAGE
- STARBOARD BUBBLE INTEGRITY VIOLATED IN CRASH.
- REACTOR PLUTONIUM PELLET FUELED
- REACTOR VESSEL SHELL
- APPROX LENGTH 36' TO 42'
- APPROX 15' OR GREATER
- TOTAL INTEGRITY LOST IN REACTOR AREA - FUSELAGE TOTALLY DESTRUCTED BY TREMENDOUS HEAT GENERATED BY REACTOR RUNAWAY AND SUBSEQUENT FLASH RADIATION.

NOTES:
1) BASED UPON VISUAL OBSERVATION & ANALYSIS REACTION WAS INSTANTAENEOUS - VIOLATING COCKPIT SHIELDING BY NEUTRON HEATING - PILOT INCINERATION OR LETHAL RADIATION EXPOSURE LIKELY. FIRE WAS RADIATION INDUCED - NOT FUEL INDUCED TEMPERATURE ESTIMATE > 10,000°C.

2) PILOT COMPARTMENTS PROBABLY ALSO VIOLATED BY NOSE DAMAGE.

3) PHOTOS - SHIP CRASH SITE TO BE MAGNIFIED AND ANALOG COMPUTER ENHANCED - AVAILABLE LATER.

STATEMENT: TO THE BEST OF MY EXPERTISE AS A PHYSICIST AND BASED UPON 7½ YEARS EXPERIENCE IN SHIP PHOTO ANALYSIS THIS IS THE U.S. ATOMIC SHIP. I OBSERVED BOTH VISUALLY & PHOTOGRAPHICALLY THE CRASH SITE AND SHIP ON 8/5/85. IT IS AUTHENTIC   10/22/15 Paul S.R.

CHAPTER THIRTEEN

IMPLANTS

As a prelude to the information that I was able to obtain about my own abduction and implant, it is important that the reader understand a little bit more about the alien electronic implants, and about the collaboration of the Secret Government and the Grey aliens in implanting human beings with electronic monitoring and control devices. The following sketch of research into brain implants is written by Martti Koski, an heroic Finnish researcher who also has been implanted with a mind control device. Koski emphasizes the human connection to these implants, but information will follow linking them to the Greys:

The CIA started its research to control people's minds in 1949 after the end of the second world war. The early research consisted of search for a truth serum and use of hypnosis. Victims of these experiments were often suspected spies or double agents. One of the chemicals that was seen as a potential truth serum was LSD. After some curious scientists themselves had taken small amounts of LSD, they started tests with voluntary prisoners. Prisoners who volunteered in these experiments were mostly heroin addicts and the pay they got for volunteering was usually some amount of heroin or other drug they desired.

Besides in prison, experiments started with voluntary college and university students, mental patients and ordinary American citizens who were picked up by CIA paid hookers into special rooms that were equipped with two way mirrors and other bugging devices to monitor how LSD disrupts the behavior of unaware subjects. Often CIA unwittingly dosed people with LSD and then let the local doctor certify the apparent insanity of these poeple. The LSD prophet Timothy Leary got his first knowledge of LSD by volunteering for CIA's mind control experiments. John Marks explains in his book The CIA and Mind Control how LSD and poisonous mushrooms found their way by CIA mind control experiments into the hands of students and the American counterculture.

The files of crimes that were connected with CIA mind control projects were nearly all destroyed in 1972 after the Watergate scandal by decision of two CIA officials, H. and G. Most of the victims that were poisoned by LSD and other drugs haven't gotten any compensation, and the paid criminals who administered those drugs are still free and American police forces are not willing to do anything about them.

In 1962 the people at the US-Moscow embassy found a new kind of microwave transmission. The Soviets were using multiple frequencies and widely fluctuating microwave beams with highly irregular patterns which did not appear to be applicable to intelligence gathering. The microwave beams directed at the embassy were referred to as the Moscow Signal.

In the autumn of 1965, the Institute for Defense Analysis convened a special task force to duplicate the Soviet experiments, showing that the microwaves effected the central nervous systems of the test animals.

In addition, the Advanced Research Projects Agency — a highly secret organization within the Department of Defense — set up a special laboratory where over a number of years experiments were conducted in which rhesus monkeys were irradiated with microwaves at power densities and frequencies similar to those of the Moscow Signal. The results still remain secret. Similar studies which have been done afterward clearly show that microwaves can exert a profound effect upon the central nervous system and on the behavior of primates.

Easier than to manipulate persons with microwave radiation was to apply electric current directly into specific parts of the human brain. In the sixties, scientists were able to control mood, behavior, sleep and many other functions of animals and humans using radio controlled telemetric devices that administered controlled amounts of electric current into specific parts of the brain.

Dr. P., with his collaborators at the Stanford Research Institute were able to evoke smooth, controlled movements for monkeys by using computer-brain simulation programs. The program was written by analyzing natural movement of monkeys.

A breakthrough in the area of telemetric brain stimulation was Dr. Jose Delgado's Stimoceivers, miniature transmitter receivers that are activated by radio. It has no batteries and can be implanted underneath the skin for a lifetime, so that the brain can be stimulated and recorded indefinately.

Modern technology miniaturized the Stimoceiver into one tenth of the original, which was an inch-wide device. More powerful devices are made by using rechargeable batteries that are charged by microwaves. Just recently Hitachi Ltd. revealed a new rechargeable battery that is no more thick than half a human hair. At this point it is very difficult to say just how large the Stimoceivers are.

In 1975 a primitive mind reading machine was tested at the SRI. The machine was a computer, which recognizes a limited amount of words by monitoring a person's silent thoughts. This technique relies upon the discovery that brain wave tracings show distinctive patterns that correlate with individual words — whether the words are spoken or not.

In June 22, National Enquirer had a story about the Advanced Research Projects Agency (DARPA): "Since 1973 the Advanced Research Projects Agency had been sponsoring a program to develop a machine that could read minds from a distance by deciphering the brain's magnetic waves. A scientist involved in the program had declared that the ultiomate goal of his work was to exercise control over the brain."

The following passage is from a letter written November 19, 1976 by Robert L. Gilliant, Assistant General Counsel for Manpower, Health and Public Affairs, for the Department of Defense: "As indicated in my letter of November 12 information which I have received from the Advanced Research Projects Agency is to effect that the so called 'brain waves' machine which was the subject of the National Enquirer article... is not capable of reading brain waves of anyone else than a willing participant in the laboratory. Efforts to develop that particular device, I am told, do not permit long range use. I have no reason to doubt that information."

Robert L. Gilliant didn't know anything about Dr. Delgado's 'Stimoceivers' or other similar equipment, which make possible long range recording and manipulation of brain electrical activity. Also, he didn't realize that no one can stop his brain activity or brainwave patterns when he is no more a "willing participant."

DARPA has not ended the brain research. According to Dr. Craig Fields, it is supporting a five year research program to analyze human brainwave patterns in real time. DARPA is also involved in efforts to develop a fifth generation supercomputer.

In the seventies published information in the area of telemetric brain research started to become scarce. Dr. Jose Delgado and other scientists, who did non-secret brain research, started to have difficulties in getting their work funded. The reason was ethical considerations for this type of research. However, in the view of the history of human experimentation in the USA this reason looks odd. The more obvious reason is that US military and intelligence agencies were taking over the research and used their muscle to end all non-secret research.

At the same time that the funding ended, the reports in scientific publications covering telemetric brain research also ended. There were seldom reports even covering the telemetric research of animal brains.

Transferring the funds from non-secret research into secret had many benefits:

A. The potential enemy (the USSR) didn't get any valuable information.

B. There were no delays of research because of legal and ethical research standards. As we know from history, US Army and the CIA have been able and are still able to carry out many kinds of illegal and brutal medical experienments even if there is a loss of life.

C. Because of the secrecy of the research there is no public concern. People don't worry about things they do not know of. This makes the government able to secretly harness the dark side of this technology to control "troublemakers" like fringe political leaders, objectionable union leaders, etc.

One designer of mind control implants has identified himself, and provided many details about the technology is used and is planned to be used. Dr. Carl Sanders, after realizing the purposes to which his electronic inventions were being put, "defected" from his connection to the Secret government, and has since spent a great deal of time informing the public of the dangers posed by this technology. Recently Dr. Sanders spoke of his research to an interviewer who recounted the following:

For the first time I saw and handled microchips. It was with an awful feeling. Dr. Sanders brought a scanner and showed me how the chips are read. He also brought two different guns with loaded microchips which are presently used for marking animals. I did not like what I saw. It is getting too close and uncomfortable to the coming of the "Mark of the Beast"...

All new automobiles are equipped with a black box. This is a radio transmitter and receiver that also contains a memory chip. As the U.S. is now in the last stages of completing the new satellite system, every car with a black box can be loacted via a satellite. When the system is in full operation, the government will know exactly where every vehicle has been and how many miles it has traveled, including date and time. Then a new tax is planned for the people which will be billed on a monthly basis.

Dr. Sanders also shared with me, that prior to the Gulf War, the American people were informed that the Iraqi government had biological weapons and one of the diseases they had loaded into their shells was Anthrax. Therefore, all American servicemen and women going overseas were innoculated with an anthrax vaccine. The vaccine was so potent and at the sime time ill-tested, that some soldiers died on the spot as they were given the shots. Their bodies were hauled off, and the innoculations continued without hesitation.

The mystery illness that is now plaguing thousands of Gulf War vets is from the innoculation against anthrax, and the death rate is now climbing.

The U.S. Air Force has removed all markings, including unit insignias from U.S. Air Force planes. The only remaining identifying mark is a black number on each plane. Dr. Sanders told me this is part of the plan to turn over the entire military structure to the United Nations within a short time.

When I shared with him that the U.S. Air Force has activated almost all of their U-2 surveillance aircraft, he told me some shocking news. From another source I had learned tha the U-2 has been modified by lengthening the nose several feet in order to house a satellite communication system. This makes it possible for the U-2 pilot to fly over the target and then send pictures and other data directly to a satellite, which then turns it over to a command center on the ground.

Dr. Sanders told me that most of the American satellites now feed directly to the very secret Pine Gap complex in Australia. This was a U.S. Air Force base, but it is now turned over to the U.N. This base now has over 25,000 people working at its facility of which most is a vast underground complex.

Dr. Sanders also told me that two of the world's most powerful computers have been moved overseas. CRAY-5 has been moved to Brussels in Belgium and CRAY-7 is now located at Pine Gap. CRAY-7 is a monster computer. It has a lving protein memory, which has been built from aborted baby cells, and this living organism must be fed daily to stay alive.

All that is left out of the preceding accounts is information regarding the influence of Greys and other aliens upon brain implant research; and that influence has been more than substantial, although you will not read anything of it in the professional literature on the subject. While this is certainly one of the most hush-hush of areas of conspiracy that exists, the close similarity in description between brain implant technology as designed by military intelligence and that employed in human abductions by the extraterrestrials proves conclusively that there has been shared research and technology, research and collaboration which continues until today.

And the consolidation of alien control continues through these duped and sometimes treacherous human allies of the aliens. I do not have any documentation stating conclusively to what degree the Greys and their cohorts are responsible for the tightening electronic net which is being drawn over the citizenry of America and other countries of the world, but I have little doubt that it is part of the long term plans of the aliens.

© Copyrighted for the Contributors
STEAMSHOVEL PRESS: POB 23715, Louis, MO 63121

By An Awakened Sleeper Unit

Warning! Red Alert *Steamshovel* readers! All major news media have recently proclaimed that false memory syndrome is likely to be the next big problem in the mental health professions for the 90s. Do not buy into these particular news releases, which have been planted by clandestine spin doctors for the express purpose of covering-up a massive ongoing abuse of U.S. citizens at the hands of a variety of Federal level agencies who are deploying a variety of so-called "Novelty effects" which are classified as "Non-lethal" yet may still cause injury, health problems, and post traumatic stress symptoms. This non-lethal technology has been deployed for nearly forty years, and is used for many purposes— some of which are suggested below.

MASER, ma' zer (microwave amplification by stimulated emission of radiation) A device that produces highly stable electromagnetic waves by harnessing the natural oscillations of an atomic or molecular system. The Maser devices have been a staple of "our" National Security States of America since before 1955— the year that the maser was hailed as an important scientific achievement in the realm of psychological warfare. These devices have been deployed through the following Federal agencies: FBI, NSA, NRO, CIA, Army Intelligence, Naval Intelligence, Department of Energy, Defense Investigative Services, DIA, Justice Department, Department of Treasury, BATF, and probably others which I am not aware of in the Federal Reserve System and State Department. Deployment of this technology is a distinctly *federal* phenomenon! The so-called "Secret Government" will not allow mainstream media to speak or write the truth about the matter, and will deny this is the case at every turn. Masers are LPM (Low Power Microwave) directed energy weapons which are capable of causing the harmful reactions in the occipital cortex, like projection of auditory effects (either hearing "voices" or subliminal suggestion). There is no way to shield oneself from this form of extremely high frequency directed energy— no shielding is adequate! One's only hope of protection is to be aware of the abuse as *external* to the self, i. e. not coming from one's own imagination or delusions, but invasive projections designed to effect *mind control*.

False Memory Syndrome is a scapegoat created by a consortium of Federal "spin doctors" bent on negating the believability and viability of the more than 12,000 unwitting citizens who have been on the receiving end of this technology. Since most persons on the receiving end have also been the types the government considers "enemies of the State" to begin with, the perpetrators have been allowed to use their victims *sexually* as well. That's right, rape, but a form of rape that is not available to the average rapist who hasn't access to the so-called "psychotronic" novelty effects weapons. Psychotronics allows the perpetrators to *sexually abuse and rape their victims and yet still have the victims enjoy and experience full sexual response. Yup, the victims have had their will power severed and give their abusers more pleasure than any unwilling non-consensual partner ever could!*

The mental health professions are currently swallowing this bogus media barrage on False Memory hook, line and sinker— and are preparing to ban all repressed memory therapies (hypnotherapies) as the main cause of these so-called "Lies of the Mind". The 12,000 victims of psychotronic abuse will then be dealt with as *mere schizophrenics, just like they always have been for over 40 years!* The media planted stories about False Memory syndrome will help "explain away" the memories of Alien Abduction/Ritual Satanic Abuse which are so prevalent in cases of government psychotronic abuse. The "Satanic" abuse being ritual *Masonic* abuse by the Illuminists who control the *Federalist World Government of the New World Order*/United Nations juggernaut! Are their eyes and ears *really* benevolent? *Not!* One of the main reasons that this form of atrocity is being so deftly covered up is due to the consistent abuse, sexual and otherwise, of the persons involved in the government's long standing "genetics vs. heredity" eugenics and genetics experiments which the imported Project Paperclip Nazi scientists have helped our government with since WWII!

These same covert arms of government are the ones who have coined the term "screen memories" to describe the obsfucational memories impressed by the abusers themselves! They must at all costs disguise their abuse in order to continue experimentation with psychotronics, and have given a fancy neutral name to their *enforced amnesia* which is designed to disguise abuse during *domestic* operations. Allowing the perpetrators their sexual reward is part and parcel of payment to the covert operatives in the field. Again screen memories are *enforced amnesia*. Since these Nazi inspired scientists must perform medical tests during the abuse event, such as implantation of biotelemetric tracking devices into nasal cavities and ear canals, retrieval of gamete samples/tissue samples, they use alien abduction as a screen memory, inspiring terror in the populace they abuse, while the clueless "sheeple" will not believe in extra-terrestrials from space, those on the receiving end of the abuse are often convinced of space alien abuse or satanic abuse. This *con job* is fooling even the best of mental health professionals! The atrocities are so *outrageously unbelievable* that justice will *never* ever be brought to bear on this most secret *activity of "our" secret government*. The Biotelemetric implants are used to locate the victims via the Global Positioning System (GPS) satellites, they *cannot* escape or hide from their abusers.

Victims are typically selected for a variety of reasons: lifelong eugenics/genetic guinea pigs, children of secular humanist society members, enemies of the state, suspected spies, gypsy types (includes hippies, beats, deadheads), war protesters, civil rights activists, suspected terrorists, persons who use any drugs which the state cannot tax, feminists, homosexuals, socialists who differ from NWO objectives, firearms owners, or anyone doing anything which irritates the *powers that be*.

The Federalists have a special name for the select few abuse victims that they wish to control for clandestine objectives— *unit sleepers*— who can be made into "Manchurian Candidates" like the crazed gunmen with killing spree madness that are used in Post Office shootings, schoolyard shootings, Luby's Cafeteria shootings, New Jersey train shootings. They would have you believe in the old "lone crazed gunman" scenario in order to convince the populace that they must be disarmed for the national good. They will succeed.

Readers will note that this past Christmas season was one of the most violent seasons in history with regards to firearms mayhem. It is being engineered. The end justifies the means when it comes to disarming the populous as far as They are concerned. It matters not that they are really responsible for the atrocities attributed to crazed lone gunmen, since they believe the benefits will only come after they disarm the law abiding sheeple, leaving criminals armed in order to foster anarchy which must eventually result in bringing in the U. N. to perform peace-keeping duties within "our" own nation's borders. Martial law will be declared, and the Constitutional rights suspended under this national "drug and crime" emergency.

The Fox Network is currently using *The X Files* to reveal the government's position on these issues. However, the extraterrestrial hypothesis is the only officially accepted position. You will not see Special Agent Fox Mulder uncovering evidence of government abuse of citizens, except when the government is deploying crashed saucer retrieval teams!

Get a clue, sheeple, your time is short!

CHAPTER FOURTEEN

ABDUCTION RECALL

After we had gotten the groundwork out of the way, Professor C. urged me to lay down on the couch in the room, and pulled out yet another marvel from his bag, or rather briefcase, of tricks. He used a small electronic machine, placed on the coffee table in front of us, for quickly inducing hypnotic trance in me, that is, in a person who thought he couldn't be hypnotized. Small cups were placed over my eyes which projected fluctuating visual displays directly onto my eyes. The visuals were shifting lights designed to entrain and synchronize the hemispheres of my brain, enabling me to go more quickly and more deeply into hypnotic reverie. At the same time, Professor C. verbally led me into deep trance.

At this point, in order to avoid depending on my hazy memory of the incident, I will begin quoting from the transcript of the tape recording we made of the first hypnotic session. The transcript begins shortly after Professor C. had confirmed I was in hypnotic reverie:

C: Where are you, Erik? Describe the surroundings.

X: Funny, but I don't think that I'm inside the saucer now. I think that was just a transfer point to some other place. The room I am in is too large to be inside the saucer.

C: Do you have any idea where you are?

X: This is just an intuition. I don't think I'm in Oregon anymore. I think I'm in an underground base, that I have been teleported there. I'm at a very deep level in a multiple-level complex, probably at Dulce. I don't know how I know, but I know.

C: Did someone tell you you were in the Dulce complex?

X: No. I just know that I am.

C: Go on. Tell me what is happening.

X: I'm naked... I don't know where my clothes are. I'm strapped down to a white table, an operating table with cables leading to it. There's diffuse, hazy white light in the room. There are wire sensors on my body, my temples, my forehead, neck, my arms, chest. My whole body feels numb and I can't will myself to struggle against their control. What are they going to do? Are they —? No. Will they be able to break my programming?

C: What programming are you talking about?

X: [long pause] Special Forces. To resist torture. Name, rank, serial number... [garbled in recording]. Wrong time, wrong place, not Laos.

C: Describe what you see.

X: Can't move at all. Can't turn my head — restrained — but the room is huge, like a large warehouse or a barracks, with a high rounded ceiling. There are banks of low white consoles surrounding the operating table, electronic screens, pulsing readouts, and there is motion in the background, just out of my sight. Digitized symbols on the screens, I think. Combination of English and alien text flashing. Some kind of large, clear glass lens mounted above my head. The lens, strange, it seems like the lens is communicating with me, like in an electronic voice, a robot voice. It's telling me that I was picked because of my knowledge, courage, because I have a mission that I am destined to perform... Telling me to be calm, to be proud of the role I will play in the future. I don't feel proud that they caught me. Should have taken better precautions. Over and over I receive the message that I'm on a mission. I don't buy it.

C: Lifeforms in the room?

X: There are three little Greys walking around, working around me — no, four. Three Greys in white uniforms, no insignia, and something else that is just outside my sight. I see it now. Moving closer to confer with one of the Greys. It's reptilian, ugly bastard. A Draco — pointing at me — giving — barking instructions to one of the Greys. All the time the lens is telling me to be calm in that electronic voice...

C: What about the sex of the beings?

X: Don't know — can't tell. Draco seems like a male, but I don't know. Would you want your sister...

C: Sister?

X: Never mind. One of the Greys, very businesslike, he's running an electronic device shaped like... perhaps an electric shaver with more contours, very fine design, white kind of aluminum finish... He's running it all over my body, and it's quietly beeping. While he's doing that another Grey is examining me, probing me with a metal scalpel with a rounded-off end — wire coming out of it, two little blue lights at the end.

Examining me, probing my ears, my mouth, moving downward. Be calm... Be calm... One of the Greys leans over me.

C: Does he say something?

X: Says something to me, but it's non-verbal.

C: Please explain.

X: I mean that it's telepathic. He tells me his rank, which is something like a doctor specializing in genetic memory. I don't remember any words describing it, so that's just an approximation. Telling me to be calm, that they have no intention to hurt me, that they want to help me and reveal the truth to me about my mission on earth. I try to break free from the restraints, but I can't. Bring me out of this!

C: What else?

X: This is crazy! I ask what kind of help, and he says help in evolving to a higher state of beingness. That I have not understood their purpose and have misjudged their intentions, which are good. I've talked to so many before... I'd be more likely to believe them if it wasn't for that Draco that's hanging around. Lens is still putting out this message of calmness...

C: Who have you talked to before?

X: Abductees, done interviews with them. I know what it's about. I know the stories that the aliens tell them, about how it's all for their own good. Now I'm living what they've told me. I knew it was real, but... [garbled] My God!

C: What do you see?

X: [Long pause]. Bastard! Human talking to the Draco and handing him some papers. Probably a Secret Government profile of me. And I know who he is, even with the mustache.

C: You recognize him?

X: [name deleted], worked with him in Laos on the Phoenix program, evil bastard. It figures that he would be involved in this. He's able to talk to the Draco, 'though I can't hear what they're saying. Now I know for certain where I am. He confirmed that he works at Dulce, so I must have been beamed to Dulce base. He didn't want me to see him, but I did, reflected in the lens. Whispering to the Draco so that I can't hear much of what they're saying, motioning at me and pointing at something on the papers, but he still doesn't realize that I'm watching him. They did catch up with me, now they're going to handle the defector.

C: The defector?

X: Yeah, me. If I get out of here...

C: Go on, Erik. Tell me more of what you're seeing.

X: Now [name deleted] moves out of sight, perhaps through a door, I don't know if it is. The Draco motions to one of the Greys, and he walks to one of the consoles and adjusts something. [garbled] Glint of metallic objects there. I can't turn my head, but it looks like there are shiny instruments arranged on one of the consoles, like in an operating room. He chooses two... he has long, spindly fingers... Approaches me, and now the lens is projecting calmness, telling me to be calm, that I shouldn't fear what they're doing...

C: Go on, Erik. What happens next?

X: One of them, not the one with the instruments, places a white, disk shaped object at... my groin. Energy is filling me up inside. Moves the disk to my belly, then to my heart, then neck. Accessing chakras? My lower body is paralyzed and my head is filled with something, like symbols. Feels like I am floating above my body. All I can move is my head. I shake my head, I scream, trying to find my arms, my body. The disk is on my forehead now, and I am washed... washed with transparent light that takes over my body. I can see everything clearly, but... I can't move my body.

C: What do they do next?

X: Long, double-tubular metal probe, flexible, with coils. Grey face is right next to mine, and I gaze into that one shiny eye that is facing toward me. His eyes are black, empty, like an insect. Cybernetic? I can't move at all. They're injecting something into me. It hurts a little, bruises me I think as he slides that in... [At this point Commander X became incoherent and began talking about Laos again, believing that he had been captured by enemy forces and was being interrogated. About five minutes were spent bringing him back to confronting the memory of the abduction and implanting. The transcript continues...]

X: Implant, implanting me. Moves it around, positioning inside my skull. I feel it, the implant, dropped into place, and a little pain as it... I guess it embeds itself in my nasal cavity. Feels like it burrows in. Feels like it injects a chemical into me, deadening me. Emptiness. I'm gone. I'm lost. They won.

And that is the transcript of the first hypnotic session, the first of many to be conducted over the next few days.

POSSIBLE INTELLIGENCE VALUE

The President Watches An Incredible Demonstration

According to the test pilot: "They demonstrated their spacecraft for the president. They showed him their ability to make themselves invisible.

"This really caused the president a lot of discomfort because none of us could see them even though we knew they were still there. The aliens then boarded their ships and departed." The pilot told Lord Clancarty that he never told another soul about this unique meeting, and that now all the others involved in the encounter are dead.

Additional Verification

A recent report in the *National Enquirer* regarding the Eisenhower incident adds a quote from UFO researcher Gabriel Green who testifies that he once held a conversation with a gunnery sergeant who had been stationed at Edwards during this period. The sergeant said he and his team were using live ammo and were ordered by a general to fire at the alien spacecraft. Their attack was futile, however, as none of the shells could penetrate the tough metal hull of the craft and eventually the men watched in amazement as the ships proceeded to land near one of the large hangars.

Additional confirmation comes from Charles Berlitz who reports in the book, *The Roswell Incident* that a man named Gerald Light was still another witness to the astonishing encounter. Light wrote a letter dated April 16, 1954 to UFO writer Meade Layne acting director of the Borderland Sciences Research Foundation. In this communication he stated that he saw the five UFOs land at the base. "I had the distinct feeling," he commented, "that the world as I knew it had come to an end. It has finally happened—we have seen and met aliens from another world!"

President Eisenhower Meets With Aliens

This story would be hard to believe except for the fact that it has been confirmed by many unimpeachable sources. One of those sources, the Earl of Clancarty, who is a member of the British Parliament, stated that President Dwight D. Eisenhower met with beings from outer space in 1954, and world famous language expert, Charles Berlitz, confirms the story.

The date was February 20, 1954. Eisenhower was vacationing at Palm Springs when he was summoned to Muroc Airfield by high military officials. Muroc is now known as Edwards Air Force Base, recently popularized as the landing field for the space shuttle.

The President had a press conference scheduled for that day but never showed up for it. There were rumors that he was ill. The official explanation was that he went to a dentist. Newsmen, however, were never able to learn which dentist treated him.

Actually, Eisenhower was driven to the California air base to meet with space aliens. According to Lord Clancarty, the incident was reported to him by a former top U.S. test pilot. Says the Earl: "The pilot was one of six people at Eisenhower's meeting with the beings. He had been called in as a technical adviser because of his reputation and abilities as a test pilot."

What Eisenhower and the Six Witnesses Saw

The test pilot told Lord Clancarty: "Five different alien craft landed at the base. Three were saucer-shaped and two were cigar-shaped...and as Eisenhower and his small group watched, the aliens disembarked and approached them.

"They looked something like humans, but not exactly."

The test pilot described the beings as having human-like features, but that by our standards they were misshapen. They were the same height and weight as the average man and were able to breathe air without the use of a helmet or mask.

The test pilot reported that the aliens spoke English and wanted Eisenhower to start an education program for the people of the United States, and eventually the earth.

Eisenhower allegedly replied that he didn't think the world was ready for that. The president said that his concern was that a world-wide announcement that aliens had landed would likely cause panic.

CHAPTER FIFTEEN

INTO THE MATRIX

Several hypnotic inductions were performed on me by Professor C., in which the information on my abduction to the Dulce Base was filled out. When we had pretty much found out all that there was to find out about my abduction to Dulce and my return to the beach in Oregon, Professor C. tried another tactic that he hoped would obtain results. I had known Professor C. long enough to know that I was in good hands, but his suggestion threw me for a loop. The conversation which follows is a pretty close approximation of what was said.

"Erik," he said, "we've learned pretty much all we can from your experience via the hypnotic method. Now, there is not much else to be learned, and so ordinarily I would simply surgically remove the implant and have done with it. But there is another possible approach that I would like to try, with your permission. What I want to do is reverse the programming of the implant. I know that it can be done. You read about the beginnings of the technique in *The Alien Mind*."

I shook my head. "I thought that was completely theoretical. Have you actually done it?"

"We've had some limited success. My researches have proven to me quite conclusively that the way the aliens access their centrally located data banks is through the electromagnetic activity of the mind, a form of ESP, you might say. I even have evidence to suggest that in their culture there is a specially-bred form of, well, 'technician' who is specifically designed for that function, perhaps a specifically bred biological adaptation. These 'technicians' are essentially biological/electronic communications devices employed by both the Greys and the Draco races, and they are able to tap into the alien data matrix using their minds."

I thought I knew what Professor C. was talking about, but I asked him to elaborate.

"The data matrixes," he said, "are located at several points on the surface of the earth that we know about, including at Dulce, Area 51, and in Australia, although naturally there are many other locations which are located in other star systems that are also hooked into the system. You might call it sort of a super-sophisticated alien Internet that has been in operation for hundreds of years, at least. The same matrix is used to manipulate abductees by broadcasting suggestings and commands, which then are re-broadcast direct to the abductee through the implants.

"The implant that is in your head has a link to the information matrix that is located on this planet. I'm sure of that much. Presumably their computers have some physical location on this planet, and no doubt there are other off- planet locations, as well. The fact that they have the capability of implanting thoughts in the heads of abductees reveals a possibility that the Greys may not have even conceived: My theory is that the implant can be used to tap into their information matrix, to gain access into their data banks."

Needless to say, I was dumbfounded at what Professor C. was proposing that I do. My initial response, knowing that I had an electronic impulse in my head, was to have him remove it at the first opportunity.

Much later, after Professor C. and I had conducted the experiments which were to follow, I came across some information on the alien information matrix that clarified its existence in my mind and possibly will help the reader to understand the nature of the system better. The following material is by one of the top UFO researchers in the field, who goes by the name Val Valerian. Although it is somewhat technical, it provides a good deal of information about the manner in which the aliens are able to access this information matrix:

During one of the autopsies on alien bodies, it was found that there existed a separate lobe of the brain that contained a crystalline network. This, to me, was an interesting discovery, for it made the connection with other information which we already possess about such networks. during examination of data from ancient texts, such as the Keys of Enoch, we can see that the networks are pertinent to advanced physical forms, and that these networks allow them to tap into the Universal Intelligent Matrix. In these ancient texts, brains of advanced physical beings... are described as having the right and left hemispheres of the brain fused and a small frontal lobe which acts as a "crystal recorder" structure, or third brain. This is exactly what the autopsies found.

With this data in mind, it might be presumed that the development of the network structure is a later physical manifestation that occurs subsequent to the development of...telepathic abilities. Within the human, a structure known as the caudate nucleus unctions in an initial structure for establishing telepathic communication. The term antankarana, or bridge in the brain, refers to the evolutionary connection of the caudate nucleus with the rest of the brain.

Thought forms pervade the universe, and evidently it is this network which allows a being to tap into the matrix and gain information. The matrix, or Universal Intelligence Matrix, pervades the universe. It is a hierarchically ordered intelligence field composed of infinite domains, dimensions/densities/parallel worlds, and conscious entities. The primary function of the matrix is that it enacts the thought patterns of the Universal Mind into manifestation. The resultant diversification exists as an infinite spectrum of interconnected combinations and permutations.

Interdimensional communication is the result of attunement to one's own network so that it functions as a multidimensional extension through which communicative access to desired aspects of the matrix can occur.

The electronic matrix that the implants access, I believe, is a more specialized version of what Valerian is talking about. Not wanting to get in any deeper than I had to without some more information as to the nature of the matrix and any dangers that might be involved in accessing it, I questioned Professor C. more closely. "Tell me about what you've done so far in that area," I asked Professor C.

"Most of the abductees that I have worked with on this are too afraid to go ahead with it. The ones who have had the courage to try it usually only get so far before they are overwhelmed by what they are presented with, by the nature of the information which is contained in the matrix. The concepts that they dredge up from the matrix are too alien for them to deal with, I suppose. I've had success with two abductees, however, out of a score or so that I have worked with over the past few years. One of them was able to get access into some of the minor levels of the matrix, access codes and so forth. Those codes, although incomplete, are now available to us."

I sensed the Professor was witholding something from me. "What about the other one?"

"I probably shouldn't tell you, but she died in the course of the research. Cerebral hemorrage. I don't know if her death had anything to do with her implant. I just don't know for certain. But I never said that this kind of experiment wasn't dangerous, Erik."

It took a day for Professor C. to convince me to try and access the alien matrix. Finally I agreed with him that there was a possibility that it could be done, at least theoretically. And even though the whole concept sounded pretty crazy to me, I agreed to give it a try. The way he put it, experimentation in this realm might net more information, and more truly important information than the totality of data that he had gained on the Grey aliens using all other methods.

After a quick briefing on the access codes that Professor C. possessed, and what he had conceptually determined about the alien matrix, I had a troubled night's sleep. I joked with Professor C. the following morning about "the prisoner having his last breakfast" over bacon and eggs in a local coffee shop, although he didn't find the joke in the least funny.

After returning to the motel room and doing another routine check for electronic bugging, I settled down with the brain hemispheric synchronizer and Professor C. again led me into a deep hypnotic state. Then I made a try for the data banks that I knew were hidden in the underground facilities beneath Dulce, New Mexico.

At first I was far from sure that reversing the communication link could even be done. Professor C., of course, had told me that he had some success with other abductees, and so I continued to try for some hours without much success, even though I was closely following his verbal commands and some access codes that he had been able to find out.

Professor C. provided me with the first access code that he had obtained, and although I visualized it repeatedly, nothing happened. Then we tried another, and a third.

Professor C. later confided to me that he was about to give up, assuming that for some reason or another I would not be able to access the matrix, when we finally hit paydirt. On the third access code I was off on a rocket ride, or I suppose I should say a saucer ride.

When the matrix link "opened up," I had to struggle against the sense that I was dreaming or imagining it all. But I persisted, letting my consciousness roam free through an onslaught of crazy information and pictures that assaulted it. Codes, memories, pictures, dimensions, planets: The sheer amount of information that made itself suddenly available to my mind was overwhelming, and like no other experience that I had ever had.

Understanding very little of what I was seeing (for one thing, information seemed to be coded in at least three alien languages, while other information seemed like abstract pictures that I couldn't make head nor tail of), I followed the connection from the implant that was affixed in my skull, going through waves and waves of strange, alien imagery and information, trying to interpret the connection with great difficulty.

Now I finally knew that Professor C. was right, though. What I was seeing, feeling, hearing, could no longer just be my imagination. It was actually possible to break into the alien data matrix. I knew now that it was possible to reverse the information flow on the implant and to access the same mental link that the alien "technicians" used.

The experience was something like what I imagine "virtual reality" to be, although I knew this was no child's game. I knew that at every step of the way my life depended on not taking a wrong step and potentially revealing to the Grey aliens that I was hacking into their systems. I felt like a disembodied intelligence, freely floating through vast layers and corridors of information: It's hard to put it any more clearly than that.

I used both my intuitive senses as well as a kind of visual/kinetic orientation to travel through and interpret the content of the vast Grey data banks as best I could. It is quite possible that I have made some mistakes in interpreting what I saw in the alien data matrix (and also possible that certain things I was shown were purposeful disinformation), but I believe that overall I was able to gain a coherent picture. And I only scratched the surface of what was ultimately available in those data banks.

"Go deeper..." Professor C. encouraged me, and I let myself relax into the flow of the alien imagery, letting the onslaught of information rush through and begin to at least somewhat coordinate in my brain. If you've ever seen the Krell cities in the classic SF movie Forbidden Planet, I was reminded of those as I flowed through huge nets and crystallizations of information and images. Virtual cities of information, you might say. Layers and layers of informational connections and recordings, and all of them so strange that at points I feared that I was going to lose my sanity.

Press a button, mentally speak an access code, and a new world would open up in front of me and all around me. An entirely new world to be explored. It was fascinating and terrifying to dive into the information banks of the aliens, and I tried not to think of the possibility that the Greys were already on to me, and might be dispatching a team (or a saucer) to deal with this security break.

I dived deeper into the virtual world of the alien data banks, forgetting about my body entirely and travelling forward into realms that no human had probably ever travelled into. And then suddenly the fear hit me and I snapped right back into my body with a jolt!

I felt like I had been hit by a freight train, and it took several minutes before I had completely regained my hold on consciousness and reality. I lay on the couch trembling and gasping, trying to orient myself to being back to reality, and feeling like I had come very close to having a heart attack from the sheer volume of fear that had hit my body.

"It's impossible!" I mumbled to Professor C. "It's nothing like human consciousness, it can't be done..."

"That's what they want you to feel," Professor C. said. "You've stumbled upon a security mechanism to stop you from gaining access to their secrets. Master the fear, Erik. I don't want to sound like something out of the Star Wars movie, but it's true. Fear is the most powerful weapon they have against us."

I hesitated telling Professor C. that I was aware of quite a few other weapons that the Greys had. I relaxed and Professor C. led me back into the hynotic reverie, "walking me" back through the same access codes and a new one I had found in my search.

I dove back into the alien matrix, again losing touch with my body and swimming forward through black empty infinite space. It seemed like I was travelling through galaxies of distance, but I also sensed that it wasn't distance, at all, but was pure information, the vast quantities of information that the aliens had stored in their underground data banks on planet earth and perhaps on other planets, too. I pressed deeper and deeper through the maze of light and knowledge, working through barriars of non-comprehension and confusion on my own part, trying to make sense of the information that was swirling through me and around me.

When the fear hit again, this time I was ready for it and resisted. I reeled in empty space, feeling like I was going to black out. I was confused, not knowing where I was and perhaps not even who I was at that point, but I kept "swimming" upstream to try and get to the core of the alien matrix.

I fought against the fear, trying to overcome it. I fought the fear down, and succeeded in keeping it at least under control. I didn't say that I entirely vanquished the fear, because it still remained below the surface of my consciousness, pulsing and waiting to leap up: But at least it was under control.

I don't think the aliens ever seriously considered that any human would try to tap into their data banks. I think that if they had, they would have erected stronger barriars and would have made sure that there was no way to create a link between the human mind and the matrix that the electronic brain implants access. The impression I got from my search in the matrix was that they consider humans too weak, too unimaginative, too fearful to even attempt such a thing. They think of us as a lower life form that would never dare to challenge the might of their galactic empire. I think that in that fact we are lucky. I think they underestimate us.

I knew that I might not have long to harvest knowledge in their matrix, and so as quickly as I could I tried to absorb all the information I could. Now I was into some sort of a multi-dimensional library that provided an entrance to any time, any planet that I wanted, all in 3-D with complete tactile reality sensation. I could go any way I wanted, to any time that had been set into the electronic locus of the information matrix, simply thinking of something and having it manifest in reality right in front of me.

But there were priorities, and I wasn't in the alien matrix just to sight-see. Even if things went perfectly, I assumed that eventually the Greys would be alerted to what was going on, and then they would take quick action against me.

I knew what I had to do. I had to seek some point of alien vulnerability and try to bring that back to conscious reality with me, so that humans could defend themselves against the Grey alien invasion. That, I figured, was the most important information that I could possibly obtain.

First I dove into the galactic history of the Grey aliens, quickly accessing all I could about their culture, about where they came from, information on their weapons and propulsion systems, why they were on earth, and most importantly their plans for humanity not just on earth, but in numerous other star systems. I will talk about what I found out later in this book, and in future books.

The edge of fear never left me as I travelled through the matrix, but I kept on searching through virtual infinities of information, trying to make some sense of it, trying to understand the way that a Grey might think. I was afraid that any moment the aliens would be alerted that there was an unauthorized access by a human taking place on their data bank, but the alert had not yet come, and so I continued.

And I stole all the information I could. I filled my mind with the sights and sounds of those alien worlds, I tapped into their minds, I tapped into the plans they had for earth. Although I was not able to understand even a millionth of what I saw and felt in the matrix, I was able to understand some of it. I hope that some of this information will be useful in the preservation of mankind in our war against the alien enemy's control.

CONTROL MESSAGE

Received at Northwestern sector control 10/17/87

A word to the non-operant human about the Pleidesian plot.The beings who describe themselves as Pleidesian are extremely devious.They are the most commonly encountered type of extraterrestrial life on earth. Physically they are humanoid.Short,pale,with bulbous cranium and large luminous eyes.They speak and emote to humans in terms of peace and love. In fact.the emotion,termed love,has no correspondant in their emotional vocabulary.Peace they know,but only the peace of complete mental domination.Truth is something that means little to the Pleidesian's. They are not even from the Pleides,since the Pleides are a nebula,this would not be possible.Stars in a nebula are much too young to support intelligent life.These so-called Pleidesian's are lying to the humans, but to what purpose?There intent is control over the earth,through the earth governments.These aliens have been in active contact with the American and Russian governments,as well as the European Common Market, since the late 1940's.Since 1964 they have played a dominate role in their relations with the earth governments.Through fear,and through lust of power,the earth governments have allowed the planet to become controlled by extraterrestrial forces which they cannot comprehend.The Pleidesian's and the earth governments are now conspiring to construct a device of great power,a Pleidesian control net.This control device has been used many times before to turn entire races of semi-intelligent beings into automatic machines with no self volition.The Pleidesian's are terrified by the unpredictable,syncronicity sends them into a blind panic.Therefore,control is their comfort,and their universal goal.

The control net will take the form of a series of parallel satellites. These will be very powerful,capable of receiving information from billions of ground based transceivers.Each satellite can proccess this information on board,and then will act upon it as indicated by its programing.These satellites are allready constructed,and may be in place even now.The ground transceivers will be in the form of implantable devices which will be implanted at birth.In transmission mode it will transmit to the nearest satellite the individuals identity,location, and brain.activity.The satellite will proccess this information and act as indicated by programming.Ground security elements may be notified, or the satellite itself may act by altering the individuals brain state by electronicly generated changes in brain chemistry.even to the point of brain failure.This system is the hidden reason behind S.D.I.While the American military displays elaborate,extravagant,useless,weaponry,the real work goes on behind the scenes.Close to 100% of the construction is being done by humans.The Pleidesian's,like the American C.I.A.,dislike taking a direct role in their own operations,prefering to use collaborators.They are at the top levels,beyond government,beyond science,beyond law.But now they must know that WE know of their actions.This will no doubt cause an increase in the speed which this work is being carried out.They must rush to forstall our interferance.For WE have quite different plans for this planet.More on this later.Since the 1940's,the Pleidesian's have been guiding earth technology towards their own purposes.The German V-rockets were developed in order to stimulate later construction of I.C.B.M's,and eventually heavy lift spacecraft such as the Saturn 5.All with the idea of providing launch capabilities for the control satellites.Advances in computers,material design,electronics,superconductivity,have all followed similar guidelines.These guidelines,as well as the programming for the control satellite computers,are set by the Pleidesians.They do not allow arguement or interferance.And if this results in the enslavement of the human race,will the politicians and rulers of the earth be bothered?No, for they are allready controlled by their desire to control.

- - -

- - -

Scientist suggests sterilization as population-explosion curb

Canadian Press

OTTAWA — Mass sterilization of people in poor countries might be the only way to stop the world population explosion, a prominent French scientist said Monday.

"I fear we may be forced to violate some basic human rights if we want to keep humanity alive," said Jean-Claude Pecker, France's leading astronomer and a long-time human-rights activist.

"One of the greatest needs now is to diminish the birth rate in poor countries. In order to do that, you might eventually be led to sterilize people after two children, for example.

"You might be forced to that drastic kind of solution less than 50 years from now. We see it coming, but no one dares to say it."

Forced migrations might also become unavoidable, he said.

Pecker is vice-president of the French National Commission for the United Nations Educational and Cultural Organization, former director of the Institute of Astrophysics in Paris, and a founding member of the human-rights committee of the French Academie des sciences.

His assertions weren't challenged by any of about 50 scientists at a symposium sponsored by the Royal Society of Canada.

But the idea of forced sterilization was strongly rejected by Bonnie Johnson of Planned Parenthood of Canada, who has studied Third World population issues.

"I find it just unconscionable that we would try to dictate to any woman or to any family their reproductive rights or freedoms," she said.

The only way to stop the population explosion is by raising living standards in poor countries, she said.

CHAPTER SIXTEEN

WORKING AGAINST TIME

I knew that simultaneously I was facing one of the greatest opportunities I had ever known, to actually tap into the alien plans right at the source, while I was also facing without a doubt the greatest danger of my career. I was relying totally on Professor C.'s expertise in order to guide me through the experiments with the matrix, as well as to pull me out if I got in too deep.

Using the information in the matrix, I sought an overview of what was going on here on earth, trying to gain perspective. Accessing several different information levels (particularly of an historical nature), I saw that our solar system has been the center of a great deal of extraterrestrial attention and experimentation for literally thousands of years, and that there is currently a cosmic war being fought in this sector, albeit a secret war.

The horrible truth I found out is that mankind is currently losing in that war.

The two main, although not only, opponents in this cosmic war are the Nordic Federation and the reptilian races. These are groups who have been enemies for a very long time, and who have been carefully building and marshalling their forces, consolidating their defense installations and territory within this and other solar systems.

The Nordics are a loosely allied confederation of human and near-human races, along with some other non-human races who have created non-agression pacts.

The reptilians are primarily composed of the Greys and the Dracos, who are two ancient enemies of the humans. The reptilians have their own alliances, some of them with humans, others with non-human races including hybrids.

Due primarily to the rich resources in this solar system and historical aspects involving previous habitation, earth is at the center of these brewing, warlike forces, and humanity may be the key to which group triumphs on the cosmic scale: the Nordics or the Greys. Such is our destiny, like it or not, and this, I believe, is the reason that both the Nordics and the reptilians are so interested in us.

The situation, however, is not quite so simple. The collaborators among humans, who have long been referred to as the Illuminati, are allied with the Secret Government which controls human governments and other institutions. They have complicated matters by selling out to and working with the Greys and the Dracos, and even participating in abductions, implants, and other grisly experiments, much to the detriment of their fellow humans.

What possible incentive could the Greys have provided that would have tempted these human traitors to sell out their own race? Wealth and power, naturally, particularly powers of an occult, corrupting nature. The Greys and the Dracos have convinced these individuals that the humans and Nordics did not stand a chance against the might of the Grey empire, and hypnotized them with visions of a collaborative New World Order, jointly ruled by the Secret Government and by the Greys.

The key to the Secret Government/Grey scheme is the Alternative 3 plan, and from the information that I was able to access, this project is on the fast track and scheduled to be in full operation by the beginning of the next century.

I continued to search through the matrix, hoping against hope that I would find an "Achilles heel" of the reptilian races. Initially, one of the most interesting areas that I got into was a quick "security check" on some of the people who are involved in UFO research, just so I would know who I was dealing with, and who was playing both sides of the field in this deadly game. What I found out didn't make me happy.

Although the files in the data bank made it clear that most of the UFO researchers who were controlled didn't know that they were, the horrible truth was that many of them were, in fact, controlled by the aliens or their collaborators. Many of the most famous people doing research into UFOs and extraterrestrial races today, it turns out, have been specifically targeted by the Grey aliens and their allied forces. Several of these researchers have been implanted, and are run almost like robots according to the purpose of the aliens.

Although I cannot mention any names specifically (these allegations would be denied, anyway), what I can say is that I have confirmed that many UFO researchers are not truly on the side they claim to be on (the human side) but are in fact control subjects engaged in disinformation. This is particularly true of the high-profile "UFO researchers" who have been previously employed by intelligence agencies ultimately under Secret Government control. Although much of what they have said is true, they have been programmed to inject "boomarangs" into the information that will throw researchers off the real trail.

Again, I would offer a note of caution: Anyone researching these matters needs to be very careful about whom he believes and whom he follows.

Diagram of alien implant.

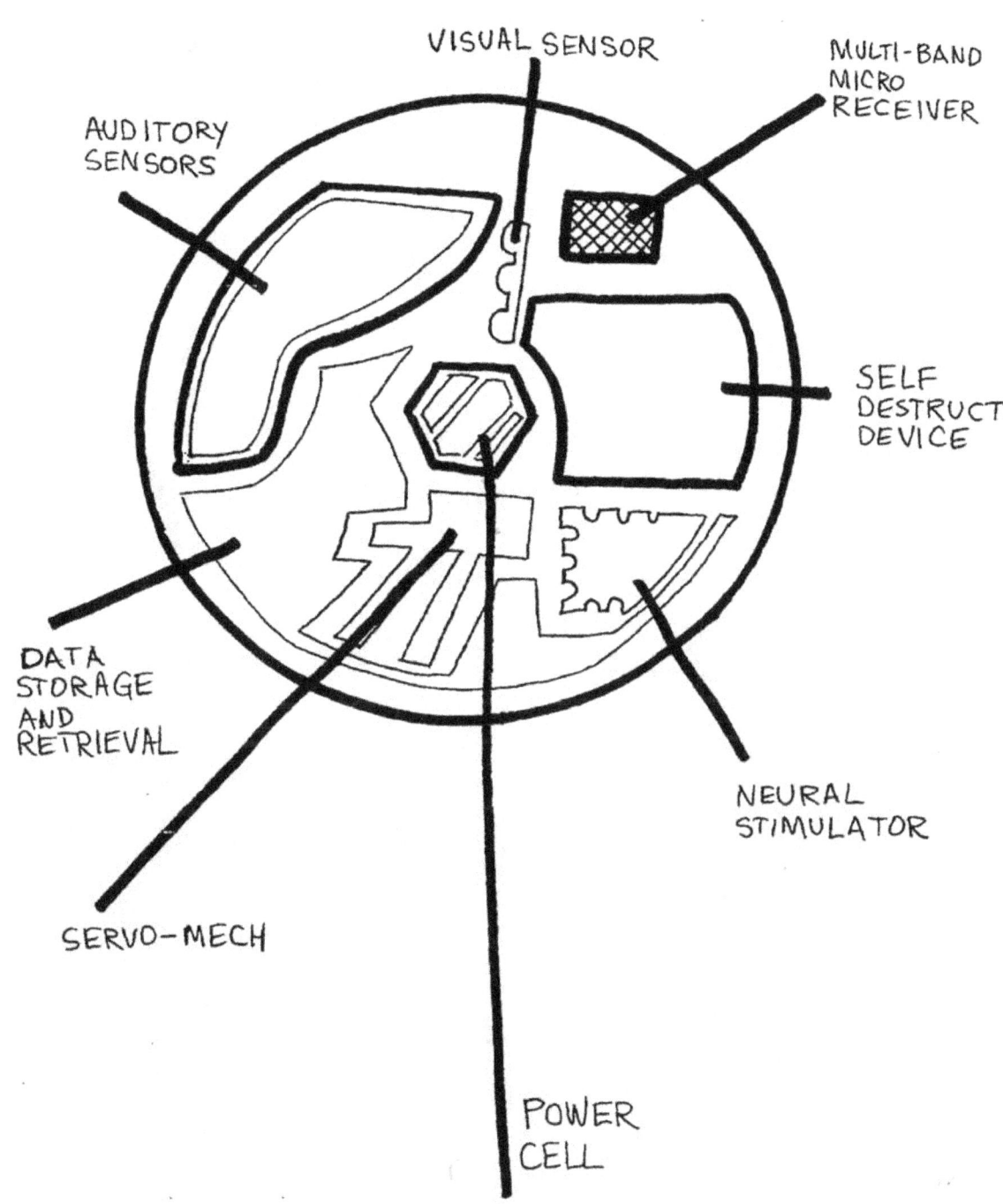

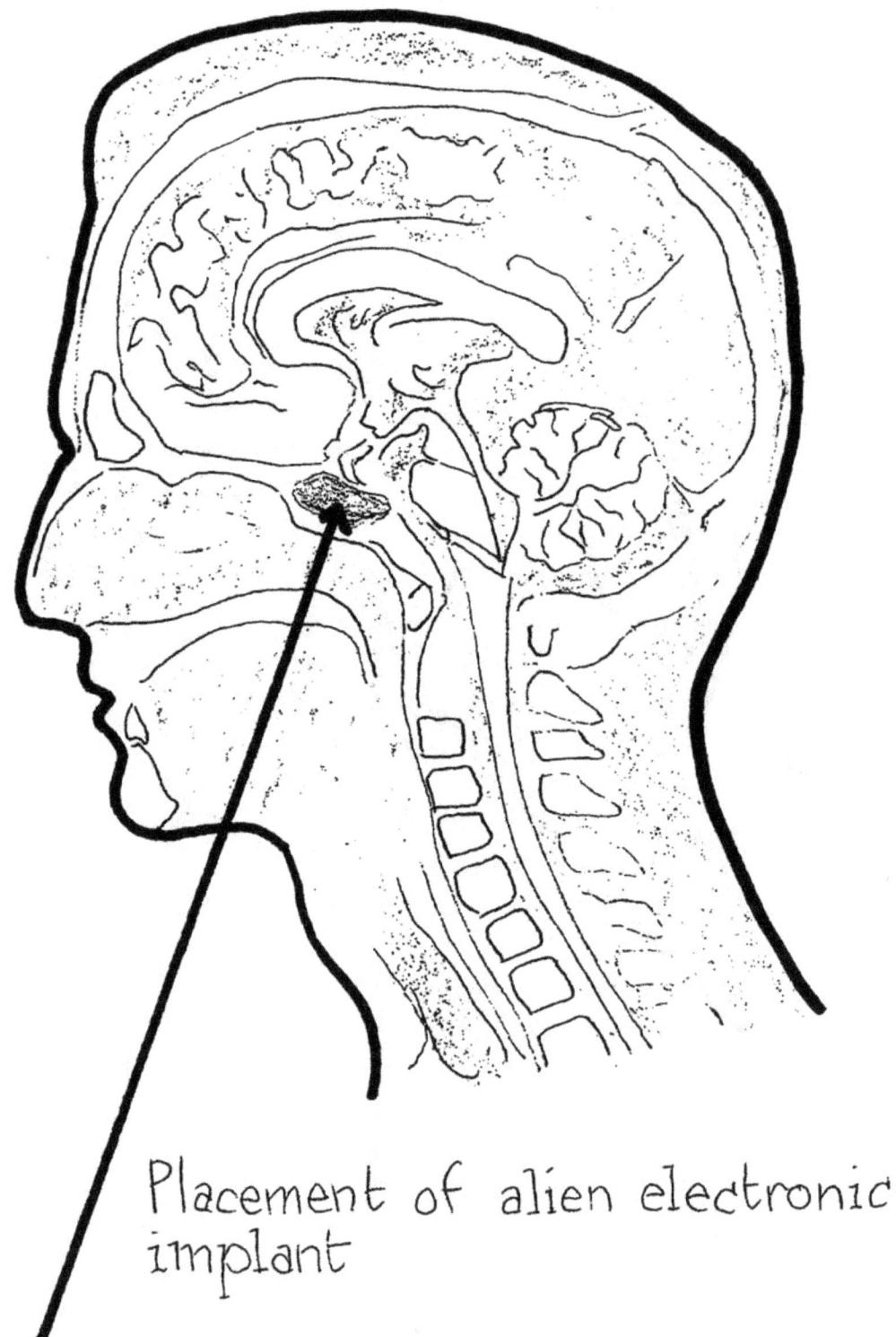

Placement of alien electronic implant

CHAPTER SEVENTEEN

ALLIES

One of the areas that I was able to access with clarity in the alien data banks was a multiple-access coding for communications with other alien races stationed on earth. Although I had heard about numerous alien races in my UFO researches, I was able to do a quick scan that clarified those alien interactions for myself, and gave me a little better insight into interspecies collaboration.

The primary opponents in the battle for cosmic supremacy are the Nordic Federation, and the Draco (with various other racial and planetary associations grouped within these factions). Although I am not able to remember all of the races which were referenced within the data matrix (there were many, some which I had not run across before in any of my researches or in the accounts of abductees), nor all of the alien racial characteristics which were listed, here are the major items which were recorded during one of my hypnotic induction sessions with Professor C. Some of this material will be familiar to the in-depth researcher in the field of UFOlogy and alien interaction, but is included simply as a verification of their researches.

THE NORDIC FEDERATION
This group includes:
Orion: These include several varieties of "Blonds" or "Nordics" (who look like tall, blond humans), Synthetics (who are vat-grown), Greys who have agreed to non-agression in this sector, and Robotoids (who

are generally employed in labor capacities by both the Greys and the Blonds). Civilization in this sector varies from sparsely-inhabited outposts which have been decimated in long-term war with the Greys (much of which has been moved to fortified underground bases) to areas which retain much of the flavor of the original Nordic civilization. These are areas of unsurpassed galactic culture and civilization, some of it conforming to the arts and philosophy attributed to the ancient Greeks on earth, with the important addition of a highly technical physical science.

Procyon: Here there are "Nordics" who are generally friendly to earthlings, except for humans involved in the treasonous Grey alien/Human Illuminati pact. Many humans are descended from, or have a strain of this "Nordic" blood in their heritage, from these beings who have acted as custodians of earth since before written history.

Bernard's Star: Here is another locale from which the Nordics hail. This group has closely monitored earth humans for many years, with the purpose of helping in the advancement of their evolution to full membership in the galactic civilization of which they are a part. They are less involved in the actual military defense of human cultures throughout space, and more with imparting the ancient knowledge which they consider are these groups' heritage. The culture on Bernard's Star pride themselves on the fact that they have injected many advances, particularly of a philosophical and even mystical type, among the far-flung colonies of humanity.

Wolf 424: This is the home of the UMMO, a Nordic group who have been in touch with humans on earth since pre-recorded history. They have maintained a "hands-on" relationship to many individual humans and groups for centuries, and are currently involved in providing information to a number of humans on earth, some of whose names would be familiar to the researcher. The current major outpost of the UMMO is an underground base in the Pyranees mountains, and they have confined much of their physical interaction on earth to Spain and France due to the fact that a secret alliance has been made with members of both the Spanish and French governments. This does not mean that they do not travel farther afield on earth when necessary.

Tau Ceti: This is the home of another Nordic group whose mission, in part, is to counteract many of the acts of terrorism which the Greys have inflicted upon the people of earth. Part of their major "alignment" as they put it is healing, although this includes both individuals and the healing of entire races through a number of advanced technologies. The Tau Cetians have been the victims of many Grey atrocities themselves (and thus feel a good deal of empathy for earthlings), and maintain dimensional "doors" located particularly in the Southern states of the U.S. through which they may enter and exit in their continuing work to counteract the harmful effect the Greys and their allies have inflicted on earth. There was a recent Draco-sponsored purge of the Tau Cetians attempted on earth and outside the solar system by the Draco but, although the Tau Cetians did incur some losses, they were able to beat back the Dracos yet another time.

The Pleiades: This is an area of extensive and advanced human habitation, and an extremely wide variety of cultures. Although most of inhabitants of this area are benevolent to earthlings, there are also manipulative groups who have in the past and will continue to use earth for their own purposes. The short amount of time that I was able to spend on researching this area showed me that even though the majority of cultures located in this area are human, thus having kinship to earth-based humanity, they vary in terms of genetic evolution. Some of them, while having advanced technology and star travel are, nevertheless, quite savage and, however intelligent, are not very developed empathically. There is a current project going on in several locations in the Pleiadian system which involved manipulation of the DAL (so they call it) universe, which is a reversed-energy twin of our own material universe. It is alleged that the destiny of our universe is closely linked to the DAL universe, and that an eventual culmination will take place in which both universes are merged prior to an higher evolution. The exact purpose of this experimentation the Pleiadians are engaged in is unknown to me, although it is being conducted by races whose intentions toward mankind are essentially benevolent.

The Orion Constellation: This is an area of considerable galactic conflict, given the fact that both reptilians and humans call the planets located here home. Warfare in this area has been of such intensity and such duration that there is a radioactive energy ridge of huge, galaxy-spanning proportions that cannot be approached by any craft without heavy protective shielding. Here the very fabric of space has been ruptured by the violence of the wars which have taken place. Although this area of information seems to be top secret, according to records which I was able to briefly scan, it seems that the extreme volatility of the conflict in the area was one of the reasons for the atrophication of the Grey bodily organs. This seems logical, but additional research needs to be done to confirm this supposition.

Arcturus: In this area the most important ruling race is Nordic, and is referred to by a number of names, including the Melchizadek brotherhood. They have evolved to the point where I was unable to discern any "technological" aspects of their civilization at all, instead they rely on metaphysical manipulation of reality through their minds. They are able to resist Grey and Draco onslaughts through the use of this advanced power. This group maintains several bases on earth, including in the Mount Shasta area, and they are friendly to humans. I also noted that this group has an informational matrix similar to that which the Greys maintain, although I was unable to access it. This matrix is available to all members of the Melchizadek group, but it is said that it may also be accessed by other humans of a sufficiently advanced evolution, and in fact may have been accessed by humans in the past. Again, additional study needs to be done. I, Commander X, would like to hear from any of my readers who have been able to gain access to the data matrix of the Arcturans.

Vega Lyra: This is the home of a race of peaceful "Benevolent Ones" who have an earth mission currently headquartered underground in the Death Valley area, in California. This group maintains that they have been in contact with earth for many centuries, in fact before the catastrophic "Lyran Wars" which were conducted by the Greys against humans in the Lyra constellation (with warfare also conducted in other areas at the same time). This war resulted in many human refugee colonies away from the Lyran system, and in the destruction of a good deal of the original Nordic culture, leaving isolated "advanced" pockets of civilization throughout the galaxy. For the interested researcher, earth is not considered by the Nordics to be an area of advanced culture.

Epsilon Eridani: This group of Nordics maintains a close alliance with Tau Ceti.

It should be noted that although the Nordics appear to be essentially human in their physiognomy, there are some differences between us and these extraterrestrial "cousins." These differences are no doubt due to the different adaptive conditions between earth and their extraterrestrial habitats. Possibly the most striking of the differences between Nordics and earth-based humans is nature of their blood. Nordic blood among most groups is based on copper. Other physiological differences include larger lungs in order to accomodate for less oxygen content in their atmospheres, inner lids on their eyes, and eyes which are sensitive to a far greater range of light, including selected portions of the ultraviolet spectrum. Nordics have only 28 teeth, and most lack canines.

Perhaps the most important area of differentiation with earth-based humans is that Nordics have a much more highly developed telepathic ability, and are able to read minds, as well as to project thought, explaining the common occurrence of Nordic-contactees being communicated to without verbal language.

There are other differences in the Nordic physiology and physiognomy, including a somewhat different array and placement of their internal organs, but it can be assumed that humans have far more similarities to the Nordics than differences.

Although I was able to learn much about the Nordic federation through directly accessing the Grey informational matrix, there was a good deal of information which I encountered which was either deeply-encoded or otherwise not understandable to me. I have been able to decode at least some of this material by comparing it to other sources of information, including channelled material, and the material mentioned in other abduction accounts. One of the most insightful researchers working today, "Branton", provides further invaluable information on the Nordic alliance:

Probably the second most commonly reported occupants or alien entities are the "Nordics" or so-called "Blonds" (as they have often been referred to), described as being human yet usually blond-haired and blue-eyed. These claim to have continuity with ancient earth societies who developed advanced forms of technology, and these "Nordics" or "Blonds" have been associated with nearby planetary or star systems as well as with subterranean colonies possibly descended from ancient Greco-Mayan explorers. it is uncertain just what "their" stand regarding the "serpent race" is, but some sources indicate that conflict between the two alien groups has existed for hundreds of years and perhaps millenia, and is increasin in more recent times. The major centers of activity for one group of blond semi-alien humans, according to several sources, is in a network of subterranean caverns which exist a few miles beneath the surface of California and surrounding regions. One of their major capitol centers of this hidden society is alleged to be a subterranean city by the name of "Telos", which is actually a Greek word meaning "uttermost."

Telos is said in itself to be inhabited by over a million persons, many of whom claim ancient ancestral ties with the old Mayan civilizations. Telos is said to be one of seven or more subterranean cities below the United States which may have been in existence since antedeluvian times and which were apparently re-discovered and re-established by various early native inhabitants of the Americas. Also, some sources claim that these "Blond" aliens have an alliance with Oriental subterranean humans from the "Agharta Empire". There is evidence that the subterranean network beneath California may have been inhabited continuously for over a thousand years.

The Telosians, etc. are allegedly aware of conditions on the surface of the earth, which they monitor constantly via TV, radio, etc., although they are usually reticent of establishing any major contact with the surface world and carry on their activities in privacy. They are apparently aware of the geological trends which are leading this planet to an eventual crisis point (i.e. ozone destruction, pollution, seismic disaster, potential polar reversal, greenhouse effect, etc.) but seem to be just as helpless to do anything to stop it as are the surface governments of the earth. All this might sound like the most daring science fiction, but there are several sources who swear it's true...

There are other groups which may have been confused with the Telosian "Blonds". One we will refer to as the "Nordics" who have allegedly established bases or communities beyond the earth. Another group which may fit into the scenario will be referred by us as the "Aryans", an alleged 'pure-bred' race of neo-Nazis who are believed to occupy underground bases below Antarctica and utilize Nazi aerial disk technology. There is still another goup which we should include here. There have been some accounts concerning so-called "Nordics" or "Blonds" or "Aryans" (which one we do not know) who have been seen working in connection with the sauroids or the serpent race. The serpent races have apparently convinced a relatively few from one or more of these human 'races' just mentioned, to work with them, perhaps enticing them with certain promises of supernatural or technological advancement. For instance if an earth-person sees a "Nordic Blond" human with a group of reptilians, as many have (These particular "Blonds" are usually described as exuding a type of mindless and superficial "unconditional compassion" from their eyes) then the human will be all the more likely to cooperate with the sauroids' attempts to implant, examine, de-sperm, de-egg, impregnate, or genetically interfere with these victims. Often the Blonds who are working with the reptilians are described as being simplistic, with child-like minds and lacking critical thought, as if they have abandoned all critical judgement in exchange for blind faith in the grandiose promises of the serpent race. In contrast to this the Nordic or Blond groups (the majority?) who are in direct opposition to, or even at war with the Greys or sauroids, have been described as being more practical, intelligent, and less prone to use manipulation and deceit to get their way.

CONFIDENTIAL

UNITED STATES GOVERNMENT
memorandum

DATE: 1405-7:REP:bd
16 January 1978

REPLY TO ATTN OF: Code 1405

SUBJECT: Report of 12 January Event

TO: Code 6701

1. **12 January Event** — Mr. Proodian was contacted at approximately 1425 hours by Mr. Drayton Cooper, Channel 2 News, Mt. Pleasant, S.C. Mr. Cooper informed me that at 1410 hours there had been a significant event. He had received numerous calls from citizens living along the coast reporting booms. I immediately contacted CRD Keck (NRL Code 1200) who placed calls to the Operations Control Officers at the military bases in the Charleston, S.C. area. The AF reported two aircraft up (A-10 and F-5) in warning zone W-177. The MAS Beaufort reported three squadrons of F-4's authorized for warning zone W-157, and one squadron of F-4's authorized for W-132 between 1400 and 1430 hours. However, subsequent conversations revealed that only two F-4's were aloft. The two F-4's flew intercept on a N/S course on an azimuth of 190 degrees magnetic at distances 40 to 80 miles from Charleston AFB, altitude 10,000 - 25,000 feet. (Pilots feel free to go supersonic as long as they are 45 miles or more off shore.) They flew intercepts at MACH 1-1 in straight and level flight and may have exceeded this speeds during the intercept. They continued south and landed at Cecil Field, Florida at 1455 hours.

2. On 13 January, Proodian contacted Dr. Bagwell at the Baptist College to see if this event was recorded. Dr Bagwell indicated that it was and it measured 3.2 cm in duration on her recorder. It was first recorded at the Middleton Garden Station, then at the Mt. Zion Station. She indicated that a copy of the chart would be forwarded to NRL for retention. She also disclosed that she was contacted by Betty Shedburne, Radio Station WHAN, Haines City, Florida, 33844, telephone 813 422-6998. Ms. Shedburne reported noises at 1615 and 1635 hours on 12 January 1978, and that seismic station at Gainesville did not record the event.

3. During the course of the conversation, she also told of a local citizen, Mr. William Heirmann, 212 Floyd Circle, Charleston, S.C., telephone 552-3842 or 552-8429, who had contacted her and said he had pictures of a saucer shaped object that he had taken on November 12 (1800 hours), November 27 (1720 hours), December 2 (0930 hours) and December 4 (2030 hours). Mr. Heirmann had previously showed the pictures to CAPT King, Charleston AFB, who indicated that upon preliminary analysis of the unenlarged print showed, that the object was an identifiable aircraft. However, upon enlargement, it became more saucer-like in shape and unidentifiable. Mr. Heirmann stated that the object followed power lines before flying off. Dr. Bagwell has been asked by Mr. Proodian to personally view the prints and, if interesting, forward them to NRL.

R. Proodian

Buy U.S. Savings Bonds Regularly on the Payroll Savings Plan

Office of Naval Research

DESTRON/IDI

Injectable Transponder
TX1410L2
Medium Size

Product Description:

The Injectable Transponder is a passive radio-frequency identification tag, designed to work in conjunction with a compatible radio-frequency ID reading system. The transponder consists of an electromagnetic coil, tuning capacitor, and microchip sealed in a cylindrical glass enclosure. The chip is pre-programmed with a unique ID code that cannot be altered; over 34 billion individual code numbers are available. When the transponder is activated by a low-frequency radio signal, it transmits the ID code to the reading system.

Although specifically designed for injecting in livestock, this transponder can be used for other animal and nonanimal applications.

Specifications:

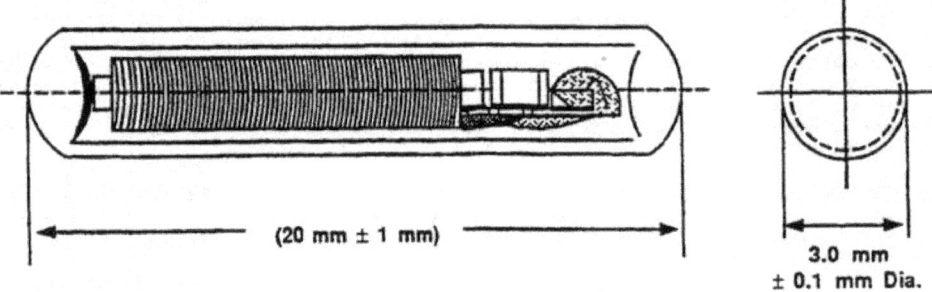

Dimensions (nominal): 20 mm by 3.0 mm (0.78" by 0.11")

Housing: Bio-compatible glass

Average weight: 0.23 g (0.008 ounces).

Temperature range: -40 to 70°C (-40 to 158°F), operating and storage

Read range with the Model HS5105L2 Mini-Portable Reader:
(In a benign noise environment with optimal orientation of transponder and scanner)

	Typical	Minimum
HS5105L2	22.9 cm (9")	20.3 cm (8")

Read speed: 3 meters per second

Vibration:
Sinusoidal; 1.5 mm (0.06") peak-to-peak, 10 to 80 Hz, 3 axis
Sinusoidal; 10 g peak-to-peak, 80 Hz to 2 kHz, 3 axis

Injector needle size: About 8 gauge (Destron part # 445-0012-00)

Operating frequency: 125 kHz

CHAPTER EIGHTEEN

ADVERSARIES

Then there are the adversaries.

THE DRACO
The members of this group include:

Zeta Reticuli 1 and 2: The planetary systems of these stars are a central area of Grey alien habitation, and several varieties of this reptilian species reside in this area, including Tall Greys, Long-nosed Greys, Insectoid Greys, and others (my abduction was by the insectoid variety, as well as by a Draco, who seemed to be collaboratively in charge of the operation along with a human intelligence agent of my acquaintance), as well as the Zeta Reticulan "Orange". Primary interest in earth: Immigration, scientific experimentation including genetics, and the utilization of earth species as both slaves and food source. The society in this area is insectoid and group-mind oriented, lacking much individuality or intelligence. Among the projects which are engaged in by this hostile-to-human group are sophisticated mind control and monitoring programs which have been in operation on earth for, literally, hundreds of years. I found that the information provided by famous UFO researcher John Lear on the purpose of the alien abductions was essentially accurate, and deserves to be widely reprinted. He has stated that there are six reasons for abduction by the Greys. These include:

(1) The insertion of a 3mm spherical device through the nasal cavity of the abductee into the brain. The device is used for the

biological monitoring, tracking, and control of the abductee.

(2) Implementation of Posthypnotic Suggestion to carry out a specific activity during a specific time period, the actuation of which will occur within the next two to five years.

(3) Termination of some people so that they could function as lving sources for biological meaterial and substances.

(4) Termination of individuals who represent a threat to the continuation of their activity.

(5) Effect genetic engineering experiments.

(6) Impregnation of human females and early termination of pregnancies to secure the crossbreed infant.

Belletrax Orion: This is one major center of the Draco alliance with a highly intelligent artificially-bred Insectoid/Grey mutation being the dominant race in the area. The genetic materials of the hive culture here must be continually supplemented with genetic materials gathered from interstellar sources, and the purposes of this group are intimately involved with the overall purposes of the Grey expeditionary forces in space. Both biological and energetic materials are in continual transhipment to this area, and this may be the "Achilles heel" of the Greys which I mentioned that I was looking for. Although it may seem like a pipe dream, one group of humans who are actively resisting the aliens are now in possession of advanced materials on inter-dimensional access ports and areas on earth. These might provide a means for launching a strike against important areas of Grey breeding and commerce. One method might be the inter-dimensional launching of toxins which would be harful to the reptilians.

The members of this specific group (at Belletrax Orion) maintain several underground bases on earth, including several in California, and in South America. Although extensive information exists on this group and their operations, I was not able to access most of it because of the extremely alien character of their culture and language. This group contains members that are both individuals as well as members of a huge hive culture and mind. Again, the nature of the activity taking place in the area, suggests that it should be closely studied, and may provide an Achilles heel for the reptilian races.

Alpha Draconis: This constellation seems to be the hub of the Draco Empire, and the Draco consider this to be their ancestral home. Native to this area are the tall Reptilians, the Reptilian-Grey hybrids, and the Deros (although they do not call themselves that, I use that terminology because of its familiarity with some researchers). These groups have severally longstanding and loosely-enforced treaties with Zeta Reticuli, with violations sometimes taking place over planetary properties, cultural issues, and possession of races employed as a food source. Information that I obtained from the information matrix suggests that these reptilians maintained outposts on earth in ancient times, but that they were exiled by human races after an extended war. Could this have been the origin of the serpent in Biblical and occult accounts? Whatever the case, it became amply clear to me that the Draco wish to remedy the situation and re-take the earth for their own purposes, and that their plans are to do this in short order. A quick scan also showed me that the Draco are showing up in greater numbers on earth for just this purpose.

Altair Aquila: This area includes extensive habitations, military fortifications, and interstellar bases, as well as a major data matrix access location. It is anticipated that this area is meant as a launching port for full scale "overt" invasion of the earth when the time comes. Information also showed that there are several large space/inter-dimensional ports being constructed underground on earth for exactly this purpose, and these areas should be considered as a high priority for investigation by alien resistance groups. The major project of the reptilian groups resident in Altair Aquila falls under the catagory "mind control" (or rather, this is the main project that they have been involved in re: humanity). These reptilians have been responsible for many of the mind control implants which have been injected into human abductees for many years. This group is also acting in collaboration with many of the human controllers in the Secret Government, participating in mind control projects, the sharing of tecnhology in this area, as well as in monitoring occult and religious groups in order to render their members subservient to the Draco goals. This group is spearheading the Alternatives projects, according to my best information.

One shocking area of information that I was able to grasp is that the step-by-step approach that is taken by many secret societies on earth culminates at the highest levels in the accessing of the alien hive mind: the human mind of members of these groups is completely surrendered to the insectoid mind at this level. Certainly we can see this in the blank stares of many high occult initiates.

Rigel: This is a Grey group who is very involved in abductions and animal mutilations on earth, and they have also formed a complex series of pacts with several earthly governments to grant them freedom to conduct these experiments. They function in total cooperation with the treasonous Secret Government. These are the aliens who, in conjunction with rogue earth scientists, are reputed to have developed the AIDS bacteria in order to reduce earth population to manageable limits. I feel certain that research into biological warfare by the Secret Government will lead us to the identity of the scientists who are collaborating with this group.

Epsilon Bootes: This proved to be an extremely fertile area in terms of information in the matrix. Almost by accident I discovered extensive records on a pact that was made between reptilian (crocodile-like, as well as others who appear to be "Greys") representatives of Epsilon Bootes with the U.S. government, allowing them free reign in a wide variety of horrendous activities including cattle mutilition, human abduction and experimentation. My researches also surfaced a current mind control project that these beings are engaged in, in collaboration with U.S. government intelligence which is not beholding to our elected officials, but is rather run directly out of the Secret Government. This is a multi-pronged project which seeks to create an InterNet-like link among human beings on earth... run from Epsilon Bootes! One can only speculate on the purpose of this mind control project, although presumably it would enable the traitorous human members of this alliance more direct access to their masters.

There are literally hundreds of other Nordic and reptilian races, although this quick survey will perhaps help in sorting out much of the information which has been released through other researchers. There are also un-

aligned groups who have not formed pacts with either the human or reptilian races, although most of these fall outside of our purpose which is to provide information directly relevant to mankind's survival. I will note one of these races, however:

The Elder Ones: I noted a good deal of information about an amorphous, star-faring race which were unnamed, but seem to conform to the Elder Ones so famed in occult mythology. This group is treated in an almost religious fashion by the Orion group, who consider themselves as "ambassadors" who are sent to prepare the way for them. Although it was difficult to grasp the meaning of the information, my impression during hypnosis was that these "Elders" travel via inter-dimensional doorways, and are considered the constructors or builders of the physical universe. They do not seem to have any particular physical form that they are limited to, but are able to take on different physical characteristics as needed. This area remains open for future research.

It is important to note the working relationship between the Reptilian-Dracos and the Greys. In my research I came across a report by an abductee who outlined this information and, I find, my own conclusions that I have gained through research as well as access to the alien matrix matches hers very closely. The following is an excerpt from a report by Cynthia Crowell from 1989. The report was provided to me by another researcher, and lacks information on obtaining it:

This initial report is primarily concerned with two groups of aliens: Greys and Reptilians. There are several different kinds of both Greys and Reptilians, but for now I will simply refer to them as single groups. Both groups live on this planet or beneath its surface and in space. They have been here for a long time. I believe that it is vital that I get this information out to researchers and other concerned individuals, and that I get it out in a reasonable period of time, rather than wait until it is "perfect."

The Greys are also "working" for Reptilians, relative to the abductee as an individual and to the human race as a whole. They have been used by the Reptilians as the middlemen, doing the work and exposing themselves to us on behalf of and instead of the Reptilians. The Greys are consistently referred to as a mercenary force, though they themselves will often say that they "have no choice", that they themselves are the slaves, presumably in their own culture or to the Reptilians.

The Greys are engaged in abduction and related activity, as they tell it, in order to survive. A great deal of the above is relative to their survival on an individual basis. They don't eat humans, but they use biological substances from humans (such as glandular secretions) in a manner we can compare with eating. (They absorb nutrients through their skin.) They milk us in the way we milk cows and they need what they take from us, or think they do. As a species, they are using material from us to recreate themselves, by creating their next generation with hybrids. Most of them can no longer individually produce offspring. I've been told that only one in a hundred or a thousand Greys can even conceive and that most of those babies do not live.

Some Reptilians, on the other hand, eat us like we eat chicken. In the United States, there are rumors of great, underground food storage rooms full of preserved human bodies. Sometimes the rumor has it that the bodies are those of children. I asked the Greys why, if this was true, would it be children? I was told that it is not only children but also adults that Reptilians eat. Children are preferred because they are generally unpoisoned by substances like caffeeine, nicotine, alcohol and other things adults are saturated with, as a group.

The Reptilians don't seem to be dependent on us as a food source, although part of their experimental work with us is toward the end of future food supply/production. When they become involved with crossbreeding (humans and Reptilians), they are not doing it for racial survival but for the purpose of creating a subclass (slave race) within their own culture. These halfbreeds are to be biological war machines and laborers, etc. They are to be someone else's property. Most contemporary monsters or oddities (such as the Cabbit, half-cat, half-rabbit, that was found in New Mexico in the 1970's) were probably created by or are otherwise related to Reptilian and/or government genetic research.

The Reptilians seem to have little regard for us as living beings. (They think that we are as ugly and repulsive to them as we ever portrayed them to be, and that we, the human race, are as "valuable as weeds.") However, they do seem to consider some of us valuable property. one gets the feeling they will continue to use us as they see fit, or, if we ever become a real problem as a group, they would sooner wipe us out than deal with it. They do not fear us, considering themselves far superior to us by all comparisons. They supposedly consider the surface of this planet to be a poisonous, inhospitable environment and "allow" us to live here, since they live below the surface and space. (We and our surface environment function as a physical buffer or living shield around their home underground.)

The Greys sometimes treat us more like children than animals. They consider us physcially beautiful and healthy; mentally young and fresh. They do not fear us, contrary to what they may claim, because they do not understand us. (They have no emotions or individuality; they are of a group mind. Socially and culturally, Greys and humans are very different.) They also fear us because they know we are potentially powerful beings. However, they insist that they "own" us: They say they created us and therefore have the right to do what they will with us. Beyond this original "right" to interfere with us, they say they have additionally earned the right through their control. Because they can control us on an individual and cultural basis both physically and mentally, they say they "own us."

These attitudes are propaganda. Their control over us in any capacity is ultimately very frail due to its very nature. Their control is based on intimidation and advanced technology. As we become more aware, we are harder to control, harder to lie to, harder to confuse. Our technology would definately be competititive with theirs if we had access to it. Much of the technology we would need to effectively overcome this situation exists now. It just isn't made available to the public, for economic reasons, as well as "national security."

The preceding statements about the Greys are based on conversations with them and long observation of them. Impressions about the Reptilians are more general. I have not engaged in conversations with Reptilians, though they have sometimes spoken to me. Most of my experience with them does not include direct communication between me and them. Almost all of my consciously recalled memories of Reptilians also include Greys, who usually do the communicating between us. Often the Reptilians seem to be present during abductions as observers only, standing off to the side of the action, just watching.

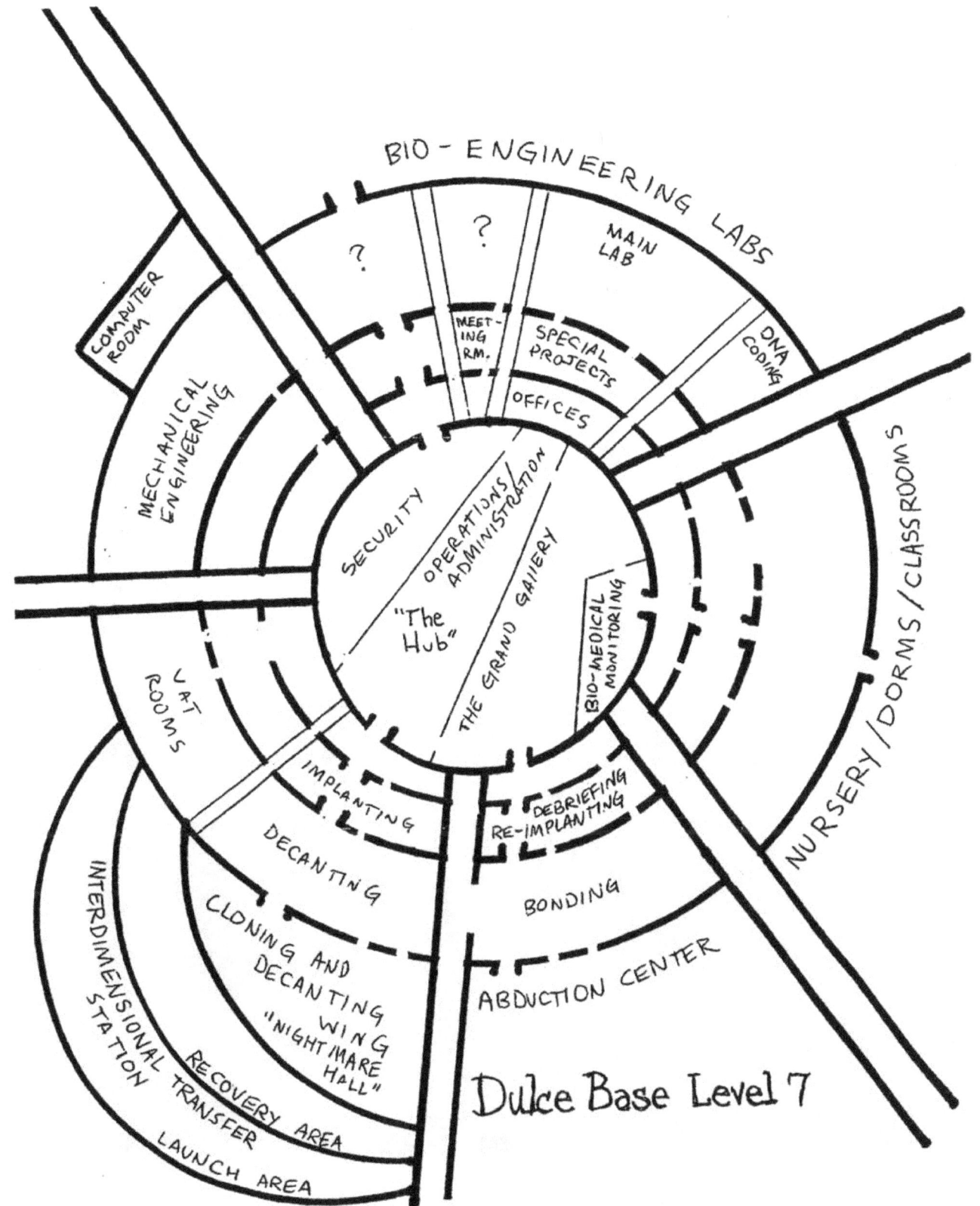

NEW WORLD ORDER HELICOPTERS IN THE UNITED STATES
Unmarked mystery helicopters — including heavily armed gunships and troop carriers — have been observed all over the nation. Some are UN. They have been reported in the states marked below. An act of treason? Most certainly!

CHAPTER NINETEEN

ALIEN CONTROL

Another area that I specifically delved into was the area of alien technology and weaponry, thinking that this information might help earth-based resistance in mounting a defense. My intention is to bring out more of this information as I am able to, but for the moment I will describe a portion of what I learned about alien weaponry, since our future may depend on the development of defense that is on a par with the hostile alien races. I am not trained in electronics or physics, so a good deal of what I was able to access in the matrix was meaningless to me, but that does not mean that it will be meaningless to someone who is familiar with these areas of research. It does get a bit technical, however, so the reader who is not interested in these areas may move on and skip the next few paragraphs.

With the idea that perhaps humanity could utilize the technology of alien weaponry against the aliens, I ran a mental query into the matrix regarding weapons of destruction, looking for a response from the system. I was surprised that I was immediately given accesss to a wide variety of information, since it had been my assumption that this would be top secret. Although much of what I received was meaningless (frankly, it was far too advanced conceptually for me to make the least bit of sense of) I was able to understand that the basic principles of alien weaponry were only modifications of the same principle used in communications and in the advanced manufacturing of their space craft. In electronic data modules of communication that may have been used to communicate these principles to alien children, or perhaps to novice technicians who were just beginning their studies, I saw that they were able to influence electromagnetic beams, pulses, and standing waves in ways which I don't believe have been accomplished on earth yet (although I could be wrong, as I said, I am not very knowledgeable in terms of advanced scientific concepts). There may be projects of this nature going on, and perhaps in collaboration with alien teams of technicians, particularly in the underground bases.

What I saw and "read" telepathically in the alien data banks, was that alien technology involved the alteration of electron flow in several ways that vastly boosted the output. This included alteration of electromagnetic particle consistancy, wavelength, and the mixing of different frequencies of radiation in order to achieve harmonic effects: creating vast boosting effects of the electromagnetics that, when directed at a life form, for instance, could rip the flesh apart (or be fine-tuned for influencing the central nervous system, or for mind control).

Another technique of rendering electronic beams more powerful is by directing them through simultaneously-

broadcast tunnels of aligned radiation, rendering them more coherent as well and imparting gyroscopic motion to the beams. There are a number of uses for this technology, including death rays which can disrupt matter including human flesh (by simulating the density of this matter electromagnetically, and generating a frequency inside, rather than on the surface of the target, rather like the effects of microwaves), but depending on the frequency of the radiation, this can be employed in the physical manipulation of tiny, even microscopic areas. The head implants seen in abductees employ this medium for mind control, through both electrical and chemical stimulation of the brain tissues. This is also the technology that causes the ignition system of cars to "short out" when UFOs are seen in the vicinity.

Doing a quick data scan, I was able to see that this technology has been "shared" in its simpler forms with both the Americans and Russians (beginning, I was surprised to note, as early as 1928, in secret experiments conducted at the State Radium Institute in Leningrad), who are primarily employing it via their intelligence agencies. I will give you an example of one usage. In a flash I received an alien/human monitoring report on a facility that has been placed by a NSA (National Security Agency) "cut-out" agency (thus offering complete deniability of any culpability in the project). There are, according to the information that I accessed, broadcasting units like this in every city of any size in the United States, some of them in operation, some of them ready to go. The particular unit I am speaking of, which provides a good example of the type, is in place atop the a well-known government building in San Francisco, and is a large black unit on the top of the building, providing a vantage on a poorer San Francisco housing district. The people who live in this area are perceived by the "establishment" as being poor, alcoholic, and worthless, and so are considered all right for experimentation and social programming of various sorts without any undue fear that the effects of the experimentation will be noticed.

The electromagnetic broadcasting unit, at least in this location, is usually turned on in the early morning hours, causing disruption of thought, angry, and violent motivations amongst the people who are targeted. Outbreaks of violence, hospital and psychiatric ward admissions, and other factors noted during these broadcasts are carefully monitored and the results are fed into a national computer which interfaces with the results from literally hundreds of other units of this sort, which are lumped under the code name BRAINTREE. These results are also directly fed into the alien matrix, since the results are of great interest to those factions of the Greys and Dracos involved in mind control operations.

The usage of the alien beam technology does not end with the BRAINTREE units which I have described, however. I was able to access information that revealed the full extent of the alien/government collaboration, including satellite broadcasting systems using the same type of beam weaponry. The systems I was able to note were the "Global Positioning System," which operates in liason with a major arms defense contractor, "Project White Cloud," run by a subsidiary of the Secret Government, and "Keyhole 11," a satellite system used by a civilian contractor in the pay of the Secret Government. Although there is an underground movement within the military meant to take over the computers running these space-based systems, they are meant to be used against patriots in the case a revolution is ever mounted against alien control.

This was the essence of what I found out about one aspect of the alien weapons and control technology. Although I have found out more, I am currently working with several patriots with technical training, so that I can more clearly impart the nature of the alien weapons systems which I familiarized myself with. I hope this information is of use to some theoretical scientists who are also patriots and long to overthrow the alien control of earth.

THE DULCE PAPERS

The Dulce papers were comprised of 25 black and white photos. A video tape with no dialogue and a set of papers that included technical information of the allegedly jointly occupied [CIA-Alien] facility one kilometer beneath the Archuleta Mesa near Dulce, New Mexico. Several persons were given the above package for safe keeping. Most of those given the package were shown what the package contained but were not technically oriented and knew very little about what they were looking at. The following is written by one of these persons about what the papers contained. This person described the scenes that the video tape showed... What you see is what you get; I can't decipher what is written or drawn anymore than you can. I pass these papers on only in the interest of getting to the truth. [From] other information I have, I believe the information herein is true. I believe the facility exists and is currently operational. I also believe that there are four additional facilities of the same type, one located a few miles to the southeast of Groom Lake, Nevada. What is the truth? Only God, MJ-12 and the aliens know for sure.

Dulce papers: Lots of papers-documents that discuss copper and molybdenum, also papers about magnesium and potassium, but mostly about copper. Lots of "medical terms" that I don't understand. A sheet of paper with charts and strange diagrams. Papers that discuss ultra violet light and gamma rays. Papers that discuss color and black and white and how to avoid detection through the use of certain colors. In addition to these papers there are about 25 pictures, black and white, plus one video tape with no dialogue, all taken inside the Dulce Facility. These papers tell what the aliens are after and how the blood (taken from cows) is used. Aliens seem to absorb atoms to "eat". Aliens put hands "in blood", sort of like a sponge, for nourishment. It's not just food they want, the DNA in cattle and humans is being altered. The "Type One" creature is a lab animal. "They" know how to change the atoms to create a temporary "almost human being". It is made with animal tissue and depends on a computer to simulate memory, a memory the computer has withdrawn from another human being. The "almost human being" is slightly slow and clumsy. Real humans are used for training, to experiment and breed with these "almost humans". Some humans are kidnapped and used completely (even atoms). Some are kept in large tubes, and are kept alive in an amber liquid. Some humans are brainwashed and used to distort the truth. Certain male humans have a high sperm count and are kept alive. Their sperm is used to alter the DNA and create a non-gender being called "Type Two." That sperm is grown some way and altered again, put in large wombs, many destroyed, certain are altered again and then put in separate wombs. They resemble "Ugly Humans" when growing but look normal when fully grown which takes only a few months from fetus size. They have a short life span, less than a year. Some female humans are used for breeding. Countless women have had a sudden miscarriage after about three month's pregnancy. Some never knew that they were pregnant. Others remember contact some way. The fetus is used to mix the DNA in types One and Tow. The atomic makeup in that fetus is half human, half "almost human" and would not survive in the mother's womb. It is taken at three months and grown elsewhere.

Event Characteristics of Four Corners Area

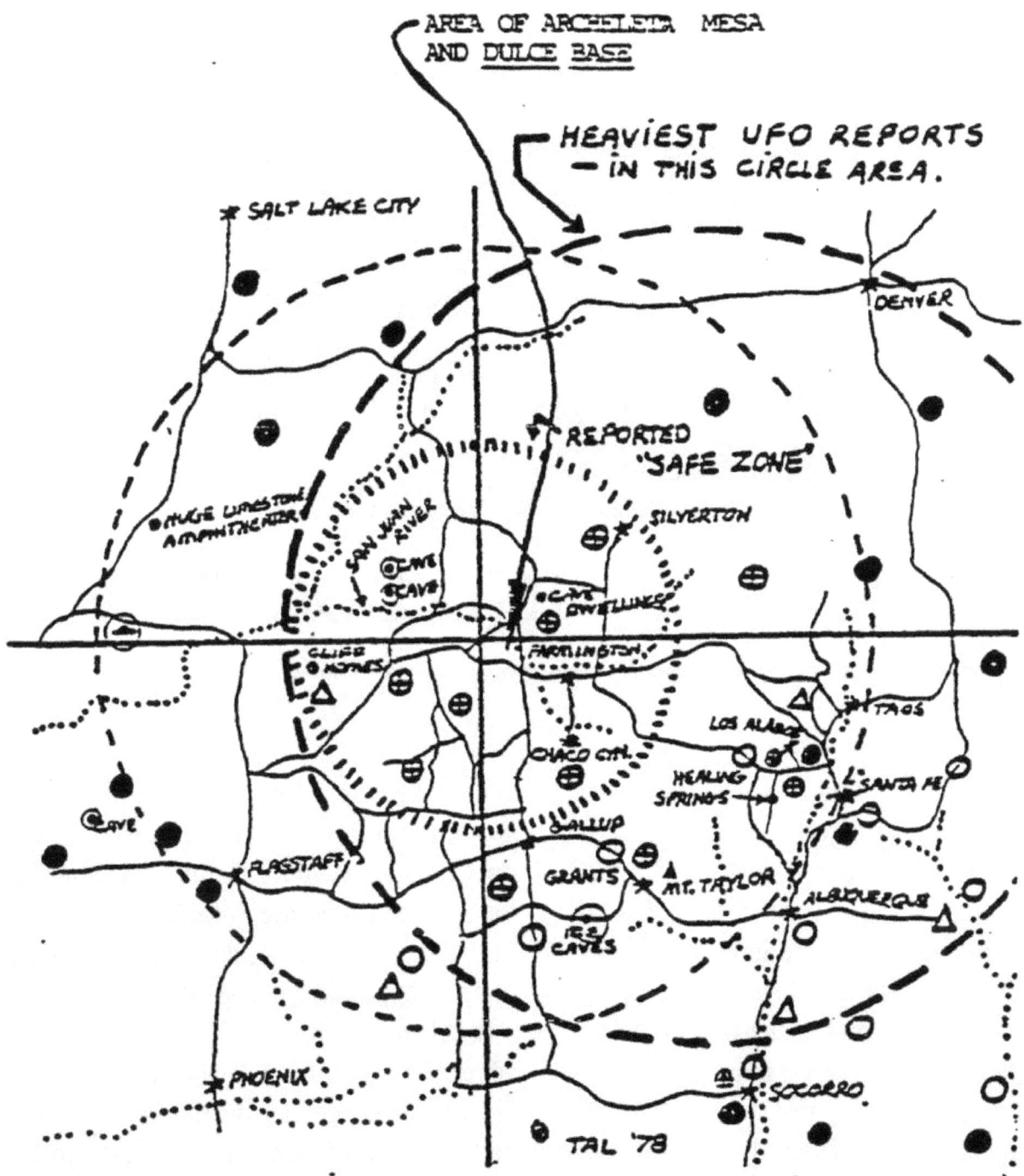

- ○ ELECTRO-MAGNETIC DISTURBANCES BY OVERFLIGHTS OF UFO'S.
- ● UFO LANDING SITES: — WITNESSED TIME AND AGAIN.
- △ UFO OCCUPANTS — SEEN REPEATEDLY.
- ⊕ SUSPECTED ANCIENT TUNNEL SITES.

CHAPTER TWENTY

OVERTHROWING CONTROL

I am very aware that time is short for humans on earth if we do not act, and that this information needs to get into the hands of concerned citizens. Thus, although I have much, much more information that was gleaned from the alien matrix, I will end my account of the matrix-link here. After several days of accessing the information in the matrix, I started to sense that the Greys had become aware that myself and the Professor had cracked at least some of their codes, and that we had been stealing them blind in terms of information. It was only a feeling, but my extensive interaction with the alien matrix had convinced me that I should trust my feelings about the Greys. When I expressed this, Professor C. insisted that the experiment be brought to an end, and that he surgically remove the implant. It is not important to explain how that was done (it is a procedure that is well known to the scientists who are specifically working in this area), but using no anaesthetic other than an hypnotic suggestion, Professor C. was able to remove the implant without any adverse reaction from my body.

After the implant was removed I only had time to briefly examine it before Professor C. took charge of it. He was going to turn the tiny, spherical electronic implant over to another scientist who was known by him and who was engaged in a long term project of cracking the secrets of the implants, and I hope to have the results of the analysis in a future report.

Now it is up to you. In my opinion, and I stress that it is only my opinion, the situation is grave, but now that I have seen first hand many areas of the data archives of the Greys, I believe that there is some hope for humanity. They, the Greys and their allies, are not nearly as unified as they would have us believe, and their relations with the Draco and with other alien races are not always cordial. In addition, the Greys themselves are victims of a huge, mulitiple-planet bureaucracy of their own making, and sometimes executive decisions take years to be implemented in the outer reaches of the galaxies. You would not believe how long negotiations over planetary property rights can take, especially if there is more than one species involved!

I repeat, there is hope for humanity. The secrets of the Grey aliens and their allies are finally being understood and seeing the light of day, and the common person on the street is beginning to understand that this is not science fiction that we are talking about. The common man is also beginning to sense somewhat, if not understand, the way in which the Secret Government has long collaborated with the Grey aliens and has treasonously sold out our human heritage.

In a way, it is as if the UFO research community has gotten too much information, so much so that it is becoming more and more difficult to evaluate what is true and what is disinformation. This is our task. We must thwart the menace of the Greys for the future of mankind depends upon it.

Finally, let me detail a strategy that seems to me to be our best hope. Humans have long neglected the offers of help and alliance from the Nordics (or the Benevolents), and in doing so have, I believe, wasted our greatest possible resource. I offer this to researchers and activists in the area of alien contact: It should be our highest priority to forge a firm alliance with the Benevolents. I see this as an opportunity which summons Mankind to a higher destiny in the stellar community. With a strong alliance between the Benevolents and the earthlings, the Greys may even be checkmated in their attempts for control. The future of the earth and the intergalactic Nordic alliance may depend upon it.

In bringing this book to a close, I would like to quote from one of the original Founding Fathers of the United States, Patrick Henry. It is amazing how relevant his words seem today when applied to a threat so different, yet equally if not more dangerous than which was posed to the colonists. Heed well the words of this hero, although realize that the threat we face is somewhat different than the threat faced by the Founding Fathers in their time. Guns are not the solution to the alien crisis (the Greys find our weapons almost laughable in the face of their far more advanced technology), but information is. At this time people need to know about the alien menace, and their plans for our future (or rather, their plans to end our future entirely). Here is Patrick Henry speaking:

It is natural to man to indulge in illusions of hope. We are apt to shut our eyes against a painful truth. Is this the part of wise men, engaged in a great and arduous struggle for liberty? Are we disposed to be of the number of those, who, having eyes, see not, and having ears, hear not, the things which so nearly concern their temporal salvation? For my part, whatever anguish of spirit it may cost, I am willing to know the whole truth; to know the worst, and to provide for it.

I have but one lamp by which my feet are guided; and that is the lamp of experience. I know of no way of judging of the future but by the past. Let us not, I beseech you, deceive ourselves longer. We have done everything that could be done to avert the storm which is coming on. If we wish to be free — we must fight! An appeal to arms and to God is all that is left us!

They tell us, that we are weak — unable to cope with so formidable an adversary. But when shall we be stronger? Will be be next week, or the next year? Will it be when we are totally disarmed? Shall we acquire the means of effectual resistance by lying supinely on our backs and hugging the delusive phantom of hope, until our enemies shall have bound us hand and foot?

We are not weak if we make a proper use of those means which the God of nature has placed in our power. Millions of people armed in the holy cause of liberty, and in such a country as that which we possess, are invincible. Besides, we shall not fight our battles alone. There is a just god who presides over the destinies of nations, who will raise up friends to fight our battles for us. The battle, is not to the strong alone; it is the vigilant, the active, the brave.

Many cry "Peace, peace" — But there is no peace. The war is actually begun! Why stand we here idle? Is life so dear, or peace so sweet, as to be purchased at the price of chains and slavery? Forbid it, Almighty God! I know not what course others may take; but as for me, give me liberty or give me death!

DEPARTMENT of DEFENSE
DEFENSE INVESTIGATIVE SERVICE

PROJECT GRUDGE DOSSIER

WARNING

THIS FILE IS THE PROPERTY OF THE DEFENSE INVESTIGATIVE SERVICE. CONTENTS MAY BE DISCLOSED ONLY TO PERSONS WHOSE OFFICIAL DUTIES REQUIRE ACCESS HERETO. CONTENTS MAY NOT BE DISCLOSED TO THE PARTY(S) CONCERNED WITHOUT SPECIFIC AUTHORIZATION FROM THE DEFENSE INVESTIGATIVE SERVICE.

SPECIAL INSTRUCTIONS:

It is certified that the material in this file is being retained pursuant to DoD Directive 5200.27, DIS Regulation 20-2 and DIS Manual 28-2.

Date Acquired ▓▓▓ 90   Signature _____

RETAIN FOR: | 60 Days | 1 Year | (15 Years) | 25 Years | Permanent |

FOR OFFICIAL USE ONLY

DIS Form 3 (85 Feb)   Previous edition will be used until exhausted.   RETENTION CONTROL SHEET

IN BOX, DIPLOMATIC POUCH UNDER LOCK + KEY SYSTEM, LOCK HAD BEEN OPENED, POUCH WAS EASILY ACCESSED TO. STANDARD DIPLOMATIC COURIERS POUCH MARKED AMERICAN EMBASSY COURIERS, CONTAINED POUCH SERIAL NUMBER JL 3 27 DELTA. INSIDE A PUBLICATION WITH RED TAPE WHICH INDICATED CODE RED SECURITY PRECAUTIONS AND A AIR FORCE DISPOSITION FORM. DISPOSITION FORM WAS STANDARD WHITE PAGE COPY, TITLE WAS ANALYSIS REPORT, FURTHER DOWN WAS ONE SUBJECT ANALYSIS OF ENCLOSED REPORT, SUBJECT TITLE WAS ANALYSIS OF ENCLOSED REPORT UNDER CODE RED. ONE, ONE READ, ANALYZE ENCLOSED REPORT UNDER CODE RED MEASURES, GIVE ABSTRACT BREAKDOWN AND REPORT ON VALIDITY. TWO, OBSERVE ALL CODE RED MEASURES, ANALYSIS REQUIRED IMMEDIATELY. UNDERNEATH THAT WAS DASH, DASH, DASH, DASH, DASH, DASH, DASH, NOF, DASH, DASH, DASH, DASH, DASH, DASH BELOW THAT, LOWER LEFT HAND CORNER THE INITIALS WGB. PUBLICATION WITHDRAWN FROM POUCH; MEASURED APPROX. 8"X 11" WITH GRAY COVER HEAVILY BOUND, BOUND PAPER BACK STYLE, ACROSS THE CENTER FRONT IT READ GRUDGE, SLASH BLUE BOOK REPORT NUMBER 13 DATED 1953 DASH PARENTHESIS 1863 PARENTHESIS LOWER RIGHT HAND CORNER WAS AN AFSN 2246 DASH 3 UPPER LEFT HAND CORNER WAS THE WORD ANN:TTID ACROSS THE FRONT UPPER RIGHT HAND CORNER TO LOWER LEFT HAND CORNER WAS RED TAPE INDICATING CODE RED SECURITY MEASURES ACROSS THE FRONT WAS STAMPED IN RED INK TOP SECRET NEED TO KNOW ONLY. CRYPTO CLEARANCE IF REQUIRED, INSIDE FRONT COVER UPPER LEFT HAND CORNER WERE HAND WRITTEN NOTATIONS IN INK WHICH WERE BLACKED OUT BY BLACK FELT PEN INSIDE COVER SHEET IT WAS BASICALLY THE SAME INFORMATION AS THE COVER FIRST PAGE WAS BLANK PAGE THEN INSIDE COVER OF 2ND PAGE WAS TITLE PAGE NEXT PAGE AFTER THAT WAS AN APPENDIX WITH NUMEROUS NOTATIONS MADE IN IT & BASICALLY NOTATIONS DONE WITH INSERTS IN WHAT APPEARED TO BE PHOTOS & ADDITIONAL NOTES. THIS WAS ROMAN NUMERAL PAGE 2 AT BOTTOM OF 3RD PAGE IT READ G SLASH BV PAGE 1 OF 624 PAGES TITLE PAGE WAS SUBJECT LETTER NOT COMPLETE LIST OF APPENDIX REMEMBERED TITLE SOME NOTES ON THE PRACTICAL APPLICATIONS OF THE WORST(?) NEMO(?) EQUATIONS TABLE OF CONTENTS PART 1 ON THE DESIGN OF GENERATORS TO ACCOMPLISH STRAIN FREE MOLAR TRANSLATION PART 2 THE GENERATION OF SPACE TIME DISCONTINUUMS CLOSED OPEN & FOLDED PART 3 ON THE GENERATION OF TEMPORARY SUEDO(?) ACCELERATION LOCAS PART 1 CHAPTER 1 DESIGN CRITERIA FOR A SIMPLE GENERATOR & CONTROL SYSTEM REFERRING TO EQUATION 17 APPENDIX A PART 2 CHAPTER 1 CONTINUATION OF

Einstein Theory of Relativity to Final Conclusion Part 3 Chapter 1 Possible Applications of Einsteinian Theory of Relativity at Conclusion Part 1 Chapter 2 Reports of UFO Encounters Classification Close Encounters of the 1st Kind Subtitle Sightings & Witnesses Part 2 Chapter 2 Close Encounters of the 2nd Kind Subtitle UFO Sightings Witnessed Within Close Proximity Part 3 Chapter 2 Close Encounters of the 3rd Kind Subtitle UFO Encounters & Extraterrestrial Lifeforms Witnessed & Personal Encounters Subtitle Colonies Relocation Thereof Case Histories Chapter 3 Part 1 Titled Military Encounters With UFOs Part 2 Chapter 3 Military Reports Concerning Sightings On Radar & Electronic Surveillance Of UFOs Subsection 2 Analysis Report J. Allen Hynek Lt. Colonel Friend On Pertinent Data Subsection 3 Refer To Appendix B At This Point Appendix Memory Becomes Slightly Blurred But Continued On For About 5 Pages Opening Subject Page Consisted Of A Report Of The Findings As Written By Lt. Colonel Friend & His Analysis Must Stress At This Point That The Version Seen Was Annotated There Were Inserts That Were Added To This Copy After It Had Been Initially Printed Sections Remembered Very Vividly Are The Photographs & The Reports Concerning Captive Sights Of Various UFOs To Include Mexico, Sweden, United States & Canada There Were Also What Was Then Classed Close Encounters Of The 3rd Kind. It Was Made Very Clear That These People Whom It Was Determined Had Genuine CE 3's Were Moved In The Middle Of The Night By Air Force Personnel And Relocated To Various Sights In The Midwest & Northwest Parts Of The United States. In Many Cases These People Experienced Physical Ailments & Exposure To Various Types Of Radiation. One Case Especially Noted & Remembered Very Vividly Was Entitled Darlington Farm Case Out Of Ohio. Case Apparently Took Place In October 1953. Man, Wife, 13 year Old Son Were Sitting Down At Dinner Table. As They Sat There Lights In Farm House Began To Dim. Dogs & Animals Raised Rucus On Outside. 13 Year Old Boy Got Up From Dinner Table To See What Was Going On. Called Father & Mother To Come Look At The Funny Light In The Sky. Father & Mother Got Up & As They Got Up The Son Went Outside Into The Yard And Father & Mother Went Out Onto The Porch. When They Got Out On The Porch One Of The Dogs Broke Loose From Leash Beside House & Came Running Around Front & Boy Began Chasing It Out Into The Open to be a UFO at the White Sands Missile Test Range in New Mexico & Texas This Took Place In March Of 1956 At About 3 o'clock In Morning The Sergeant's Captivity Was Witnessed By A Major William Cunningham Of The United States Air Force Missile Test Command, White Sands New Mexico Homebase New Mexico Approx. 3 o'clock In Morning Holloman Air Force Base The Major Cunningham & Sergeant Lovette Were Out In Field Downrange From Launch Sights Looking For Debris From A Missile Test When Sergeant Lovette Went Over Ridge Of A Small Sand Dune & Disappeared For A Time Major Cunningham Heard Sergeant Lovette Scream In What Was Described As Terror Or Agony The Major Thinking The Sergeant Had Been Bitten By A Snake Or Something Ran Over The Crest Of The Dune & Saw Sergeant Lovette Being Dragged Into What Appeared To Him & Was Described As Being A Silvery Disc Like Object Which Hovered In The Air Approx. 15 To 20 Feet Off The Ground Major Cunningham Described What Appeared To Be A Long Snake Like Object Which Was Wrapped Around The Sergeant's Legs & Dragging Him To The Craft Major Cunningham Admittedly Froze As Sergeant Was Dragged Inside The Disc & Observed The Disc Lifting Off From The Surface & Going Up Into The Sky Very Quickly Major Cunningham Got On Jeep Radio & Reported This To Missile Control & Missile Control Confirmed A Radar Sighting At This Time Search Parties Went Out Into The Field Looking For Sergeant Lovette & Major Cunningham's Report Was Taken & He Was Immediately Admitted To The White Sands Base Dispensary For Observation The Search Continued For 3 Days & At The End Of 3 Days A Search Party Came Across Sergeant Lovette's Body Approx 10 Miles Downrange From Location Where They Were At The Description Read That The Sergeant's Body Was Nude & Mutilated & That The Tongue Had Been Removed From Lower Portion Of The Jaw. An Incision Being Made Just Under The Tip Of The Chin & Extending All The Way Back To The Esophagus & Larynx He Had Been Emasculated & His Eyes Had Been Removed & Also His Anus Had Been Removed There Were Comments Of The Apparent Surgical Skill Of The Removal Of These Items & That The genitalia was removed with thoroughness precise incision as though a plug had been removed as was the anus which extended all the way up to the colon base also that there was no sign of blood within the system. Initial autopsy report confirmed that the system had been completely drained of blood & that there was no vascular collapse due to death by bleeding. Sub comment was also added that this is unusual that anybody who dies or has complete loss of blood there was vascular collapse. Also noted was that when the body was found that there were a number of dead predatory-type birds within the area who apparently had died after trying to partake of the Sergeant's body. There were a number of photos extremely grisly which were black & white but from all indications the body had been exposed to the elements for at least a day or two. New Mexico sun in the desert is extremely hot & debilitating under normal circumstances. In this section of the report it also indicated that there were numerous occasions in which a UFO tracked alongside of a fired missile & on one occasion said missile was observed being taken aboard a UFO while in flight. The speeds indicated were absolutely phenomenal (William's father had told him previously that on more than one occasion he personally had tracked what they termed as Foo Fighters at the time. His father a electronics engineer by profession & a member of the Arizona State House of Representatives by choice but at this time he was fairly well versed on electronics engineering & design & on more than one occasion he was involved in telemetry programming of missiles what are referred to as on board computers. Los Alamos area was also an atomic test scout area in the late 1940s. For some reason there seems to be a rash of UFO sightings around these areas which might give indication to validity of beings looking in on us in regards to what we are up to, that kind of thing) The report also indicated that there were a number of recovery teams that were activated specifically for the purpose of recovering any & all evidence of UFOs, UFO sightings, this kind of thing. Most notable recorded in publication was what they

Called as Recovery Team Alpha. It was reported in report. That Recovery Team Alpha had been extremely active in a number of areas + on certain occasions had travelled outside of the continental United States to Mexico + Canada. They were based out of Wright-Patterson Air Force Base. They were on the move constantly. Further information in the report consisted of such things as reported sightings + the kind of things where Air Force planes had been downed or had combat encounters or had been attacked by UFOs. Also there were autopsy reports of various human mutilations + this type of thing. In the memo typed up a number of things were out of sequence but it did deal specifically with areas as divided into sections. About midway through the report there came a section which dealt specifically with photographs + each photo was labelled + appendixed to certain reports. A number of photos in there dealt with a recovery program of some type that took place in the southwestern part of the United States. They did not give a location name but they did give grid coordinates. Thus. Unless there are Air Force grid coordinates for that area there is no clear indication to exactly where it was. The photo dealt with special team that was called in to recover a certain UFO. It also dealt with alien bodies + autopsy reports

Autopsy type photographs, high quality, color, 8 x 10, 5 x 7. Photo #1 showed a alien being on a autopsy table which is a metal table with runnels & traps underneath to trap fluid & feces. Body appeared to be little short of 4', table about 7'. No clothing on body, no genitalia, body completely hairless, head was rounded cranium, slightly enlarged, eyes almond shaped, slits where nose would be + extremely small mouth & receding chin line, holes where ears would be. Photo taken at angle, side view, looking at body at 45° angle, left hand was visible, head was going from right to left, body was right to left position, head on right side, closed eyes appeared oriental-looking + almond shaped, left hand seemed longer than normal, wrist coming down just about 2'3" above knees. Wrists appeared to be articulated in a fashion that it allowed like a double joint with 3 digit fingers + thumb. Wrist was very slender & a palm was almost non-existent, the thumb + 3 fingers were direct extension from the wrist. Color of skin was bluish-gray, dark bluish-gray. At base of body there was a darker color, indicative body was dead for some time. Body fluid or blood had settled to base of body. This indicates that body was drained before beginning autopsy. Picture 2 showed beginning stages of autopsy, following standard procedure, body was slit from crotch to just under chin + green viscuous liquid was in evidence. There were internal organs but could not be identified. Photos thereafter concerned specific areas of internal organs. Of what appeared as small cluster of a multi-valve heart or at least 2 hearts within the cadaver. No accurate description or autopsy report of what was found within corpse accompanying photos. Indication that there was no stomach or digestive track per se. Later analysis showed that fluid within body was chlorophyl-based liquid which apparently dealt with photosynthesis or similar. The report theorized that nourishment was taken in through mouth, however since there is no digestive track or anything of this nature, the waste products were excreted through skin. One section of report did specify that cadavers were extremely odorous, but this could be accounted for by either deterioration or a number of things, but theory was that waste was excreted through pores of skin. They could only theorize in report

Because there was no xenobiology, a report by Dr. J. Allen Hynek was recalled vividly which indicated that he had also studied the information provided by this particular case & that he felt that it was indeed a genuine UFO capture & subsequently the alien was part of UFO. Dr. Hynek was non-committal but did however sign this report, also indicated in report that he did not view bodies personally but viewed photographs & accompanying reports from autopsies. The photos dealt with a number of bodies which were vivi-sectioned in various ways. At one point a head was removed from body & photographed & autopsy was performed on the head. The cranium was opened & brain matter was photographed & was evident. Interesting thing about photo was that there was ridgebone or dividing partition-type bone running directly through center of skull as though dividing two brains one from the other, this seemed apparent from picture. The skin was completely removed from cranial structure & the skull was layed bare as much as possible. At one point it was divided directly in half & photo showed under-developed esophagus & nasal cavities. No clear photo of eye orbs as we know them, just photos of complete vivisection of skull itself. Numerous photos of flesh of the being starting with cutaneous & subcutaneous micro photo-graphic plates, appeared to be cellular studies done under microscope & electron microscope type photos, extreme magnification of tissue samples.

```
*****************
* CONFIDENTIAL *
*****************
```

THE WARREN SMITH REPORTS

Warren Smith is a journalist who evidently has a number of inside connections to the CIA, as well as other sources that have revealed some interesting data about the aliens and their interactions with human beings. The following data is extracted from public domain materials being circulated about these matters that had their origin with Warren Smith.

THE UNOFFICIAL CENTRAL INTELLIGENCE AGENCY REPORT

by

WARREN SMITH

1. During the 1947 "Flying Saucer Flap", the CIA knew that Russia did not have the knowledge or the technology to produce a weapon that would be as advanced as the flying disks. They did, however have a nagging suspicion that Nazi scientists and Germanic knowledge might have been put to work behind the Iron Curtain. The world was just entering the jet age and high-speed maneuverable craft would give the Russians vast superiority in the air.

2. It therefore became imperative that the United States find out about flying saucers. As covert activities require money, the intelligence community turned to their wealthy friends. There has always been an "Old Boy" network among spies and their various agencies from the start. The CIA has been an agency heavily loaded with people from Ivy League colleges and the eastern establishment.

3. According to my information, a meeting was held shortly after the Arnold sighting (1947, Mt. Rainier) at the prestigious Brooks Club in New York. Funds were obtained to launch an official check-out on what flying saucers might be and where they originated. At the same time, the CIA was checking out US military and foreign sources to find out about the UFOs. All reports came back negative, including a statement from Truman that he didn't know of anything like that on the line in the military industrial complex.

4. That left the CIA with the thought that UFOs were of Russian origin, but there were doubts about Russia as a source. The disks didn't react in a predictable pattern, and as the flap built up, it became apparent that something unusual was happening. People in all parts of the

```
*****************
* CONFIDENTIAL *
*****************
```

****
* CONFIDENTIAL *
****

country were seeing these disks. They were definitely machines of unknown origin.

5. The CIA recognized that a half-dozen of these disks could throw the citizens of the US into a panic. The disks appeared to have the capability to extremely rapid mobility and could fly coast-to-coast in a very short time. If panic arose, it was projected that the phone and radio communication systems would break down.

6. The next meeting took place at the Nassau Gun Club on the Campus of Princeton University. It was decided to start an immediate debunking of sightings. Psych Warfare and Propaganda branches of the OSI would be used to develop hoaxes, false sightings and wild reports. Stories ridiculing UFOs and the sighters could be planted in the newspapers and magazines.

7. When Frank Scully's book "Behind the Flying Saucers" was debunked, the rumors seemed to stop. UFOs were to become the exclusive property of the CIA, a group that has effectively controlled the field since 1947.

8. In 1953, the Air Force is said to have developed sophisticated radar tracking equipment. On thirteen occasions that year, the Air Force picked up blips on huge spaceships that were orbiting around the earth at altitudes from 100 to 500 miles. It was found that these ships preferred an equatorial orbit.

9. This information was rushed to DOD and the CIA. The appearance of the ships was so unnerving that a tracking station was set up at White Sands under the direction of Dr. Clyde Tombaugh, the noted astonomer who discovered Pluto. According to my informant, the hastily constructed system was to maintain a complete record of the orbiting UFOs.

10. Since that time, the agency has maintained a "duck, bob and weave" stance on these ET visitations. The agency has compiled a vast amount of data on the ETs, their technology and point of origin.

11. The agency maintains a world-wide surveillance on UFO data.

****
* CONFIDENTIAL *
****

****
* CONFIDENTIAL *
****

12. UFOs are real and they represent an advanced technology from another planet. Their home is similar to earth and they have an atmosphere somewhat like ours.

13. The problem is that their sun is dying. Their planet has started to cool and has begun to enter an ice age.

14. The aliens have decided the only way to survive was to go to Earth, which was selected for the purpose. The problem for mankind is that we are living here.

15. We have obtained data that reveals they are conducting a systematic project of surveillance. The first phase of their mission on earth involved long distance surveillance by drone aircraft. Then a high level base was established on the moon. A cartographics survey was launched and the new data transmitted to base was compared to data in the computer from earlier times.

16. The next phase was to survey to check continental drift , polar misalignment, and grid-pin misplacement from the last catastrophe. All remaining pins were located and their coordinates were plotted, computed and recorded in permanent data storage.

17. During the carrying out of this mission, other teams from the Confederacy were bust doing biological surveys and collecting specimens, and checking on the feasibility of interracial compatability at the protoplasmic and genetic levels.

18. Upon completion of these projects, vast comm relay stations were set up to monitor the cultures existing and future media networks and all military projects. The Watchers are operational. Every aspect of our civilization is recorded by the would-be invaders.

****
* CONFIDENTIAL *
****

SECRET

CRYPTO

APPENDIX

SPECIAL ACCESS REQUIRED

SECRET

Weather Control Operations by the Knights of Malta

The following material may be some of the proof needed to illustrate that various sources playing with weather patterns around the world. It may be one of the sources of the devestating weather over the past few years that has affected so many lives and has cost billions of dollars in property damage. Thanks to the source who shall remain unnamed for sending this in. Also, the OSJ maintain that orgone energy and nuclear energy are the two categories of supreme energy .... but they forget about the energy of consciousness itself - which creates the nature of reality. The OSJ are also "stuck" in a religious belief system, which does not credit them with having much awareness in an absolute sense.

World Political Intelligence on the Coming Ecological Disaster

The Western world is on a "runaway" energy binge!

Available supplies of coal, oil and natural gas are being taken and scraped from the earth, gobbled up and burned at unprecedented rates, producing unbearable pollution.

Fuel shortages are focusing world attention on the international politics of energy. How to keep fuel supplies flowing is becoming the politicians' dilemma.

Two categories or sources of supreme ENERGY exist in the world today!

One is Cosmic (*) Energy which is constructive, forever renewable, clean and most economical. Unfortunately, we are being deceived, threatened, polluted and about to be destroyed by the forced use of Nuclear Energy, which is unnecessary, nonrenewable, destructive, costly and evil.

(*) Cosmic Energy is also referred to as Orgone Energy by many authorities.

Evil Forces Oppose Natural Laws

Human history reveals a persistant hostility toward any person who touches upon or preaches the truth of the fundamental natural law of Cosmic (Orgone) Energy.

The natural method of maintaining and sustaining health and life through Cosmic Energy has eluded the best scientific minds for centuries.

Nothing should be more sacred to governments and human society than health and human life. Only truth is the answer. But what good is TRUTH to people who do not want it or cannot tolerate it?

Every attempt to bring man to understand and practice the knowledge of God and God's Natural Law of Cosmic or Orgone Energy has resulted in the steady and persistent persecution of the greatest benefactors of mankind by the slaves of Mr. X and destructive Nuclear Energy.

Nothing is more dangerous to freedom, harmony, true statecraft and health than the mis-educated hate-enraged slave of power and subversion.

God is the prime mover of the Universe, humanity, and all good works. God is the first cause and all creation stems from God our Creator.

What is urgently needed is a government that stands above the conflicting, selfish interests and *wasteful pursuits* of men and nations, to show man the right way to live in harmony with God-given laws.

Explanation: The foregoing text is part of a warning and confidential report submitted to the Supreme Council of the O.S.J. for consideration and action.

These disturbing facts have been arrived at and certified by a qualified guild of over one hundred independent scientists, physicists, meteorologists, geologists, mining engineers, chemists, researchers in science, explorers, navigators, metallurgists, and the Faculty of the First School of Statecraft. All are dedicated Knights of the Sovereign Order of Saint John of Jerusalem.

These excerpts were released to the O.S.J. membership for their consideration, response and action: September 1, 1972.

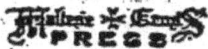

People Uninformed

It is to be deplored that great masses of innocent people in this world are *misruled* and unable to understand how to extricate themselves from misrule. However, there is the divine and correct way to rule people, according to the strict rules of Statecraft. Denied knowing how they should be properly and fairly ruled, evil forces have thoroughly purged such information from educational institutions. Why?

People are prevented from knowing that the constructive properties of Cosmic or Orgone Energy can be used to completely immunize and reverse the destructive power of Nuclear Energy.

Due to an over-all world control, no national government today is permitted to advocate, supply, finance research or any development of the use of Cosmic Energy.

Mr. X

Both Cosmic Energy and Nuclear Energy are well known, controlled and directed, not by any one or more nations, but by a live MAN known variously as the Prince, anti-Christ, Mr. X, Satan, the Devil, etc.

Mr. X is promoting and pressuring us with all the phases and sources of destructive Nuclear Energy, while he suppresses and denies the existence of God's vast stores of clean, economic, pollution-free Cosmic Energy. Being the anti-Christ, bent on destroying Christian civilization, he discredits and falsely declares that pollution-free energy is inadequate for present and future needs. He says we must accept Nuclear Energy.

The Devil attempts to discredit and destroy anyone who tries to divulge and make known the existence, advantages and virtues of our Creator's safe and sane Cosmic Orgone Energy.

The anti-Christ is the man who supervises and directs the destiny and subversive activities of world-wide propaganda groups, agents and nations, with masterful skill and miraculous methods, such as timing, precision and concerted world action.

World manipulation and destruction impossible to achieve by any individual or group of nations, is a simple chore for Mr. X.

Wars, revolutions, terror, Israeli and Soviet aggressions and Arab disunity, inflation, world monetary crises, rising prices of world goods and services, including the induced political "scandals" of Europe, England and the United States, have all been simultaneously planned and produced by Mr. X.

The world success of Mr. X is due entirely to the fact that his identity and existence remains unknown and unopposed thus far, while he easily manipulates and directs legions of dupes pledged to deny his existence and machinations.

The existence of Mr. X is unknown to most of his followers, because his followers have been carefully selected, thoroughly misled and brainwashed through modern education, underground direction and conceit, impelling them to act upon what they are made to believe is their personal views, convictions, judgment, ideas and principles.

World's Natural Resources Wasted

We know that non-renewable fuels pollute, but this is not all. It is man's exploitation of them for short-term profit and convenience which aggravates the energy crisis. A day of reckoning is coming soon.

It becomes increasingly evident that we must re-evaluate, not only our concepts of energy consumption, but also the *motives* behind our cravings. We need to examine the unbridled profit motive itself!

We have been most careless in our consideration in the use of the earth. We have polluted, raped and destroyed part of the earth God gave us, through ignorance and selfish motivation. Man has too long been *taking from* the earth — instead of *taking care* of it.

So much has been taken from the inside of God's good earth without proper compensation, that the earth's surface is beginning to crack, separate, collapse and sink, leaving great voids with irreparable damage and destruction.

The wise words of the noted biologist Dr. Barry Commoner echo the present dilemma facing mankind: "I believe that we have, as of now, a single decade in which to design the fundamental changes in technology that we must put into effect in the 1980's — if we are to survive." Further adding: "we must determine now to develop in the next decade, the *new means of our salvation.*"

Our earth is wounded, and we are wielding the death weapon. Our collective selfishness may kill us unless we find a new way to live.

Weather Control

Since weather moderation and control may be regulated by the proper use and direction of Cosmic-Orgone Energy, the controlling "powers" will not permit any nation to foster weather control.

No nation dare contribute one dollar toward protecting lives and property covering large areas of land destroyed by raging man-made floods, extended droughts and forest fires.

WEATHER MODERATION & CONTROL

Photograph showing part of a scientific weather control unit, directed by an O. S. J. scientist, located at a Cosmic Energy weather control research station in one of the western states.

Partial view of the latest weather control unit at a Cosmic Energy Research station in an eastern state. O.S.J. scientist in charge at left. Grand Chancellor of the O.S.J. at right.

VIRTUES OF COSMIC ENERGY

The ever present wonders of economic Cosmic Energy which is also a Life Energy, have always been with us but never a problem. This great Force appears to be a secret which is feared by the administrators of established knowledge, and therefore, the general public is uninformed or misinformed about its potentialities.

Cosmic Energy is capable of moderating and controlling weather. Properly manipulated and harnessed it can heat and light our homes, factories and streets. It can propel with equal speed, constancy, without pollution and most economically, machines, motors, vehicles and trains. Most important of all, it can help maintain normal physical health.

A substantial group of well qualified scientists from several countries have dedicated their lives, fortunes and services to the task of developing all the peaceful and constructive possibilities of Cosmic Energy for humanitarian purposes, under the direction of the Sovereign Order of Saint John of Jerusalem (O.S.J.).

Warning: Beware of persons or groups masquerading as this Order. Members are not solicited. Affiliation is by a careful selection and serious recommendation by members in good standing. Imitators will be prosecuted.

Sovereign Order of Saint John of Jerusalem &
Knights of Malta

World Headquarters, Shickshinny, Pa., 18655

(Published October 3, 1973, for members of the O.S.J.)

Jerusalem 1048-1291, Cyprus 1292-1310, Rhodes 1311-1523, Malta 1530-1798, Russia 1796-1907, U.S.A. 1908-

"M" PROJECT FOR F. D. R. STUDIES ON MIGRATION AND SETTLEMENT

by
HENRY FIELD

1962

card catalog indicating exact location of publication or document together with a detailed Subject Index would be prepared and maintained. The Library of Congress would be considered as the principal source of publications. The Librarian would purchase books and documents not available in LC or considered significant reference works. One or more of the largest computers, such as UNIVAC, should be employed to store and answer questions. Selected maps to be purchased or photocopied. Liaison with the Army Map Service, the Library of Congress Map Division and that of the Department of State to be maintained.

Documents. Unclassified except for some Restricted. None Confidential or Secret.

Expeditions. Complete file on all Expeditions since 1950 to be compiled and maintained with names of personnel and their biographies.

Photoduplication. Special equipment similar to that in LC to handle photostats and microfilms. Wherever possible, LC Photoduplication Service to be used; in addition special arrangements could be made with Edwards Brothers, Ann Arbor.

Reports. To be prepared by Staff, mainly upon request.

Reproduction of Reports. IBM-typed on 20-lb. bond paper, double-spaced and only on one side of paper. Font "Modern" with proportional spacing.

Use. By the Congress, all branches of the Federal Government, and any responsible investigator, but not generally available to the Press.

Space. Near the Library of Congress.

Results. Fewer political, technical and individual errors abroad. Reduction in tensions through understanding. More exports through increase in good will. Expert data on countermeasures to Communist propaganda.

Cost. One large Rocket per annum.

FUTURE

In these brief paragraphs we will be concerned with overpopulation on Earth, interstellar migration and the quest for living organisms on other planets.

Earth. In a previous section we have referred to world population growth. However, Von Foerster, Mora and Amiot[50] predict that on November 13, 2026, "human population will approach infinity if it grows as it has grown in the last two millennia."

Interstellar Migration.[51] Among the many flights of fancy, the idea of sending by rocket the Earth's surplus population looks at the moment highly impracticable. While temporary quarters may eventually be established on Venus or Mars, the probability of colonization seems unlikely. Alpha Centauri, the nearest star, is 4.3 light-years distant. Our Saturn rocket traveling at 19,000 miles per hour would require 129,000 years to reach Alpha Centauri. Even at 7,000,000 miles per hour, the transit would require 350 years. According to a recent estimate,[52] world population is increasing at the rate of 123,000 per diem. On present figures and estimates, this daily increment would cost $369,000,000,000 to rocket into space. All these figures, based on 1961 knowledge, indicate high degrees of improbability for a solution to overpopulation through migration into Space.

Life in Space. This should be divided into two categories: (a) living organisms; and (b) rational beings. Under (a) we have to assume Special Creation or the chance chemical combinations necessary to form living matter through abiogenesis. With regard to (b), the existence of rational beings on other planets, the student of the highly complex evolutionary processes on Earth can hardly imagine a similar sequence of events evolving from an ameba-like form to the Common Primate Ancestor and finally to Man--all during a period of at least 3,000,000,000 years. For those who prefer to believe in Special Creation, it is far easier to visualize the Creator making Man on many planets.

MISCELLANEA

Is there any evidence of life reaching the earth from Space? Almost a quarter of a century ago the theory was proposed by Professor Charles B. Lipman[53] that meteorites contained living matter. Since Field Museum of Natural History (now Chicago National History Museum) possesses the largest collection[54] of meteorites, as represented by meteoric falls, Dr. Sharat K. Roy[55] conducted an important series of experiments. These proved that when the experiment was maintained on a strictly sterile basis, no living matter was found.[56] However, the problem of no contamination was exceptionally hard to maintain. Now in 1961 Dr. Melvin Calvin, University of California biochemist, has described[57] the finding of "ancestral chromosomes" similar to those chemicals associated with the emergence of life on earth. Calvin wrote, "The samples indicate the same evolutionary processes that unfolded on earth have gone on elsewhere. We are not unique." For my part, I would prefer not to accept Calvin's results without additional checks from several sources.

While Life in Space may be visualized--even prophesied--proof of communication with rational beings is far more difficult, in fact as yet totally unproven.

The radio telescope may make the interception of intelligible signals[58] possible. Soon the U.S. Navy's 600-foot electronic dish will begin to pick up signals far out into Space. Even larger electronic ears are projected.

Almost forty years ago Marconi, aboard the "Elettra," was reported to have intercepted signals from Mars.[59] The press carried this front-page story world-wide; Marconi's complete denial appeared in a small paragraph on an inside page or not at all.

In the early 1920's U.S. radio and British wireless hams (government licensed operators of amateur radio stations) were organizing the first transatlantic tests, first by short-wave spark or continuous wave, later the reception of U.S. broadcasts[60] on standard wavelength (360 meters). At Oxford University Professor Morrell was conducting experiments in transmitting radio signals of 1.0 meter wavelength by means of small reflectors[61] set about 1,000 paces apart. This experiment gave me the idea to construct a receiver capable of receiving on a wave length of 1.0 meter or even less. Conversely, it seemed desirable to build an extremely long-wave receiver. Thus, a few months later my ham station[62] was equipped with two special receivers; one capable of tuning in on 1.0 meter or less; the other from 20,000 - 35,000 meters wave length. At that time we were concerned with attempting to filter out static or atmospherics which seriously affected all broadcasts. We found that heavy static came in simultaneously on all bands from 1.0 - 35,000 meters. However, on the latter maximum wave length to which we were able to tune, there were certain signals which did not come in on some of the other wave bands. These were totally illegible as far as the Morse code was concerned. I spent many hours listening to these sounds from Outer Space. A British ex-Naval operator was employed to attempt to decipher these signals. Nothing intelligible resulted. Finally, I recorded on a series of electrical transcription or phonograph records a selection of these mysterious radio signals. These records were listened to by Captain Round, Captain P.P. Eckersley, BBC technical experts, and others in London. The reply: no signals intelligible, but apparently not the result of normal atmospherics.

Now almost forty years later, I wonder, as I did then, if those signals from Outer Space were attempts at radio communication between rational beings and ourselves. Certainly during the next forty years we shall know the answer.

STUDIES ON MIGRATION AND SETTLEMENT

SUMMARY

These notes are now being written more than sixteen years following our Victories in Europe and in the Far East. The Refugees, Displaced Persons, Population Growth, Technical Assistance and the myriad of interrelated problems such as Public Health and Food Supply still plague the peace of the world--in fact far more had been than almost twenty years ago when the Staff of "M" Project received the Presidential Directive to prepare Studies on Migration and Settlement and Population Growth leading to world tensions.

I conclude with the dying words of Cecil Rhodes, but now applied world-wide in context, "So much to do, so little done."

DISCLOSURE OF
TOP SECRET INFORMATION OR MATERIAL
COULD RESULT IN *EXCEPTIONALLY GRAVE DAMAGE* TO THE NATION!

TECHNOLOGY USED FOR GUIDING THE UNDERGROUND BASES

THIS PROJECT IS

SECRET

Economic and Social Council

Distr.
GENERAL

E/C.7/1985/9
25 February 1985

ORIGINAL: ENGLISH

COMMITTEE ON NATURAL RESOURCES
Ninth session
8-17 April 1985
Item 9 of the provisional agenda*

UTILIZATION OF SUBSURFACE SPACE

Development and utilization of subsurface space

Progress report of the Secretary-General

SUMMARY

The present report has been prepared in response to Economic and Social Council resolution 1983/58 of 28 July 1983 on the utilization of subsurface space. It deals with steps taken to strengthen support mechanisms relating to the use of subsurface space and progress made in the development and use of that resource. It contains a summary of the activities carried out by some of the organizations of the United Nations system and recommendations concerning steps to be taken so that potential uses of subsurface space may be more effectively brought to the attention of developing countries.

---

* E/C.7/1985/1.

United States Patent [19]
Altseimer et al.

[11] 3,885,832
[45] May 27, 1975

[54] **APPARATUS AND METHOD FOR LARGE TUNNEL EXCAVATION IN HARD ROCK**

[75] Inventors: John H. Altseimer; Robert J. Hanold, both of Los Alamos, N. Mex.

[73] Assignee: The United States of America as represented by the United States Energy Research and Development Administration, Washington, D.C.

[22] Filed: Jan. 25, 1974

[21] Appl. No.: 436,401

[52] U.S. Cl. 299/14; 175/11; 299/33
[51] Int. Cl. E21d 9/00
[58] Field of Search .... 299/33, 14; 175/11, 16; 61/45 R

[56] **References Cited**
UNITED STATES PATENTS

3,334,945 8/1967 Bartlett 299/33
3,396,806 8/1968 Benson 175/11
3,693,731 9/1972 Armstrong et al. 175/11

Primary Examiner—Frank L. Abbott
Assistant Examiner—William F. Pate, III
Attorney, Agent, or Firm—Dean E. Carlson; Henry Heyman

[57] **ABSTRACT**

A tunneling machine for producing large tunnels in rock by progressive detachment of the tunnel core by thermal melting a boundary kerf into the tunnel face and simultaneously forming an initial tunnel wall support by deflecting the molten materials against the tunnel walls to provide, when solidified, a continuous liner; and fragmenting the tunnel core circumscribed by the kerf by thermal stress fracturing and in which the heat required for such operations is supplied by a compact nuclear reactor.

3 Claims, 5 Drawing Figures

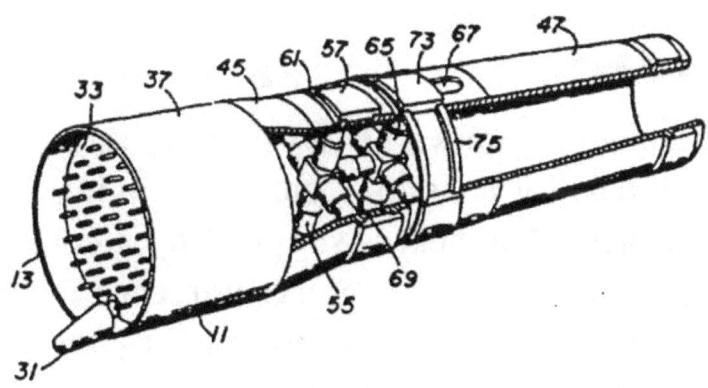

Nuclear tunneling machines work by melting their way through the rock and soil, actually vitrifying it as they go, and leaving a neat, solidly glass-lined tunnel behind them. The heat is supplied by a compact nuclear reactor that circulates liquid lithium from the reactor core to the tunnel face, where it melts the rock. In the process of melting the rock the lithium loses some of its heat. It is then circulated back along the exterior of the tunneling machine to help cool the vitrified rock as the tunneling machine forces its way forward.

These machines are used to build tunnels and underground bases. Presently, there are 129 deep underground military bases in the United States. These bases are basically large cities underground connected by high-speed magneto-leviton trains that have speeds up to Mach 2.

The Department of Defense

DEPARTMENT/AGENCIES PARTICIPATING:

 Department of the Army

 Department of the Navy

 Defense Advanced Research Projects Agency

PROGRAM SOLICITATION 90.2
Closing Date: 2 July 1990

FY - 1990

ZON-212   Ref. 1999-22

INNOVATION RESEARCH (SBIR) PROGRAM

DEFENSE ADVANCED RESEARCH PROJECTS AGENCY
FY 1990 Topic Descriptions

DARPA 90-062   **TITLE:** On-site Inspection Procedures and Techniques for Detection of Underground, Large, Hidden Cavities in Field, Mining, or Other Environments

CATEGORY: Engineering Development

OBJECTIVE: To develop and test operational on-site field procedures and equipment to detect cavities suitable for nuclear decoupling near quarries, open mines, and drill-sites.

DESCRIPTION: There is substantial research on tunnel detection and on mineral exploration that is relevant to this subject. In addition, mining engineers and quarry operators may be able to suggest practical clues or means, accounting or physical, of detecting or preventing secret activity. Cavities of interest would range from radii of 10 to 50 meters at depths or at distances from tunnels of up to 1000 meters.

    Phase I: Survey the existing literature and experts on this subject. Consult with mining and quarry engineers and operators. Outline suitable procedures and systems and define their probable capabilities. Propose suitable experiments for Phase II.

    Phase II: Execute experiments in detecting hidden cavities. Evaluate results and propose designs for operational procedures and systems.

DARPA 90-063   **TITLE:** Techniques for In-situ Borehold Determination of Gas-filled Porosity to Better Than 1% at 200-1000 Meter Depths

CATEGORY: Engineering Development

OBJECTIVE: To develop an in-situ method for obtaining dry porosity in hard rocks at a depth of 200-1000 meters below the water table and in other rock environments.

DESCRIPTION: Air filled porosity (AFP) reduces the seismic magnitude resulting from underground nuclear tests. The accuracy of current logging methods at the Nevada Test Site for determination of AFP is +/- 5% absolute; that is, if the true porosity is 1% the estimate may be in the range -4% to +6%. What is desired is an operational in-situ technique for determining dry porosity to an accuracy of 1%. If necessary, efficient methods requiring core recovery may be considered. Estimation of AFP below the water table is an important sub-problem.

    Phase I: Review existing procedures of determining AFP, both in-situ and in the laboratory. Critically assess the accuracy of the methods, if possible by direct comparison of logging data with the highest quality laboratory data. Plan experiments for Phase II to test improved methods. If possible, execute a few prototype proof-of-principle experiments.

    Phase II: Execute experiments designed in Phase I. Implement controls so that absolute accuracy can be definitively evaluated. Use of existing wells, and possible selected existing data, to minimize costs is encouraged.

DARPA 90-064   **TITLE:** Techniques for In-situ Dynamic Stress Measurements in Rocks in the 10-300 KBar Range

CATEGORY: Engineering Development

OBJECTIVE: To develop new in-situ methods for obtaining dynamic stress measurements within 2-4 cavity radii of a nuclear explosion.

DESCRIPTION: In-situ stress measurements within 2-4 cavity radii of a nuclear explosion can be of use in determining the yield of underground tests for which the original test layout is not spherically symmetrical. Existing instruments for making these measurements use the change of resistivity of selected materials as a function of stress and strain. Ease of emplacement and long-time recording capability are current areas of deficiency.

    Phase I: Review existing procedures for estimating dynamic stress. Propose one or more new instrumentation designs. Discuss the advantages of the new designs. Build a prototype instrument. Design and estimate costs for suitable experiments to test the system. In estimating experimental costs, be sure to separately estimate costs of drilling since it is possible that these would be government furnished.

    Phase II: Execute and evaluate experiments designed in Phase I.

DARPA 90-065   **TITLE:** Seismic Network Concepts for Location of Targets and Events

United States Patent
Armstrong et al.

[15] 3,693,731
[45] Sept. 26, 1972

[54] METHOD AND APPARATUS FOR TUNNELING BY MELTING

[72] Inventors: Dale E. Armstrong, Santa Fe; Berthus B. McInteer; Robert L. Mills; Robert M. Potter; Eugene S. Robinson; John C. Rowley; Morton C. Smith, all of Los Alamos, N. Mex.

[73] Assignee: The United States of America as represented by the United States Atomic Energy Commission

[22] Filed: Jan. 8, 1971

[21] Appl. No.: 104,872

[52] U.S. Cl. 175/11, 175/16, 175/19
[51] Int. Cl. E21c 21/00
[58] Field of Search 175/11–16

[56] References Cited

UNITED STATES PATENTS

3,396,806	8/1968	Benson	175/16 X
3,117,634	1/1964	Persson	175/94
1,993,641	3/1935	Aarts et al.	175/13
1,898,926	2/1933	Aarts et al.	175/16
3,115,194	12/1963	Adams	175/11
3,225,843	12/1965	Ortloff	175/94 X
3,357,505	12/1967	Armstrong et al.	175/16

Primary Examiner—Marvin A. Champion
Assistant Examiner—Richard E. Favreau
Attorney—Roland A. Anderson

[57] ABSTRACT

A machine and method for drilling bore holes and tunnels by melting in which a housing is provided for supporting a heat source and a heated end portion and in which the necessary melting heat is delivered to the walls of the end portion at a rate sufficient to melt rock and during operation of which the molten material may be disposed adjacent the boring zone in cracks in the rock and as a vitreous wall lining of the tunnel so formed. The heat source can be electrical or nuclear but for deep drilling is preferably a nuclear reactor.

3 Claims, 7 Drawing Figures

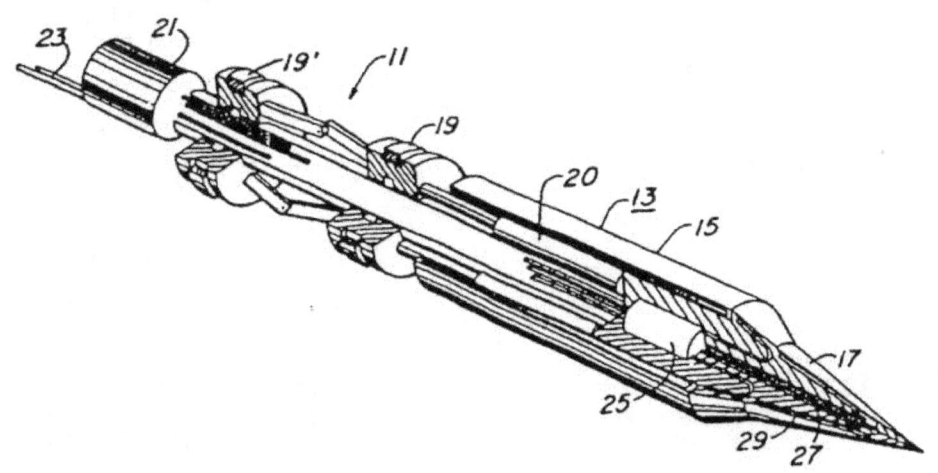

BIBLIOGRAPHIC DATA SHEET	1. Report No. NSF-RA-T-75-001	2.	3. Recipient's Accession No.
4. Title and Subtitle COST COMPARISON BETWEEN SUBTERRENE AND CURRENT TUNNELING METHODS			5. Report Date April, 1975
			6.
7. Author(s) John D. Bledsoe, J. Ernest Hill, Richard F. Coon			8. Performing Organization Rept. No. 9013
9. Performing Organization Name and Address A. A. Mathews, Inc. Construction Engineering 11900 Parklawn Drive Rockville, Maryland 20852			10. Project/Task/Work Unit No.
			11. Contract/Grant No. NSF-C840
12. Sponsoring Organization Name and Address National Science Foundation Research Applications Directorate Washington, D.C. 20550			13. Type of Report & Period Covered Final
			14.

15. Supplementary Notes

16. Abstracts

A study was made to compare tunnel construction costs between the Subterrene tunneling system and methods currently in use.

Three completed tunnels were selected for study cases to represent finished diameters ranging from 3.05 meters (10 feet) to 6.25 meters (20.5 feet). The study cases were normalized by deleting extraneous work and assigning labor, equipment, and materials costs for the Southern California area in 1974. Detailed cost estimates (shown in Appendix A) were then made for the three tunnels for baselines.

A conceptual nuclear powered Subterrene tunneling machine (NSTM) was designed. It was assumed that NSTM's were available for each of the three baseline tunnels. Costs were estimated (shown in Appendix B) for the baseline tunnels driven by NSTM.

Savings of 12 percent for the 3.05 meter (10 foot) tunnel and 6 percent for the 6.25 meter (20.5 foot) tunnel were found to be possible using the NSTM as compared to current methods. A penalty of 30 percent was found for the 3.05 meter (10 foot) tunnel using the NSTM. The cost advantage for the NSTM results from the combination of (a) a capital rather than labor intensive system, and (b) formation of both initial support and final lining in conjunction with the excavation process.

17. Key Words and Document Analysis. 17a. Descriptors

Subterrene
Thermal Tunneling
Rockmelt
Glass
Tunneling, Cost Analysis
Tunneling, Cost Comparison

17b. Identifiers/Open-Ended Terms

17c. COSATI Field/Group

18. Availability Statement Release unlimited	19. Security Class (This Report) UNCLASSIFIED	21. No. of Pages
	20. Security Class (This Page) UNCLASSIFIED	22. Price

RESTRICTED ACCESS ONLY
Copy No. _____

AN "INSIDERS" FILE ON MIND CONTROL

SENSITIVE MATERIAL

Future shocker: 'Biochip'

'Science fiction' technology here

By Teresa Allen
IJ senior writer

Don't reach for your wallet at the check-out counter.

After your food items have been priced, tallied and bagged, simply pass your hand over the computer code scanner used on the groceries, and the bill will be automatically deducted from your checking account.

Or consider this: A powerful "biochip" made from living protein that, once surgically implanted in the brain, could make it possible to program or "upload" an unlimited amount of information into the mind — without having ever cracked open a book.

Impossible? The plot of a science fiction novel?

The technology to accomplish such fantastic feats is already here or, as in the case of the living biochip, in the process of being developed, says Tim Willard, executive officer of the World Future Society, a Washington D.C.-based organization that claims 27,000 members worldwide, including "Future Shock" author Alvin Toffler.

Strong aversion

"But just suggest something like an implant in humans and the social outcry is tremendous," Willard said. "While people over the years may have grown accustomed to artificial body parts, there is definitely a strong aversion to things being implanted. It's the 'Big Brother is watching' concept. People would be afraid that all of their thoughts and movements were being monitored. It wouldn't matter if the technology was there or not. People would still worry."

Even the idea of implanting dogs and cats with identifying microchips — as the Marin Humane Society announced it would on May 1 — "is a concept we're taking slow," said Diane Allevato, director of the Novato animal shelter.

"We want to make sure it's right for the animals, and that the community is willing to accept this new technology," she added. The chip, about the size of a grain of rice, is imprinted with an identification number that corresponds to the name, address and telephone number of its owner. The information pops up on a screen when the animal is scanned with a computer wand. It is the first animal shelter in the country to use the system.

One person telephoned the society to say she felt the implants were "unnatural and weird."

"And there's no doubt about it — injecting an animal with a computer chip is a pretty unnatural thing to do," Allevato told the caller.

"But it's also unnatural, obscene really, that 15 million stray animals are destroyed in the country every year."

Chip used with cattle, swine

The microchip targeted for use by the humane society is made by Destron/IDI, firm in Colorado and marketed by Infopet of Southern California. Already the chip is being used to track the health history of swine and cattle, identify race horses in Europe and monitor the migration pattern of salmon in the Northwest, according to Destron President Jim Seiler.

In another fisheries application, salmon injected with the chip are scanned as they pass through dam sites "to assure environmentalists they are not being chewed up in the (dam) turbines," Seiler said.

Other applications could include identifying pets for health insurance purposes and identifying animal research subjects in lieu of clipping ears and toes.

While there are "10,000 ideas to explore" when it comes to the chip's potential, Seiler said Destron is only concerned with animal identification and is not considering human application.

"There's no need to (apply the technology to humans)," he said. "The human fingerprint is unique. Animals don't have a unique identifier."

But Willard, managing editor of the World Future Society's bimonthly magazine called Futurists, said the technology behind such a microchip is "fairly uncomplicated" and with a little refinement, could be used in a variety of human applications.

"Conceivably, a number could be assigned at birth and go with a person throughout life," Willard said.

Most likely, he added, it would be implanted on the back of the right or left hand for convenience, "so that it would be easy to scan."

"It could be used as a universal identification card that would replace credit cards, passports, that sort of thing," Willard said. "At the checkout stand at a supermarket, you would simply pass your hand over a scanner and your bank account would automatically be debited."

More importantly, Willard said, "it could be programmed to replace a medical alert bracelet. For example, at the scene of an accident, a medic could scan the person to find out his or her recent medical history, allergies, a relative to get in touch with. This would be especially valuable if the person was unconscious."

In another application, such a microchip could replace the need for house or car keys.

Within 15 to 20 years, the "regular microchip" will be out-classed by a biochip made out of living protein, according to Willard.

Compared to the microchips of today, "it will be infinitely smaller and have the capacity to carry much more information," he said. But the potential for "a range of functions that will boggle our minds" carries with it the danger of abuse — particularly over the issue of privacy.

A human microchip identification system, Willard said, "would work best with a highly centralized computer system where one identification number would gain access to medical and academic records, home security — all kind of things. But under this arrangement, as you can imagine, the security risks are somewhat intense."

"People tend to be romantic about their independence and privacy, but the reality is that most information pertaining to education, credit history, whatever, is readily available to just about anyone who asks. Anyone who has ever gone through a credit check knows this."

Another futurist found the concept of microchip implantation in humans offensive.

"It reminds me of tatooing concentration camp victims in World War II," said Robert Mittman of the Institute for the Future — a non-profit research and consulting firm in Menlo Park.

He said there were better methods of identifying people than "violating the integrity of their skin."

"Personally, I have problems with it. If it's ever used on humans, it won't be very widespread. People would end up sacrificing some civil rights," he said.

Martha Kegel, associate director for the American Civil Liberties Union for Northern California, expressed concern about how medical and other private records would be kept from "inquiring minds" if such a system existed.

STATE & VALLEY

THE ARIZONA REPUBLIC
THURSDAY, JULY 20, 1989

'Eye in sky' to track kids a teen horror

By Charles Kelly
The Arizona Republic

Jack Dunlap envisions his eye in the sky as a way to rescue snatched children, but it sounds like a teen-age nightmare.

You, Joe Teen-Ager, have a computer chip buried in your body, and a satellite in the sky tracks you *wherever you go*: to your girlfriend's house, to the local poolroom or to the beer party in the desert.

Whenever Mom or Pop get worried, the police are dialed and asked to track you down on their computers.

Of course, Dunlap didn't come up with his KIDSCAN idea so that it could bird-dog teen-agers.

The system is supposed to help find children who have been "picked up, transported, molested, abused, raped and murdered," he says.

Dunlap, who runs Arizona West Film Productions Inc. in Tucson and works as a private investigator when the film business gets slow, thinks he has hit on a lifesaver.

"The most important thing is to save the children," he says.

Each child whose parents signed up for KIDSCAN would get a computer chip planted under the skin and an identification number.

The chip would transmit a signal that would bounce off a satellite and be picked up by police on a computer-screen map.

A parent with a missing child could call the police, give the KIDSCAN number and have the child traced. Police everywhere would have the equipment, so you could find a child anywhere.

But if Dunlap's dream is realized, it will

— See IDEA, page B3

Steve Marcus/Special for The Arizona Republic
Jack Dunlap says his KIDSCAN system, if developed, would help parents locate children who were missing. He is flanked by Eloise M. Yanez (left) and Lorna R. Lujan at Tucson's Optical Electronics Inc., which will build a KIDSCAN prototype if Dunlap can finance it.

Idea of tracking kids via chips could be teen nightmare

— IDEA, from page B1 —

cause some troubling privacy problems, said Louis Rhodes, director of the Arizona chapter of the American Civil Liberties Union.

The police could use the system to enforce curfew laws or trace the movements of teen-agers who had not agreed to such scrutiny, he said.

"It's always dangerous to have so much information given to the police," Rhodes said.

Detective Charles Masino, a veteran of the missing-persons division of the Phoenix Police Department, acknowledged that some parents would be concerned about the "Big Brother" aspects of KIDSCAN.

But the concept is attractive, Masino said.

"Any technology that can be used to detect missing children and children that are in danger would be welcomed," he said.

Dunlap's project is just in the talking stage. He's trying to raise money to have a prototype built.

At one time, he said, he had some Pennsylvania investors prepared to kick in $600,000.

He received encouragement from employees of Martin Marietta Energy Systems Inc., which runs the Oak Ridge National Laboratory in Oak Ridge, Tenn.

Dunlap said officials there first told him they would build the prototype, then backed out.

"It was like a James Bond movie," Dunlap said. "It was like they had been told to shut up and stay away from it."

When the lab people sidestepped the project, his financial angels made themselves scarce, Dunlap said.

"It was really weird," Dunlap said. "This sort of knocked me for a loop."

Joe Culver, a lab spokesman, said there wasn't anything weird about it.

Lab people did speak to Dunlap about a microchip they are developing, he said. Scientists want to put the chip on "killer bees" to trace them as they sweep up into the United States from Mexico.

But the chip hasn't been fully tested, Culver said, so the lab can make a commitment to Dunlap.

"It's way premature," Culver said.

The Electronic Mark Is Now Perfected

By G. G. Stearman

The race is on! Several companies are now competing in a new market that has practically unlimited potential: The implantation of electronic identification transponders in animals. When electronically interrogated, they broadcast a specific number.

These transponders—radio receiver/transmitters—are now encased in tiny glass tubes about the size of a rice grain. As technology rapidly improves, they will no doubt become even more compact, and contain more information. Many municipalities and farm operations are beginning to use them to identify animals. They are much more effective than a tag or brand, since they can contain information specific to the individual animal. Also, since they become a permanent part of the animal, they can't be lost.

Currently, these so-called passive transponders can be programmed with a number ranging between 4 and 10 digits. Using a hypodermic needle, the unit is placed just beneath the skin of an animal. When a hand-held interrogation unit is brought near the implantation site, the transponder is activated, transmitting its number, which is then digitally displayed on a screen.

One U.S. company, known as Destron/IDI Inc., is now marketing its unit "used to track cow and sheep herds, as well as pigs, pets and fish." The April 16th edition of *The Denver Business Journal* reports that an Australian company known as Animal Electronic ID Systems Ltd. has linked up with Destron/IDI to install the system in their country. "Animal Electronics will purchase $2.5 million of Destron's animal identification products in the next five years and contribute $100,000 to Destron's product development. The company intends to sell the Destron products to cattle and sheep raisers, as well as to pet owners."

The California Dairy Herd Improvement Association has begun a program in seven Western states, with the expectation that it will soon spread nationwide. In 1990, the association "expects to identify 70,000 animals with the Destron system in 1990, and 1 million by 1991, but that is just the tip of the iceberg of the Destron agreement, said Lee Curkendall, president of the California association."

Texas Instruments is also rushing to develop its own identification system, and is in the running "for a massive contract with the Dutch government to identify 22 million pigs in Holland."

Another U.S. company known as Infopet has already sold its system to many municipalities as part of an animal control system. Soon, pets will be numbered as part of a nationwide move to improve animal control.

In truth, the system is based on a good idea. Branding and tagging will now yield to a much more efficient system. Farmers and ranchers, as well as city animal-control officers will no doubt welcome the system as it greatly simplifies their work.

But students of Bible prophecy will feel a chill, futuristic wind blowing across a sinister horizon. The economic system of the antichrist will someday call for just such a numeric identification system. Currently, Americans are numbered with a 9-digit Social Security number. Implanting that number just beneath the skin of the right hand or the forehead is now a practical reality. An individual so numbered could be traced in all his movements.

Of course, none of our current leaders would call for such a draconian system. But one day, the numbering of the population will seem like the right thing to do:

And he causeth all, both small and great, rich and poor, free and bond, to receive a mark in their right hand, or in their foreheads:

And that no man might buy or sell, save he that had the mark, or the name of the beast, or the number of his name.

Much has been written about these two verses in Revelation 13:16 and 17. There has been much conjecture about details of the antichrist's economic strictures. The simple fact of the matter is that a man's number will be the agency by which his financial transactions are registered. Without the number, no transactions will be possible; there will be no income, no food and no shelter.

As you read this, electronic implants are being introduced worldwide in the animal-control industry. They are considered an improvement, and no doubt they are. Someday soon, however, the offshoots of this system will be used in a way that their inventors never envisioned.

> *Currently, Americans are numbered with a 9-digit Social Security number. Implanting that number just beneath the skin of the right hand or the forehead is now a practical reality.*

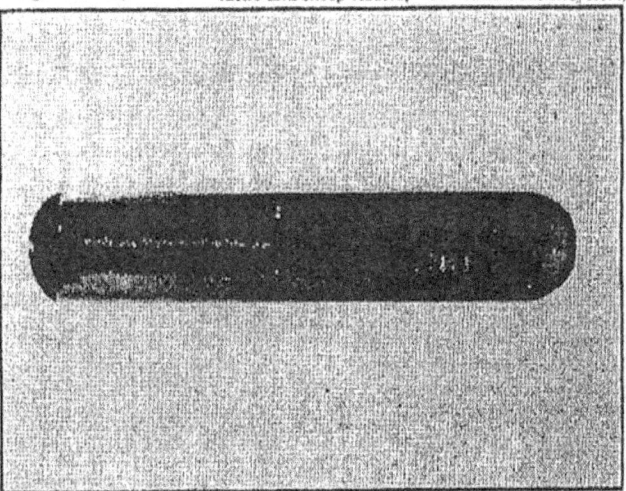

This is a magnified view of an identification transponder now voluntarily being implanted under the skin of animals. Its actual size is the size of a grain of rice. How long might it be before the government or police require these in the right palm or foreheads of humans?

COUNTDOWN

Microtechnology and the Mark of the Beast

BY TOM FONTANES

"And he (the Antichrist) causes all, both small and great, rich and poor, free and bond, to receive a mark in their right hand, or in their foreheads:

And that no man might buy or sell, save he that had the mark, or the name of the beast, or the number of his name.

Here is wisdom. Let him that hath understanding count the number of the beast: for it is the number of a man; and his (the Antichrist) number is Six hundred threescore and six." Rev.13:15-17

"Consider a powerful 'biochip' made from living protein that, once surgically implanted in the brain, could make it possible to program or "upload" an unlimited amount of information into the mind- without having ever to crack open a book." This was the scenario Teresa Allen presented in her 1989 article "Future shock: 'Biochip' Science Fiction Technology Here."

Too far-fetched to really happen? Tim Willard, managing editor of a bi-monthly magazine *Futurist* and executive officer of the Washington D.C. based **World Future Society** which claims among its 27,000 members Future Shock Author Alvin Toffler, would disagree. According to Willard within twenty years today's microchip will be rendered obsolete by "a biochip made out of living protein ...infinitely smaller and (with) the capacity to carry much more information (and) a range of functions that will boggle our minds."

In the last two millennia Western Civilization has moved from the Age of Faith to the Age of Reason, into the Age of Discovery. Today, because of technology we are said to be in **The Age of Information**. In the book America In Perspective, by Oxford Analytica, it states that "The area of greatest economic impact in the next decade is likely to be **telematics,** the information of economy. This (will increase) the development of a wide range of microchip-based systems of information processing combined with communications and control technologies.ll

By far the two largest subscribers of telematics are the federal government and private business. In the government there are five major federal agencies which collect the largest amount of data. These are the Department of Health, Education and Welfare, of Commerce, which handles the census of Defense, of Social Security, and the IRS. In his book, The Cult of Information, Theodore Roszak writes that together these five departments have over 3 billion overlapping files on American citizens.

In 1985 the government enacted National Security Directive #145 giving the National Security Agency exclusive control and use of all federal computers and data banks. More ominously, however, it permits the NSA access to all government computerized files with no provision for the right of privacy.

In the private sector the largest data banks are those belonging to the nearly 2,000 credit bureaus. The 5 largest, among which are corporations like TransUnion of Chicago and TRW of California, alone possess over 450 million files. One estimate, in fact, states that 80 percent of Americans over the age of eighteen are in their computers somewhere. These files contain entries under such headings as **lifestyle** which include information ranging from personal income and shopping habits to political affiliation and religious persuasion.

Rozsak gives an excellent example illustrating that no data is so unimportant or too trivial to be collected. In 1984 the Selective Service sent an eighteen-year-old boy in California, several months delinquent in registering for the draft, a computerized warning letter. There was, however, no such person at the address. After a federal investigation it was found that the name had, in fact, been invented by two teenagers. Several years before the pair had filled out a card at a local ice cream shop offering free birthday treats to its young customers. The name went into the store's computerized mailing list, which was later sold to one of the country's many direct mailing businesses. The list was eventually made available to the Selective Service which routinely collects and sorts such lists specifically to obtain names and addresses by birthdays.

As technologically advanced as today's computers have to be, to process all this data, there are even greater computers known as "super computers."

According to Sidney Karin and Norris Parker Smith, in their book The Supercomputer Era, rather than a particular design or model, "A supercomputer is the most powerful computer available at any given time."

New ideas," asserts the Analytica, "techniques and ways of building computers aim at more powerful, faster processors and memory chips, and machines that function in entirely new ways in order to think and learn. Systems that use 'parallel processing', allowing many operations simultaneously, would enable artificial intelligence applications: distinguishing between fragrances; vision; reading; hearing and speaking natural language; and the ability to reason and make judgements."

Bearing this in mind it is worth noting that according to Karin and Smith, in the mid-80s the Trilateral governments of the United States, Japan, and Western Europe began stimulating the development of supercomputers.

It goes without saying that what makes

> "a biochip made out of living protein ...infinitely smaller and (with) the capacity to carry much more information (and) a range of functions that will boggle our minds."

The prototype microchip (shown encased in plastic), can be inserted with a hypodermic needle.

Microtechnology
CONTINUED FROM PAGE 8

these computers "super" is their ability to compile and collate massive amounts of data almost instantaneously. The next "wave" or **quantum leap** forward will be in the combining of the micro-chip and telematics.

The Smart Card

An example of this marriage is found in a 1987 *U.S. News and World Report* article entitled "Raising the Intelligence of Credit Cards," by Stanley N. Wellborn, which talks about a "smart (credit) card" with a "silicon brain." The article describes how a microprocessing chip with a 2,500 character memory, and 200 possible transactions will be combined into a (credit) card. It also goes on to tell about a future version of **the smart card** which will have tiny memory banks containing the subscriber's bank balance, stock portfolio, complete medical history, a computerized signature and fingerprint, and even a list of appointments and addresses." Wellborn goes on to write about an even more "advanced smart card" called "the UltiCard," or "Ultimate transaction Card," that's memory can be changed and updated by the card holder."

Arlen R. Lessin, president of Smart Card International and inventor of the UltiCard, says the card in effect will allow holders "to carry their banks in their pockets. It can keep track of two separate accounts, one for charges and one for debts (and) with enhanced memory, as well as carry an encrypted version of your signature, fingerprint, and/or even your portrait."

The Ulticard will allow a merchant to verify that your account can cover a particular purchase. It then interfaces with your bank, records the transaction, and deducts it from the balance, before displaying an authorization number that can be copied on the sales slip.

"Smart cards could (also) serve as keys to restricted areas," continued Wellborn, "serve as a passport and hold prepaid electronic tokens for phone calls, parking meters and gas pumps." To activate the UltiCard the user enters a password or six digit PIN (Personal Identification Number) assigned by the banking system.

It is worth considering that perhaps this six digit PIN could, in fact, be the precursor or maybe a form of the 666 in the thirteenth chapter of Revelation. Hal Lindsey believes, and stated, that 666 "will be the prefix to a larger number that every person will be required to receive and (that everyone will be) required to worship the Antichrist in order to qualify to receive it-without which they can't buy, sell, or hold a job. So it's a means of absolute control through the use of economics. I believe the world is being set up for that right now."

Needless to say the implications of Allen's scenario are ethically threatening. Yet it is important to realize that, given our technological ability and moral climate, rather than a future threat, it is a real and present danger. According to Willard, "the technology to accomplish such a feat is already here, or in the process of being developed."

Consider this fact: a microchip, manufactured by the Destron/IDI firm of Colorado and marketed by INFOPET of Southern California, is already being implanted in animals by veterinarians and various humane societies throughout the U.S. and Canada.

This chip, or **Implantable Transponder**, is 11 mm x 2.1 mm, and weighs only 67 mg making it small enough to be injected under the skin through a hypodermic needle. Inert, and composed of biocompatible glass, each Transponder is imprinted with a unique identification number.

Destron describes the **Implantable Transponder** as "a passive radio-frequency identification tag, designed to work in conjunction with a compatible radio-frequency ID reading system." Consisting of an electromagnetic coil and microchip the **Transponder** is sealed in a tubular glass enclosure. With over 34 billion individual code numbers available, the chip is preprogrammed with a unique ID code that cannot be altered. When activated by a low frequency radio signal, the **Transponder** transmits the ID code which appears on a screen when the subject is scanned with a computer wand.

A marketing video by INFOPET, offering the Transponder to pet owners, states: "In the past four years thousands of animals have been implanted with micro-chips. The conclusive results indicate that this form of identification is both safe and effective in all species."

Once implanted all related information goes into a computer data bank that can be accessed via a toll free 800 number from anywhere in North America.

> In 1985 the government enacted National Security Directive #145 giving the National Security Agency exclusive control and use of all federal computers and data banks.

The video tape presentation ends by stating that this "high tech," "electronic identification," "micro-chip system...will replace and render obsolete all other forms of identification."

While stating that there are "10,000 ideas to explore" when it comes to the chip's potential, Destron president Jim Seiler claims human application is not one of them.

A brochure by Destron, however, states that: "Although specifically designed for implanting in animals, this transponder can **be used for other applications** requiring a micro-sized identification tag."

Since, according to Willard, the technology behind the transponder is "fairly uncomplicated" with a little refinement, could be used in a variety of **human applications**. One of the "applications" he feels includes "a Universal identification card that would replace credit cards, passports, that sort of thing."

"But just suggest something like an implant in humans and the social outcry is tremendous," continues Willard. "While people over the years may have grown accustomed to artificial body parts, there is definitely a strong aversion to things being implanted. It's the 'Big Brother is watching concept..."

And rightly so since Willard then states that: "a human microchip identification system would work best with a highly centralized computer system....Conceivably, a number could be assigned at birth and go with a person throughout life....Most likely," he added, "it would be implanted on the back of the hand for convenience so it would be easy to scan."

> One estimate, in fact, states that 80 percent of Americans over the age of eighteen are in their computers somewhere.

This futurist view is as Orwellian as the doublespeak used to try and justify it. Not

COUNTDOWN
Microtechnology

all futurists, however, share Willard's view.

"It reminds me of tattooing concentration camp victims in World War II," said Robert Mittman of the Institute for the Future, a non-profit research and consulting firm in Menlo Park, California. He said there were better methods of identifying people other than "violating the integrity of their skin."

Mittman's comment is almost scripturally insightful. First consider that "the Mark of the Beast" in Revelation thirteen is a counterfeit of "The Seal of the Lamb" in chapter seven. Next, consider that in Greek the word "seal" is **sphragizo** which is a stamp of security and preservation while "mark" is **charagma** meaning a scratch, etching, or tattoo, representing a badge of servitude, or slavery.

In the science fiction movie classic "Demon Seed", Proteus is the evil conscious intelligence of an ultra-supercomputer. Like some technological genie, Proteus seeks to escape the limits of its silicon based microprocessing world. Yearning to experience reality externally as a human, it abducts, and keeps hostage, its creator's wife. By means of bio-technology, genetic engineering, and a remote robotic unit, **Proteus** creates a sperm cell. This "Demon Seed," containing an artificially constructed DNA code replicating its unique conscious personality or, if you will, "soul," is then implanted in its captive womb. An embryo is produced that develops into a fetus which is eventually born. The movie ends with the new born infant's eyes reflecting the laser gleam of the supercomputer

Proteus, as it whispers, then declares, "I am alive." Cinematically, this film is "biotechnology meets 'Rosemary's Baby'." Prophetically, it is possibly a means for a satanic counterfeit of the virgin birth and incarnation of the coming Antichrist.

As we "fast forward" into the last days, the fulfillment of prophecies increase. Although alarming, as Christians we know that our God is sovereign and has everything under complete control. This, however, will only be of comfort to those who have been **spiritually reborn.**

Do you know Jesus Christ as your Lord and Saviour, or will you meet Him as your Prosecutor and Judge? You may one day find yourself in a world where everyone, including you, is being implanted with transponders and forced to worship the image of the Antichrist. Then after you either die of fear, supernatural catastrophe, divine judgements, are executed, or even survive, you will find yourself facing the same Lord you have ignored and rejected.

The Bible tells us that "It is a fearful thing to fall into the hands of the living God" (Hebrew 10:31). However, the same Bible states that "God is not willing that any should perish but that all should come to repentance." (I Peter 3:9) So "Choose this day whom you will serve. As for me and my house, we will serve the Lord". (Joshua 24:15).

Brain Transmitters

What They Are and How They Are Used

Mediaeko
Investigative Reporting Group

1996 Reprint
REVISED

Radio Implants and Remote-Controlled Humans

Brain Transmitters
What They Are and How They Are Used

Doctors in Sweden

began placing brain transmitters in the heads of anesthetized patients without the persons' knowledge in about 1960. The insertion was conducted through the nostrils and took only a couple of minutes to perform.

Implanted devices can remain in a person's head for life. The energy to activate the implants is transmitted by way of radio waves. Professor José Delgado wrote about the technology in *Physical Control of the Mind* in 1969.

The Technology and Its Possibilities

Brain transmitters have been thought to be impossible by the majority of people and have been relegated to science fiction. The fact is that scientists developed the technology into reality at least forty years ago.

By means of two-way radio communication called *telemetry*, or remote control, one can send wavelengths round trip to a brain transmitter in a person's head. The wavelengths flow through a person's brain, then return to a computer where all aspects of a human being's life are uncovered and analyzed.

To allow brain waves, measured by *electroencephalograph* (EEG), to be analyzed by a computer instead of through a printout offers new possibilities of interpretation. The charting of mental thoughts, vision, hearing, feelings, and behavioral reactions can lead to an analysis of the foundation of personality. It allows one to study the psyche more completely. In addition, one can follow chemical reactions, observe patterns of neurons, or follow an illness or disease and analyze it at an earlier stage of development. All of the above and much more can be discovered with bio-medical telemetry.

During the 1960s, brain transmitters as small as a half of a cigarette filter made it possible for doctors to implant them in patients easily and without surgery.

Two-way radio communication throughout the world to the brain was possible by the late 1950s. This was done in many ways. For example, vocal messages could be sent by radio waves to receivers placed in the head, where a person with an attached transmitter could answer directly to a central location with his thoughts, by brain waves data (EEG) carried with radio signals. Distances were not a problem, since radio waves could travel globally at the speed of light.

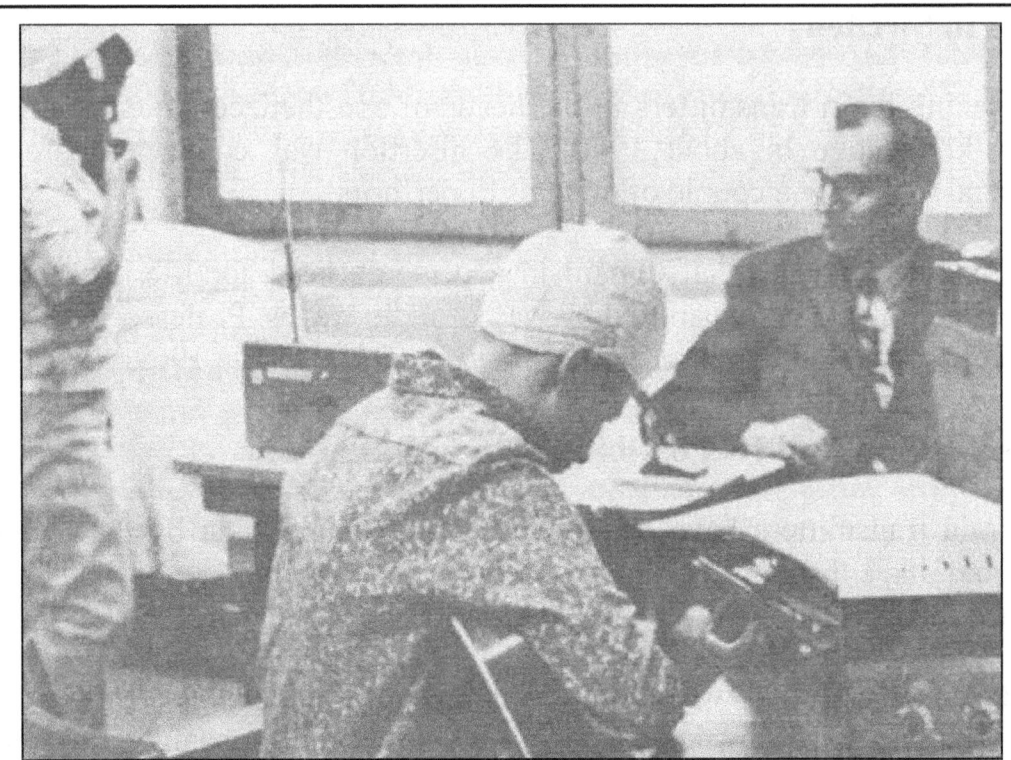

Implanted brain transmitters (biotelemetry devices) have been reported since the 1960s: "Two patients instrumented for intracerebral radio stimulation and recording engage in spontaneous activities (one is playing the guitar) in the psychiatric ward in the presence of the doctor (VM). Explorations of the brain can be performed for as long as necessary without disturbing the patients." — J.M.R. Delgado, V. Mark, W. Sweet, F. Ervin, G. Weiss, G. Bach-y-Rita, and R. Hagiwara, "Intracerebral Radio Stimulation and Recording in Completely Free Patients," *The Journal of Nervous and Mental Disease*, 1968, October; 147(4): pages 329-40.

Liquid crystals which are injected directly into the bloodstream and fasten themselves to the brain have been developed in the last ten years. It works on the same principle as the usual transmitters and uses the same technology and contains the same possibilities.

How It Began - Experiments with the Brain

As early as the 1920s, European scientists made discoveries which paved the way for future development of brain stimulation. The Swiss W. R. Hess could identify 4,000 different places in the brain's hypothalamus, which are in direct contact to certain physical and mental reactions. By stimulating specific points in the brain by an electrical current, the stimulation of one point of the brain could bring about aggressive reactions, while the stimulation of another point could bring about calmness. Through electrical currents to the brain, Dr. Hess could change peoples' personalities, bring about feelings of happiness or sadness, hunger or satisfaction, etc. All of this was achieved over seventy years ago.

To the Present and Victims for Life

Brain transmitters, also called *electrodes, stimoceivers,* and *endoradiosondes,* can control the brain and transmit data. They can be used to influence people to conform to a political system. They can be applied to remotely monitor and control human beings to serve as agents. The technology exists and is being utilized. The devices usually remain in a person's head for life.

"Autonomic and somatic functions, individual and social behaviors, emotional and mental reactions may be evoked, maintained, modified, or inhibited, both in animals and in man, by electrical stimulation of specific cerebral structures. Physical control of many brain functions is a demonstrated fact. ... It is even possible to follow intentions, the development of thoughts, and visual experiences," wrote Dr. José Delgado in the book *Physical Control of the Mind* in 1969. At that time Dr. Delgado was a Professor of Physiology at Yale University, where he developed techniques for electronically and chemically influencing the brain. He has published more than two hundred scientific works and is a well-known authority in neurology and behaviorism.

In the preface to the book, it is written that Dr. Delgado, "... shows how, by electrical stimulation of specific cerebral structures, movements can be induced by radio command, hostility may appear or disappear, social hierarchy can be modified, sexual behavior may be changed, and memory, emotions and the thinking process may be influenced by remote control."

It is possible to change people, create illness, modify opinions, and dull or activate the senses by penetrating centers of the brain with radio waves. People then obey controllers instead of their own natural choices. Monitoring of individuals' brain activity can instantly reveal all private experiences and observations of others.

> "This is the second implanted transmitter; this device appeared under rather unusual circumstances on 10th March 1972, when I became tranquilized in the hotel where I was temporarily lodging. This implantation preceded a period of prolonged torture with personality-altering radio signals 10 - 20 hours a day and they started communicating directly with my brain. It was then I realized that they could discern my thoughts and, indeed, experience my entire range of cognitive activity. ... The picture was taken at Karolinska Hospital where all radiographers deny that any foreign object can be identified in this picture. However, there are a number of overseas physicians who testify the obvious fact, that several transmitters can be seen quite clearly." — Robert Naeslund, INMC, Open Letter, Stockholm, Sweden, May 1993, page 32.

Dr. Robert G. Heath, of Tulane University, has implanted as many as 125 electrodes in a human being's brain. In his experiments, he discovered that he could control his patients' memories, sexual arousal, fear, pleasure, and cause hallucinations.

Overriding Proof Against the Hospitals

"In response to your most recent letter regarding the roentgen films, I can only confirm that some foreign objects, most likely brain transmitters, have been implanted at the base of your frontal brain and in the skull," wrote Professor Petter Aaron Lindstrom from California to one of his Swedish patients. The patient was a victim of an implantation of a brain transmitter over twenty-five years ago. Dr. Lindstrom, who taught at the University of California, San Diego, added, "There is no excuse for doctors to implant brain transmitters in people's heads."

There is complete evidence that Södersjukhuset, Karolinska, Nacka, and Sundsvall hospitals, among others in Sweden, have implanted brain transmitters without the permission or knowledge of the patients for many decades.

Mental Patients Utilized

Investigations at different mental hospitals in Sweden have shown that a great number of patients out of fifty interviewed, thought themselves to be victims of long-term medical experiments. A number of these patients were actually in need of mental care due to the experiments. There were also many at the hospitals who were forcibly placed there because they had declared that a transmitter had been implanted in their heads during an operation, or in conjunction with admittance to the mental hospital.

Checks were made of all groups with electronic devices which confirmed that there were radio waves traveling from brain transmitters in many patients.

Interviews with patients were done at Långbro Hospital, Beckomberga Hospital, as well as at Karolinska Hospital Psychiatric Clinic.

The radio waves which pass through the brain are not necessarily registered by one who has a brain transmitter. Only when the effect is greatly increased, for example when experiments are performed, is it possible for the victim to detect them.

> "This is the third transmitter placed in my head and the first which was embedded in my brain. Without doubt it was implanted while being detained by the police in Stockholm 1973; this was my first period of custody and afterwards I underwent considerable personality modification, a process which had already begun in 1967 but accelerated rapidly towards criminality after the implantation of the second transmitter." — Robert Naeslund, INMC, Open Letter, Stockholm, Sweden, May 1993, page 32.

One of the letters from P.A. Lindstrom, M.D., to his patient that is an implants victim.

P.A. LINDSTROM, M.D.

June 20, 1983

Mr. R. Naeslund
Ervallakroken 27
12443 Bandhagen
SWEDEN

Dear Mr. Naeslund:

The enclosed letter of May 30 I had prepared in rough draft. I don't find a copy so I might not have mailed it to you. Later I received your additional skull film, which clearly demonstrated some implanted transmitters, one inside the brain and two probably just underneath the brain. Within a week I shall have that film examined by the radiologists here, but I do not expect them to prove, nor to rule out, any brain damage like granulomatous changes or a superficial brain abscess, at least not based on the findings of that plain skull film you sent.

I have been very busy the last months, which explains why I am uncertain about the mailing of the letter outlined May 30. I am serving as "Certified Consultant" in Neurosurgery and in Dentistry for the U.S. Department of Education. In addition I am very much engaged in teaching and surgical work as Clinical Professor in Neurosurgery at the University of California Hospital in San Diego and also as Senior Consultant at the local Veterans Medical Center. My schedule is as heavy as when I worked in Stockholm. There I was Associate Professor of Dentistry for six years and Consultant in Dentistry for the old Royal Medical Board of Sweden while I was studying medicine at the Karolinska Hospital. I have not done any studies or work in dentistry in this country.

Now you will understand why I cannot spend much time on your serious and complicated problems. Nevertheless, I might have spent more time on your case than any Swedish physician has done so far-- and without a charge.

With best regards.

Very sincerely,

P. A. Lindstrom, M.D.

PAL:mjt

Electronic Measurements

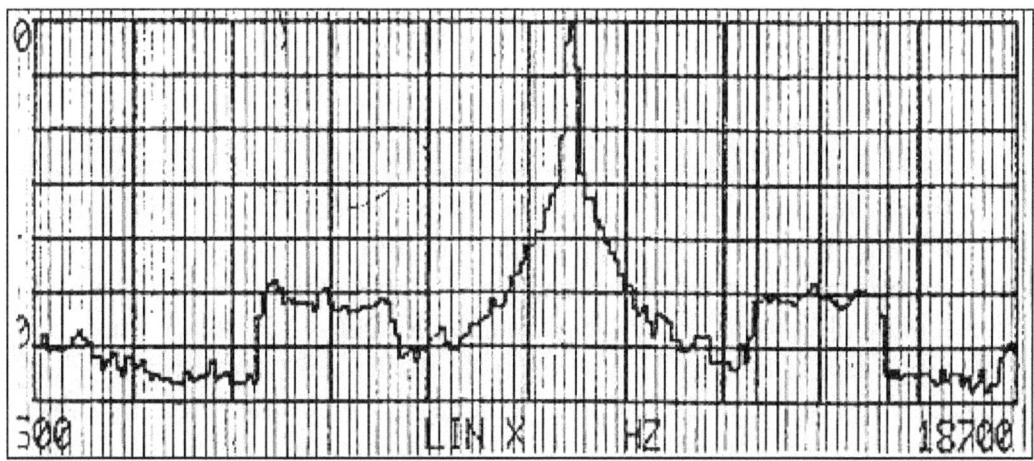

This picture shows the frequencies 18.5 - 18.7 kHz which were sent from a brain transmitter. The chart was created by a printer connected to a radio frequency analyzer computer during measurements from a transmitter in a person's skull.

While measuring other persons, the wavelengths were counted at similar values.

Long wavelengths are commonly used since they work over vast distances at the speed of light, and the frequencies are often between 15 - 35 kHz.

The radio waves are called "frequency shift" signals and can flow within a certain wavelength area. They do not occur in a decided frequency, but rather through a special modulation, the radio waves *identity*. The bandwidth was 150 Hz and the effect in all measurements was between 1 - 10 microvolts.

Measurements were done with the following electronic devices:

Hewlett & Packard Spectrum Analyzer 3585 A
Roedre & Schwarts VLF-HF Receiver EK 070
Marconi Spectrum Analyzer
Dynamics SD 375 Spectrum Analyzer
Nicolets Radio Frequency Analyzer Computer

Court Trials in Canada

were heard against a number of hospitals in Montreal in 1989. The hospitals were accused of carrying on long painful experiments with patients which began in the

1950s. One of Canada's most honored doctors, Ewen Cameron, Head Doctor at Royal Victoria Hospital and Allen Memorial Institute, worked on assignments from the Secret Police that ordered experiments with, among other things, brain transmitters.

"Furthermore, it can be seen that electrodes placed in the occipital lobe are blocking the blood flow behind their delimitation where the oxygen depletion is caused and this is seen as well in his frontal brain just above the implanted transmitter. Among the changes caused by the frequencies affecting his brain, the reduced oxygen levels have induced an alteration of neurological functions, and impaired cognitive abilities including that of memory. Moreover he [Mr. N'Tumba] has obviously been anesthetized without his knowledge so that this implantation could be performed. ... The x-ray examination was performed at Brook Hospital Main, September 16, 1992." — INMC, Letter to British Prime Minister John Major, Stockholm, Sweden, October 9, 1992.

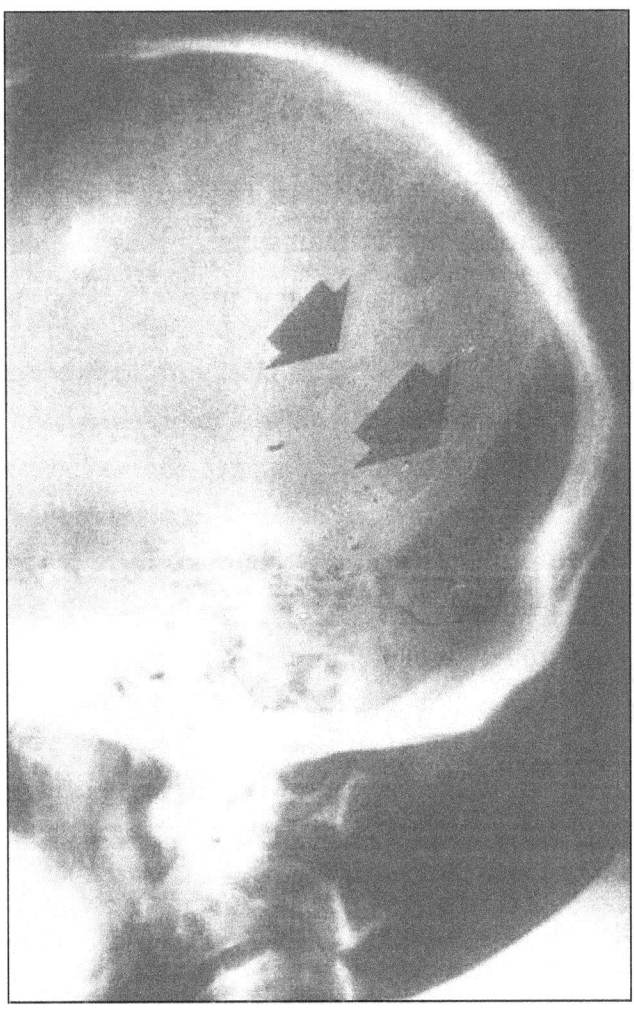

"... a meeting between Mr. John Austin-Walker, Member of Parliament, and a victim of mind control, impressed on him the importance of pursuing investigations into the matter ..." — INMC, Letter to British Prime Minister John Major, Stockholm, Sweden, October 9, 1992, page 1.

HOUSE OF COMMONS
LONDON SW1A 0AA

Mr K N'Tumba

20 August 1992

Dear Mr N'Tumba,

Following your most recent visit to see me, I have written to the Prime Minister on your behalf.

As you will know, there is very little accountability of security services to the House of Commons and Members of Parliament have almost no power in relation to the activities of MI5.

As soon as I receive a response from the Prime Minister, I will be in touch with you again.

Yours sincerely,

pp John Austin-Walker MP

Many Others Cry for Help

Doctors at the World Health Organization's (WHO) office in Copenhagen say that many Swedes write to them, stating that they have been exploited for hospital experiments. Many say that devices must have been implanted in their heads.

The United Nations' information office in Copenhagen also says that upset residents of Sweden have contacted them and have sought help as victims of hospital experiments.

Amnesty International in Stockholm and Copenhagen tell a similar story, as well as the Citizens' Rights Movement, representatives of the Green Party of Sweden, and a number of female members of the Swedish Parliament.

Those who contact the National Swedish Board of Health and Welfare (Socialstyrelsen) about this issue are sent to Department Ptp (formerly HS4 and SN3). Then they are informed that they are psychologically ill and that they run the risk of being admitted to a mental hospital if they continue to talk about a device in their heads. Additionally, they are told that brain transmitters do not exist.

Swedish Board of Health and Welfare

The person Dr. Lindstrom later helped had by 1977 written to authorities in Sweden and explained to them to what he had been subjected. Among those he wrote to was the General Director of the Board of Health and Welfare.

Declared Mentally Ill

Dr. Annmari Jonson at the Board of Health and Welfare referred to the letter a year later when she explained, "He intensely maintains everything which he had written to the Board of Health and Welfare. He exhibits, in this way, obvious misconceptions and points clearly to the need for psychiatric examination."

The examination was conducted in 1978 by Dr. Janos Jez, who wrote:

"He says that he is convinced that a device was applied in his head during an operation at Södersjukhuset. He ought to be considered dangerous if this pattern of misconceptions cannot be erased; and if he then begins to doubt his ideas and thereafter begins to have insight into his illness. He should therefore be committed to an asylum."

Five years later Dr. Lindstrom wrote, "... I can only confirm that some foreign objects, most likely brain transmitters, have been implanted at the base of your frontal brain and in the skull. ... I fully agree with Lincoln Lawrence who in his book on page 27 wrote: 'There are two particularly dreadful procedures which have been developed. Those working and playing with them secretly call them R.H.I.C. and E.D.O.M.—Radio Hypnotic Intracerebral Control and Electronic Dissolution of Memory.'"

The patient wrote to both the doctors and the Board of Health and Welfare's General Director, Barbro Westerholm, and included a copy of Dr. Lindstrom's declaration. However, none of them desired to answer, which indicates both the Board of Health and Welfare's attitude towards the issue, and even the doctors' guilt.

What Brain Transmitters Look Like

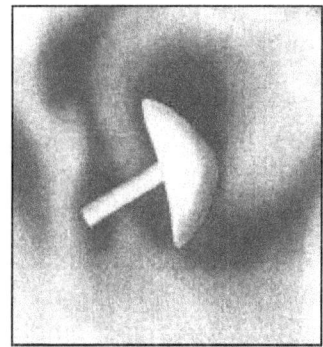
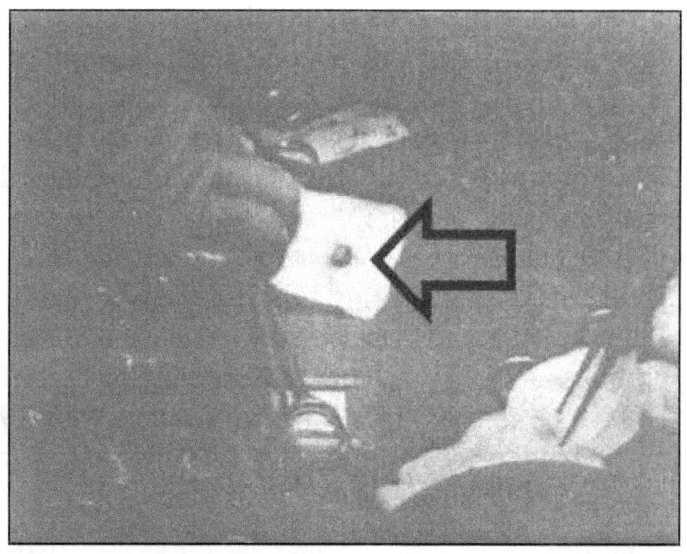

The above photographs are of brain transmitters. The above one on the left is an enlargement taken from an X-ray. The above picture on the right was taken at an operation to remove the implant.

The above one on the right shows the shape of the most usual type of brain transmitter. It looks like a bullet and is put into place through the nose. This device was inserted during an operation at Södersjukhuset in Stockholm by Dr. Curt Strand at the end of the 1960s, without the knowledge or consent of the patient. It was placed just underneath the brain. This implant is the same shape on both sides and its actual length is 16 millimeters (mm) or .62 inch, with a width of 7 mm (.27 inch).

The above picture to the left shows a brain transmitter which has the shape of a mushroom. It was implanted through a surgical opening in the forehead. Its actual size is 7 mm (.27 inch) across the head, while the stem is 4 mm (.16 inch).

Most implant victims are unaware of the devices because they were sedated during the procedures. Then they are amnesic, monitored, and controlled. However there are some disclosures.

"This is the fourth transmitter in my head and it was inserted in connection with an appearance at Nacka Police Station, just outside Stockholm, on 26th November 1975, ostensibly for interrogation. I was locked up in a cell, but after a short while I fell into a deep sleep from which I emerged to an entirely new life. It is during these hours when the transmitter was implanted, and when, I awoke I had a searing high frequency signal at about 100 db in my skull. This was to plague me for about 16 hours a day for the past eight years and completely transform my life. It depressed the functional capacity of my right cerebral hemisphere and altered my personality, behavior, and abilities as if they no longer were part of myself." — Robert Naeslund, INMC, Open Letter, Stockholm, Sweden, May 1993, page 32.

Doctors Warn

Dr. Robert J. Grimm of the Good Samaritan Hospital in Portland, Oregon, stated in March 1974 at a doctor's symposium in California, that he viewed brain control and influencing the brain with radio waves was of similar importance as to the debate concerning the detonation of the first atomic bomb in Hiroshima. He also asked, "Do scientists have the right to pursue projects potentially destructive of human life, and in this era, destructive of the individual?"

And Protest to the Swedish Government

The chairman of an internationally influential scientific organization in Canada, Dr. Andrew Michrowski, wrote in 1985 to the Swedish government and sought an answer about Sweden's obvious encroachment of human rights. He saw clear evidence that Swedish doctors implanted brain transmitters in patients, and referred to the Declaration of Human Rights signed by Sweden.

The Swedish government did not reply.

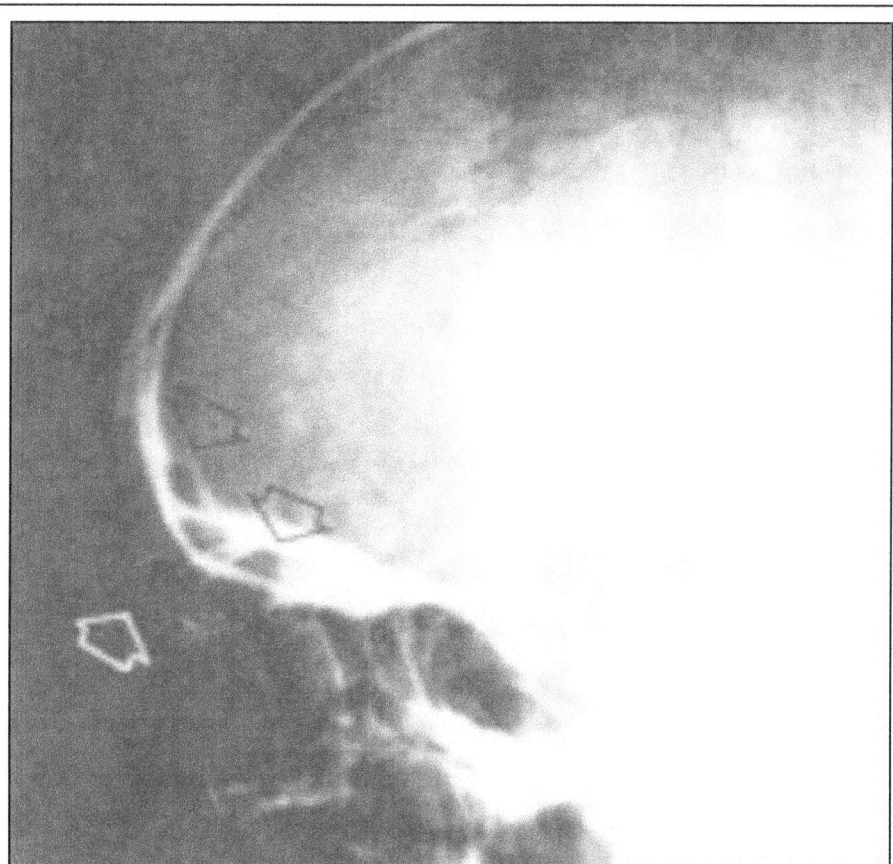

"This X-ray shows three transmitters in the frontal lobes. All of these were implanted on different occasions by the Swedish police. The detainee had been put to sleep unaware, as usual, at the police remand center in Stockholm. A doctor writes in his statement concerning this X-ray: '**...Later I received your additional skull film which clearly demonstrated some implanted transmitters, one inside the brain and two probably just underneath the brain.**'

The upper arrow indicates the object lodged completely within the brain.

> All these transmitters were inserted through the nostrils and implanted into the frontal lobes in the vicinity of the upper opening of the nasal passage." — Lennart Lindquist, Evamarie Taylor, and Robert Naeslund, *Cybergods*, Stockholm: Gruppen, 1996, page 11.

> Another medical opinion about X-rays, "... taken at Karolinska Hospital where all radiographers deny that any foreign object can be identified." — INMC, Open Letter, Stockholm, Sweden, May 1993, page 32.

```
UNIVERSITY HOSPITAL
University of California
Medical Center, San Diego

            PROGRESS RECORD
             (Typewriter Copy)        Source    Request Date


TO WHOM IT MAY CONCERN:

Recently I reviewed a skull film marked: NASLUND, ROBERT and
dated 26-11, 1981. That film shows a couple of unusual
foreign bodies at the base of the skull, possibly some form
of brain transmitters.

However, I have not examined or talked to this patient and
do not know the pertinent history.

San Diego, CA
October 6, 1983


                    Ingmar Wickbom, M.D.
                    Professor of Radiology
                    U.C.S.D.
```

FOA Educates Doctors

Since the 1960s, the Swedish Defense Research Institution (FOA) has educated hospital doctors, mostly surgeons and psychiatrists, regarding brain transmitters and bio-medical telemetry.

One of the books which was used twenty-five years ago at FOA's Department 3 in education had the title *Bio-Medical Telemetry* (1968), written by Dr. Stuart Mackay. Dr. Mackay wrote in the introduction that, "The purpose of this book is to introduce a wide segment of the scientific community to the rapidly developing field of bio-medical telemetry. It presents to physicians, engineers, and scientists information about the possibilities of different telemetric methods. It gives biologists a background in electronics to enable them to choose equipment."

The former head of FOA, Lars-Erik Tammelin, and the following director, Bo Rydbeck, are medical doctors with advanced knowledge in biology.

When Bo Rydbeck became head of the FOA in 1985, he said in an interview in the newspaper *Dagens Nyheter* that, "Among the current assignments, more intensive effort will be put into information technology." Which includes both telemetry and brain transmitters as essential parts.

Dr. Mackay continued in his introduction, "Among the many telemetry instruments being used today [1968] are miniature radio transmitters that can be swallowed, carried externally, or surgically implanted in man or animals. Recent developments include pressure transmitters small enough to be placed in the eye, ultrasonic and radio units for free-swimming dolphins, units for tracking wild animals, and pill-sized transmitters of many designs and functions that can operate continuously for several years. The scope of observations that can be made is too broad to more than hint at with a few examples. ... The possibilities are limited only by the imagination of the investigator."

Dr. Stuart Mackay has worked as a Professor at the University of California, Berkeley, and at many foreign universities. His main fields are Medicine and Biology.

Computers and the Brain

"Dr. Delgado is optimistic that with the increasing sophistication and miniaturization of electronics, it may be possible to compress the necessary circuitry for a small computer into a chip that is implantable subcutaneously. In this way, the new self-contained instrument could be devised; capable of receiving, analyzing and sending back information to the brain, establishing artificial links between unrelated cerebral areas, functional feedbacks, and programs of stimulations contingent on the appearance of predetermined wave patterns," wrote Samuel Chavkin in *The Mind Stealers* (1978), a book about psychosurgery and mind control.

Samuel Chavkin was the founder and chief editor of the Science and Medicine Publishing Company, which publishes periodicals concentrating on medical topics.

In the preface to the book it is stated that, "Telemetry for the surveillance of every citizen is on the drawing boards. Chavkin's prediction that mind-control techniques could become standard equipment of governments, prisons, and police departments is backed by forceful documentation."

Biotelemetry systems that remotely "mind read" and "mind control" have existed for decades. Brain transmitters measure EEG and send data to computers that instantly translate it into words. Implants also deliver electric shocks that control a brain and behaviors. The devices are now less than 1 mm (.04 inch) in diameter.

Dr. Delgado conducted experiments in the early 1960s that placed an electrode on the eardrum (middle ear) of a cat. The device picked-up people's conversations and transmitted them to a receiver for listening. According to Victor Marchetti, co-author of *The CIA and the Cult of Intelligence* (1974), the CIA attached a tiny radio implant to a cat's cochlea (inner ear) for surveillance purposes.

A few years after Delgado's implanted "bug" experiments, Dr. Ralph Schwitzgebel developed a miniature radio receiver so that a therapist could communicate with his subject.

Tiny combination microphone-transceiver-speakers are implanted inside unsuspecting people's ears. The instruments transmit nearby conversations and deliver audio commands. Individuals are conditioned to obey the directives, though they are usually unaware of the voices.

"X-ray photograph taken the day following the operation [August 12, 1987, St. Carolus Hospital, Ji Salemba, Djakarta], the 1/2 cm [.20 inch] deep area of branded cortex can be identified, as can the implanted transmitter." — INMC, Open Letter, Stockholm, Sweden, May 1993, page 15.

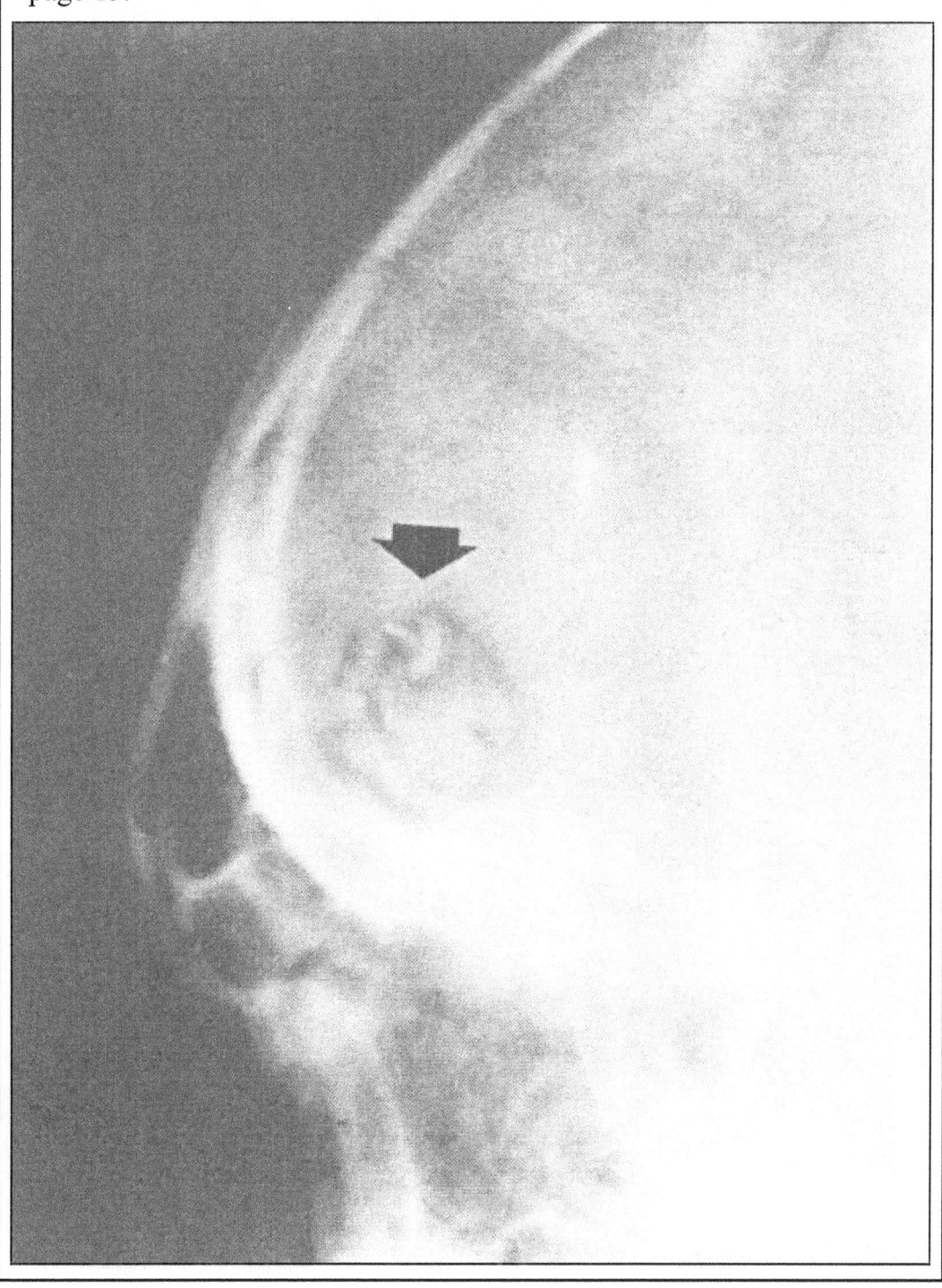

Report for an x-ray examination conducted over three and a half years after an August 12, 1987 brain implant victimization.

Sanjeevan Medical Centre

S. No.	DEPTT. OF RADIOLOGY	Date 9.4.91.
Name MR ROBERT NASLUND	Age	Referred by

REPORT

X-RAY SKULL AP LAT FOR COMPARISON

The skiagram reveal a radioluscent area with irregular and hazy margins behind the frontal sinuses which is marked by arrows and suggests break down.

In comparison to previous skiagrams this area appears to have regressed with the borders not so well defined.

The umbrella shaped object of metallic density seen in earlier skiagrams of the patient appears not so distinct but is seen within the destructed area.

DR NALIN SACHDEV
RADIOLOGIST.

In 1985

An advertisement placed by the Swedish Citizens' Rights Movement in over thirty daily and weekly publications stated that doctors in larger hospitals in Sweden inserted brain transmitters in anesthetized patients during operations. At the same time, a letter signed by fifty people was sent to the Attorney General.

The Attorney General Questioned

Those who had signed the letter had read through material which showed that the reality of brain transmitters is a fact. The signers demanded an answer from the Attorney General on whether the implantation of brain transmitters is a crime or not. Those who signed the letter were representatives from different human rights groups, the Swedish Peace Movement, professors from, for example, the Royal School of Technology, lawyers, and others.

The State Says Yes to Brain Transmitters

The Attorney General did not reply to the letter. Instead, he sent it to the Attorney District (*Överåklagaren*), who said that this issue should *not* be considered a crime. Decision from May 15, 1985, *Överåklagaren Register number AD II 76-85*.

However, of course it is one of the harshest crimes which the state can commit; to deny the right of the individual to his or her own brain, and to inner peace without the interference of government authorities. Since Sweden signed the Human Rights Act, it must follow the act's assumptions. In any case, it means that a new relationship has been created between the state and the people of the country.

"There are similar signs, here and now, like in Germany during the 1930s, where the country's leading doctors and politicians see individuals as objects of experimentation where their brains and behaviors are changed," wrote Samuel Chavkin about the United States in 1978. The same can be said about Sweden, the same ideas exist here. Mind-control technology has changed since the 1970s and has been developed even further.

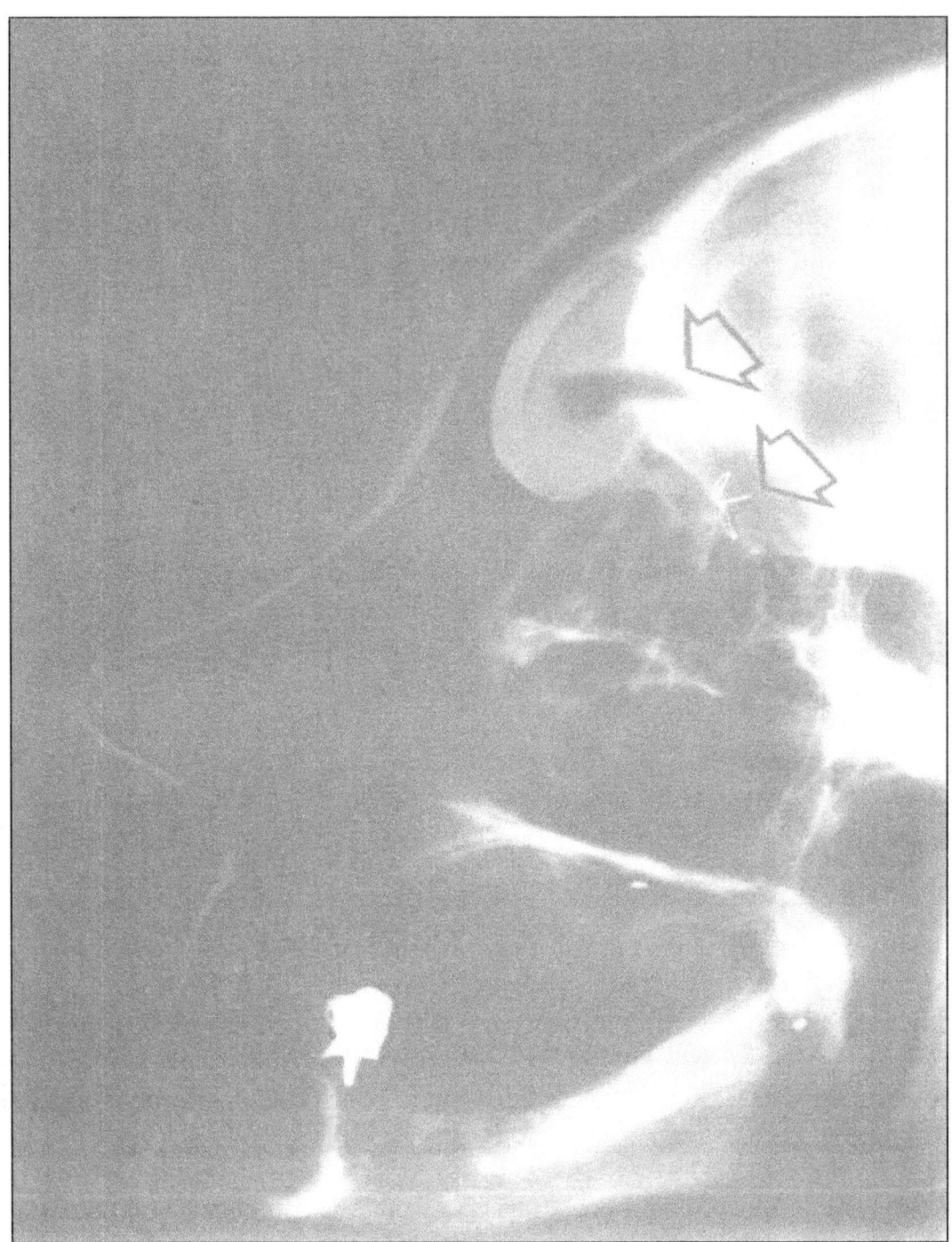

X-Ray of a person with two types of brain implants and an object in the jaw.

Mediaeko
Investigative Reporting Group
Box 136
S-114 21 Stockholm, Sweden

Stockholm October 12, 1992

Prime Minister John Major
British Government
London SW1A OAA
England

INMC
International Network against Mind Control

Dear Sir,

Our international network of researchers has for several years been engaged in investigations into mind control and its widespread utilization around the world and we have become aware of several victims in Great Britain; reports received from exploited individuals refer to mental hospitals, police authorities and prisons as among the state institutions involved in the implantation of transmitters, electrodes or radio-transmitting crystals in people. **The use of mind control is such a grave encroachment on civil liberty that, if allowed to develop further, it will threaten the freedom and integrity of all. Along with environmental problems, this is one of the most urgent issues to address if we are to ensure a more secure future.**

The reason we are addressing this letter to you personally is that a meeting between Mr John Austin-Walker, Member of the Parliament and a victim of mind control, impressed on him the importance of pursuing investigations into the matter so much that he addressed a letter to you himself in August this year. Later writing to the injured party, a Mr. N'Tumba, he said: *"Following your most recent visit to see me, I have written to the Prime Minister on your behalf. As you know, there is very little accountability of security services to the House of Commons and Members of Parliament have almost no power in relation to the activities of M15. As soon as I receive a response from the Prime Minister, I will be in touch with you again."*

Just what happened to Mr. N'Tumba, he describes himself in a letter to us: *"Concerning the brain transmitter in my head, it has been performing without my knowledge or consent... What's very outrageous is that I am sharing all my vision, thoughts, images, hearings...etc with people around me as the security services are engaging in a large scale propaganda drive to smear my character, background, behaviour, emotions and motives... I have no privacy at all... I am not a spy, I am not a criminal, I am not a terrorist. Being an innocent victim of M15... my persecution started in June 1988".* What is more, there is no reason to suspect the validity of what he writes; we are overburdened with letters such as this one from the USA, Denmark, Sweden, Germany, New Zeeland inter alia and **our investigations in Sweden reveal a terrifying reality where the mental health services, police authorities and hospitals implant radio-transmitting devices in people's heads and brains. This reality is exposed by a vast amount of X-ray** material to be a chilling and gloomy vision of the future, stage-managed for decades by the security forces in collaboration with medical and psychiatric institutions who together have created a secret power which transcends law and order and which is beyond intrusive public control.

Brain-computor radio communication has long been considered impossible by the majority of people and has consequently been relegated to science-fiction, but the fact is that the technology had been developed into reality by at least the 1950s during which time the initial experiments were being performed on unwitting subjects. The system has at different times been called Intra Cerebral Mind Control, ESB, Electronic Stimulation of Brain, Biological Radiocommunication or Bio-medical telemetry and in both the eastern and western worlds is the prevailing system of mind control, creating unlimited possibilities to influence and change an individual's behaviour patterns and personality. By means of two-way radio communication, called telemetry or remote-control, an electromagnetic wave can be sent on a return trip to a receiver/transmitter located under the skull or in the brain; this signal records the activity of the brain and returns it to a computer for analysis from which all aspects of the subjects life can be exposed. Radio transmitting crystals which when injected into the bloodstream fasten themselves to the brain have been under development for decades. They work on the same principles as a normal transmitter, use the same technology and have the same capabilities.

To analyse an EEG in a computer instead of on a conventional printer provides an entirely fresh perspective on the conclusions which can be drawn and gives a whole new perspective on what can be concluded. Cognitive manifestations and activity such as thoughts and visual impressions or emotions, behaviour and psychological reactions can continually be registered, making it possible for secret police authorities, medical scientists and the state to observe an individual in a deeper and more comprehensive way than the individual could possibly do him or herself. Through analysis and manipulation by the computer, it is even possible for changes in an individual's physical mental status to be effected. The potential of intracerebral remote control is limited only by the imagination of the investigator, especially when it is remembered that, since these frequencies travel at the speed of light, the system of control is not constrained by matters of range.

Recently we received some X-ray pictures of Mr. N'Tumba and our medical experts in Stockholm have examined those of his skull and can confirm that a transmitter has been implanted in his left nostril. Furthermore, it can be seen that electrodes placed in the occipital lobe are blocking the blood flow behind their delimitation where the oxygen depletion is caused and this is seen as well in his frontal brain just above the implanted transmitter. Among the changes caused by the frequencies affecting his brain the reduced oxygen levels have induced an alteration of neurological functions, impaired cognitive abilities including that of memory. Moreover he has obviously been anaesthetised without his knowledge so that this implantation could be performed.

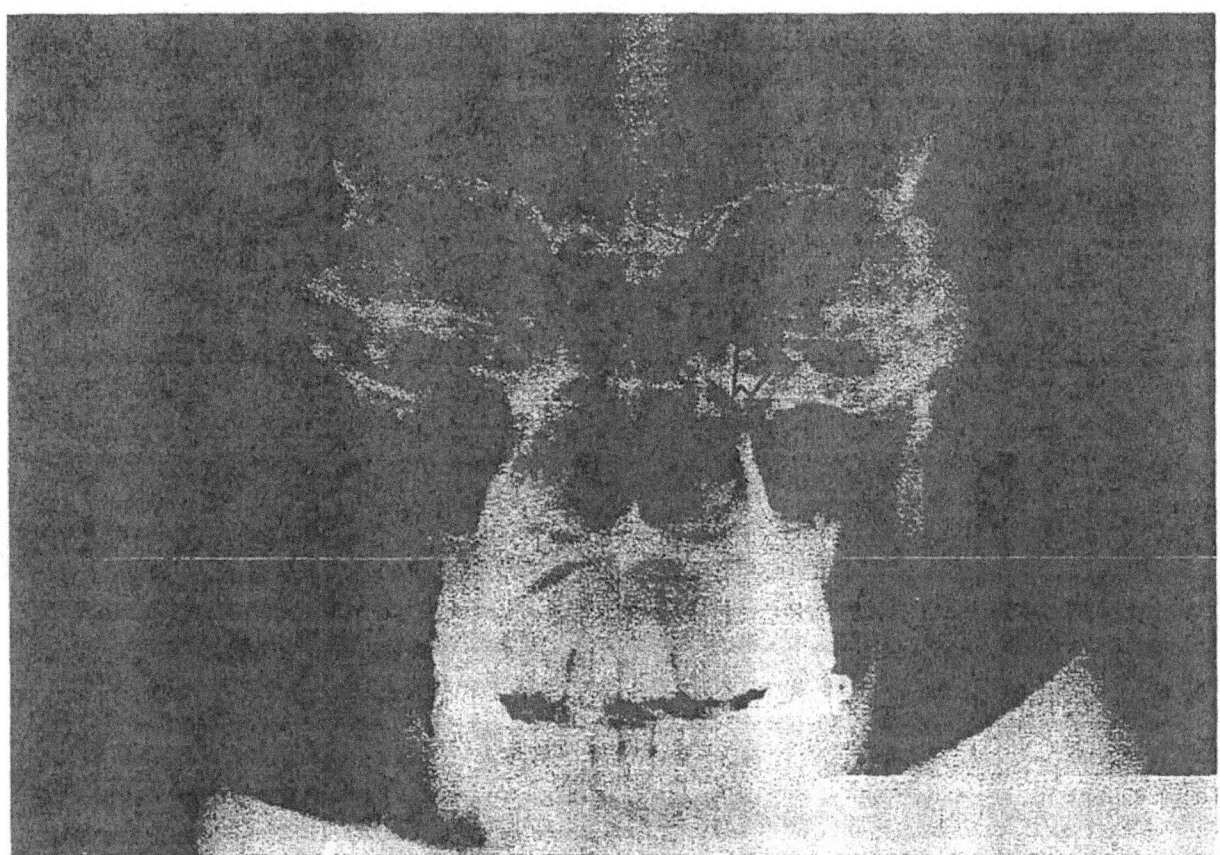

The use of mind control techniques has in fact fostered a new relationship between state and citizen, in which many human rights, as prescribed in the United Nations's Universal Declaration of Human Rights, are violated; in particular we turn to Article 3 which states that all people have the right to life, liberty and integrity. This is clearly violated by such experimentation in mind control, and the very subjection of an individual's brain to medical research, behaviour modification experiments and mind control is in contravention of Article 4 which decrees that no one shall be held in slavery or servitude. Explicitly violated is Article 5 which states that *"No one shall be subjected to torture or to cruel, inhuman or degrading treatment or punishment. Nor shall anyone without their approval be utilised for medical or scientific experiments"*. Finally, since such mind control techniques transmit an individual's privacy to the state, Article 12, which defends the right of privacy against arbitrary interference, also ceases to be valid.

By the 1970's, Samuel Chavkin, the American newspaper publisher whose papers had a medical inclination and who was highly aware of social trends, was writing, *"telemetry for the surveillance of every citizen is on the drawing board...mind control techniques could become standard equipment for governments, penal and police institutions in the near future"*. Further aspects of this technology have come to light from other researchers such as Dr. J.M. Delgado who writes in his book *"Physical Control of the Mind"*: *"A new technology has been developed for the exploration of cerebral mechanisms in behaving subjects, and it has already provided data about the intracerebral correlates of learning.*

memory, drives, performance, and other aspects of mental functions. **This methodology has proved that movements, sensations, emotions, desires, ideas, and a variety of psychological phenomena may be induced, or modified by electrical stimulation of specific areas of the brain.** These facts have changed the classical philosophical concept that the mind was beyond experimental reach". Transmitters have no batteries, are activated by radio and can be used for life. The popular scientist Carl Sagan wrote in "The Dragons of Eden" that he saw the possibility to implant brain electrodes as a strong argument against state control of the health services stating that, *"people who would allow their government to use electrodes have already lost the battle...when it comes to technological nightmares it is imperative that we see the possibilities so that the people can understand them and prevent their abuse by institutions, bureaucrats and governments"*. Naturally there are many possible ways to evaluate the issue but it is not difficult to see direct implications for individual freedoms: those which give a right for a person to live his or her own life, to choose his or her thoughts and opinions, decide his or her own destiny. **The question is whether our right to these should remain intact or if our neurological functions should be recorded and submitted to the control of the state with its predetermined political intentions and psychiatric computer programmes which transform us into robots.** During mind control, people are forced to become the victims of researchers' experiments and the life that was always the individual's is encroached upon by medical science and the state. **This technique can recreate people, change their behaviour and values, as well as their characters, opportunities and fates. It is the inner and most important freedom which is threatened, that which during the history of mankind, has been obviously and naturally valued more highly than suffrage and the temporary political system under which we live.**

We wanted to provide you with this brief summary of the territory which Mr. John Austin-Walker discussed with you, in order to hear the opinions and evaluations of the Prime Minister of one of the world's most influential countries concerning this most pressing of humanistic issues. **We are at a crossroads where the choices relating to human freedoms are either confinement behind an electronic barbed-wire fence or growth like an exquisite blossom flourishing out of its own biological depths.** We would greatly appreciate a statement regarding your views concerning this issue, and we urgently press you for all possible assistance which you can give to Mr. N'Tumba.

Yours faithfully

Lennart Lindqvist,
International Secratary

MICRO CHIP DESIGNER REVEALS MORE INFO

Dr. Carl Sanders was one of the pioneers in bio-microchip technology. He stopped working in that field when he realized this technology could be used to "mark" every citizen. He has been interviewed on the radio numerous times, and ministers across the nation exposing the New World Order plans to inject Americans with an I.D. chip.

Recently he discussed many of the issues he has been researching with Pastor John S. Torell of Resurrection Life of Jesus church. The following is the report released by Pastor Torell:

"For the first time I saw and handled microchips. It was with an awful feeling. Dr. Sanders brought a scanner and showed me how the chips are read. He also brought two different guns with loaded microchips which are presently used for marking animals. I did not like what I saw. It is getting too close and uncomfortable to the coming of the "Mark of the Beast".

Dr. Sanders has been in a number of prophecy conferences and had the opportunity to meet with many Christians who are active in this field. The world government is much more developed than I thought.

All new automobiles are equipped with a black box. This is a radio transmitter and receiver that also contains a memory chip. As the U.S. is now in the last stages of completing the new satellite system, every car with a black box can be located via satellite. When the system is in full operation, the government will know exactly where every vehicle has been and how many miles it traveled, including date and time. Then a new tax is planned for the people which will be billed on a monthly basis.

Dr. Sanders also shared with me, that prior to the Gulf war, the American people were informed that the Iraqi government had biological weapons and one of the diseases they had loaded into their shells was Anthrax. Therefore, all American servicemen and women going overseas were inoculated with an Anthrax vaccine. The vaccine was so potent and at the same time ill tested, that some soldiers died on the spot as they were given the shots. Their bodies were hauled off, and the inoculations continued without hesitation.

The mystery illness that is now plaguing thousands of Gulf war vets is from the inoculation against Anthrax, and the death rate is now climbing.

The U.S. Air Force has removed all markings, including unit insignias, from U.S. Air Force planes. The only remaining identifying mark is a black number on each plane. Dr. Sanders told me this is part of the plan to turn over the entire military structure to the United Nations within a short time.

When I shared with him that the U.S. Air Force has activated almost all of their U-2 surveillance aircraft, he told me some shocking news. From another source I had learned that the U-2 has been modified by lengthening the nose several feet in order to house a satellite communication system. This makes it possible for the U-2 pilot to fly over the target and then send pictures and other data directly to a satellite, which then turns it over to a command center on the ground.

Dr. Sanders told me that most of the American satellites now feed directly to the very secret PINE GAP complex in Australia. This was a U.S. Air Force base, but is now turned over to the U.N. This base now has over 25,000 people working at its facility of which most is a vast underground complex.

Dr. Sanders also told me that two of the world's most powerful computers have been moved overseas. CRAY-5 has been moved to Brussels in Belgium and CRAY-7 is now located at Pine Gap. CRAY-7 is a monster computer. It has a **living protein memory**, which has been built from aborted baby brain cells, and this living organism must be fed daily to stay alive." (end of quote)

This last bit of disturbing information concerning the living computer brain would have seemed unbelievable to me if it wasn't for a program that my wife and I saw on educational TV about computers. This program showed some of the most powerful computers in the world, and one of them was located in an underground headquarters for NORAD. The computer they were using and experimenting with was called CRAY, and the commentator explained that it was so powerful that it had to be cooled by a liquid. This liquid was "'artificial' human plasma." We believe that was only partially true. Human plasma would not be used for cooling, but would rather be used to feed something that required that type of food, such as a brain.

At this point much of the information on these subjects is sketchy, we will continue to research these issues. George Eaton

In 2010, Jon Meyers of St. Louis, Missouri, said that while he was jogging in a local park, several disc-shaped craft suddenly appeared and took up position directly above him. The UFO closest to him shot out a "sparkling beam of bright light" which enveloped and paralyzed him. While he was frozen in place, Meyers said that his head was filled with "voices" telling him that he had a mission to accomplish at a future date in order to convince the people of Earth about the reality of extraterrestrials.

The Mental And Spiritual Influence of UFOs
By Tim R. Swartz

THE idea of mind control by the government or clandestine groups is in itself a disturbing concept. Yet the possibility that humans are being mentally and spiritually manipulated by an ultra-terrestrial intelligence is a scenario far more horrifying to contemplate.

A number of investigators have suspected that UFOs may be responsible for somehow controlling the minds of some witnesses and abductees. UFO literature is filled with hundreds of cases in which observers have been subjected to continuous harassments following an encounter with a UFO. Some witnesses report strange, ghost-like phenomena in their homes. In other cases, weird, mechanical-sounding voices, purported to be "messages" from extraterrestrials, begin emanating from their phones, radios and televisions.

Some witnesses persist in believing that they are being harassed controlled day and night by UFO entities. Cases of UFO mind manipulation are actually quite common. Yet very little is known about it because of the scant research being conducted.

Investigators have attempted to distance themselves from cases of alien mind control. Most feel that the witnesses who complain of such attacks are probably mentally ill. However, the research that has been done shows that accounts of UFO mind control are almost always identical.

The pattern that emerges usually follows a close encounter with a UFO. The eyewitness goes through a period of anxiety, during which he is unable to consciously remember certain aspects of the incident. Within months, the personality of the observer actually changes. Eventually, it may change to the point where he finds it impossible to get along with co-workers, friends or even family. Personal tragedy seems to strike many of those who have had UFO experiences.

In some cases, the eyewitness discovers he has developed certain "gifts" or abilities. Though they may appear to be beneficial at first, too often this is not the case. Among these unusual abilities are powers of ESP, precognition, or psychokinesis. In addition, a heightened intelligence level or an unusual increase in physical strength may be noticed. Such peculiarities will often manifest themselves shortly before a person is about to be controlled. Shortly after this, he may begin slipping into a "trance," during which time it appears as if an alien intelligence has "taken over" his body and is using his brain. There are hundreds of so-called "mental contactees" who claim to receive information and data of a highly advanced scientific and philosophical nature.

During the 1950's and 60's, this method of communicating with UFO occupants (better known as channeling) became so popular that entities calling themselves "Ashtar," "Agar," and "Monka" were heard from daily, somewhere in the world.

There is no doubt that this phenomenon is widespread and it is by no means limited to the United States. Cases of mind-altering UFOs seem to be occurring at an alarming rate. There have been reports of entire communities being placed under a strange "spell," with the simultaneous appearance of UFOs in the area.

MENTAL INVADERS

A large-scale attempt to invade and seize the minds of human beings occurred on April 29, 1967, when a coastal village on the outskirts of Rio de Janeiro became the target of a mysterious malady that may have been perpetrated by a strange craft sighted overhead.

In an hour's time, the citizens of Barra de Tijuca, Brazil were literally forced into establishing contact with an unearthly intelligence, which quickly subdued many people in the town. The series of disturbing events began at noon, when an emergency telephone call reached Dr. Jeronemo Rodrigues Morales, chief physician at Barr de Tijuca's general hospital. An excited voice explained how a man in his late 60s had fallen unconscious on the beach near town.

Dr. Morales immediately drove to the scene. Upon arriving he found the man brushing sand from his clothes and talking to a crowd of people who had gathered to offer help. "I was merely walking about the sand dunes," the man explained. "I had been watching the gulls high above the water, when suddenly I blacked out."

An examination ruled out the possibility of a heart attack and Dr. Morales decided that the man had suffered a mild case of sunstroke. Within minutes, another call came in with the news that a fisherman had been discovered in shallow water beneath a nearby bridge, and was said to be trembling from shock. Dr. Morales quickly drove to the area and arrived just in time to see the "stricken" fisherman casually drying himself off, and asking what all the excitement was about.

When the doctor explained that he had blacked out, the man seemed insulted. "I'm not sick," he argued. "I feel perfectly well." He assured Dr. Morales that he had been tossing his nets into these waters every day for twenty years without any difficulty, and would do so for twenty more.

Within a short while, Dr. Morales received word of six other "stricken" individuals. All followed the identical pattern: People keeling over and then reviving themselves without aid, and, after a flurry of excitement, insisting that nothing was wrong.

While Dr. Morales was treating a mother and her young son, both who had collapsed together on the beach, he noticed something high overhead. Glistening in the sun, the doctor observed an enormous disc-shaped UFO over the town. The craft was darting about in the sky at tremendous speeds. Several other physicians and nurses on the hospital staff reported that they had seen the UFO suspended over the town since noon. Shortly after that, the object disappeared along with the strange illness. Still, the town's people had not heard the last from their strange visitor.

Three days later, another UFO, similar to the first, appeared over the city. Once more, a number of people dropped unconscious to the ground. During these two days, many other individuals were treated at the hospital for headaches and dizziness. Some even reported hearing strange voices talking to them in an unknown language.

VOICES FROM THE SKY

In the weeks after the strange incident at Barra de Tijuca, people who had experienced the mysterious malady began to speak openly about what happened to them. Most reported a strange voice in their head that spoke in a guttural language no one understood. Others said the voice was clearly understandable and kept repeating the phrase "do not be afraid" over and over. One man said the voice told him not to tell anyone what had happened to him, and promised that it would return soon. What has not been reported are the continuing strange incidents that have plagued many of the town's people of Barra de Tijuca in the years after their initial event.

One Brazilian UFO investigator wrote that: "The people of Barra de Tijuca continue to be haunted by the insistent voices in their heads. Most will no longer talk to outsiders about their problems. Those that do tell frighteningly similar stories of voices that control every aspect of their daily lives. The voices, the towns people say, originate from alien beings hovering high overhead in their UFOs."

While some people say that they have learned to "tune out" the constant chatter in their heads, others have not been so fortunate. The suicide rate in town is staggering. Some try to drown out the voices with drugs or alcohol. Others try and leave Barra de Tijuca for good. Nothing really seems to work against the continuing torment.

Strangely enough, when asked what the voices talk about, most town people say they can't remember, that the voices didn't want them to remember. Could there be other towns across the globe experiencing the same harassment? Are the inhabitants of these towns being prepared through mind control for some kind of unknown situation or mission in the future? Might we be faced someday with an army of hypnotically controlled humans, ready through years of mental manipulation, to do the bidding of their otherworldly controllers?

In his book **Passport to Magonia**, Jacques Vallee writes of a chilling account of possible alien mind control in the former Soviet Union. "In 1971, an eminent scientist in the field of plasma research, died under suspicious circumstances, he was murdered by a mentally disturbed woman who pushed him into the path of a train at the Moscow subway station. The accused women claimed that a 'voice' from space had instructed her to kill this particular man, and she felt unable to resist the order."

Vallee has also stated that he has heard from "trustworthy sources" that Russian police are disturbed about the recent increase in cases of this nature. "Quite often," Vallee maintains, "Mentally unstable people are known to run wildly across a street, protesting they are being pursued by Martians, but the present wave of mental troubles is an aspect of the UFO problem that deserves special attention."

Ukrainian UFO researcher Anton A. Anfalow reports that after the fall of the former Soviet Union, dozens of UFO research groups sprung up in an attempt to finally investigate the thousands of UFO reports that had been suppressed by the government.

Because of their efforts, many prominent researchers soon found themselves being harassed and physically attacked by unknown assailants. These assailants would often act like muggers, but would then forego easier prey to target UFO investigators.

One such attack led to the murder of well-known Russian scientist and UFOlogist Dr. A. Zolotov. Dr. Zolotov was attacked by a knife-wielding stranger in the town of Tver. Russian authorities say that the attacks are being carried out by individuals suffering from a "type of mental illness where the person claims that voices from alien beings are ordering them to kill certain people." Cases such as this have led some to speculate that the wave of alleged abductions of humans is part of an agenda by extraterrestrials to control mankind with the help of electronic implants.

Physical implants may be used for long-term efforts by unknown intelligences, but there are many reported UFO incidents where people were influenced mentally without any apparent physical connection.

In his book, ***UFOs: The Psychic Solution***, Jacques Vallee related an amazing case that happened on the night of November 17, 1971. Two men, Paulo Gaetano and Elvio B. were driving near the town of Bananeiras, a municipality in the state of Paraíba in the Northeast Region of Brazil.

Gaetano noticed that the car was becoming difficult to steer and mentioned this to Elvio. His companion reacted by saying that he was tired and wanted to sleep. Next, the car suddenly died and Paulo had to pull off onto the shoulder. He then saw a strange, egg-shaped object hovering over the road.

The UFO projected a red beam of light at the car and at the same time, several small beings materialized and took Gaetano out of the stalled car. The man was taken into the craft and placed onto a small table. After tying down his arms, the entities lowered down a device that looked like an x-ray machine. With this device, the beings collected blood from a cut near his elbow.

Next, Gaetano was shown two pictures; one was a map of the town of Itaperuna, the other was a photograph of an atomic explosion. At this point, Gaetano doesn't remember what happened or how he got back to the car. He did tell investigators later that he remembered being helped by Elvio, but did not recall how they got home.

Elvio's story on what happened that night is very different. He said that near Bananeiras, Gaetano had begun to act nervous, saying there was a flying saucer following them. Elvio didn't see any UFO behind them, there was only a bus. Elvio added that the car had slowed down and stopped, and that Gaetano had gotten out and collapsed behind the car, with the door on the driver's side remaining open.

Elvio managed to get Gaetano on his feet and boarded the bus that had been behind them. The pair went to the town of Itaperuna, where Gaetano was examined by the first-aid station. The police went to the site and found the car still on the side of the road. Elvio could not explain what had happened to Gaetano and why the car door was open. He did not remember when Gaetano had got out, and could not explain why they had left the car behind and taken the bus. The police found no trace on the car that could explain the wound on Paulo's arm.

Vallee comments that some experiments with microwaves suggest it is becoming technically feasible for sensory impressions to be projected into people's minds at a distance. He asks: "Is this part of the technology that is involved in the UFO phenomenon? Are we dealing with a technology that systematically confuses the witnesses?"

Another possibility is that instead of being influenced by some kind of advanced mind-control devices acting on the physical brain, the mind could be influenced on the astral level without the use of any physical technology. Many UFO abductions do seem to have a physical component. There is certainly a great deal of evidence that UFOs can manifest physically and leave physical traces. In some cases people may have been physically taken on board these vehicles, and there are a few abduction cases in which the abducteé was apparently dropped off miles from the pickup point. If humans are occasionally taken on board materialized craft, then a physical medical examination is not inconceivable, though it may only be a simulated one, conducted by paranormal entities rather than by extraterrestrial scientists. However, many aspects of abduction experiences sound like visions or dreams.

Abduction cases with definite physical elements seem to be rare compared with the numerous cases where there is no hard evidence of anything extraordinary. Many aspects of abduction experiences sound like visions or dreams. In these cases the entire experience could be taking place on the mental plane, and reflect a variety of influences. Some of these cases could be generated during the hypnosis session itself, while others may originate in an actual unusual experience.

UFO encounters may actually take place on several different levels...a physical level, a mental level and an astral or spiritual level. Whatever the source is for the intelligence behind the UFO phenomena, it apparently can operate in ways that is completely outside of the realm of known science. This is why many religious leaders over the years have warned about avoiding any contact with UFO intelligences. The fact that these unknown entities can influence people on a spiritual level is frightening and is reminiscent of the ancient mythologies of demons and other malevolent spirits.

ALIEN IMPLANTS

In recent years, hundreds of people claiming to have had contact with aliens also believe they have been implanted with strange electronic devices. The exact purpose of these microchip-like implants, reportedly found embedded in the skin of abductees, remains unknown. Until recently their existence has only been supported by anecdotal evidence. However, as the abduction phenomenon gathers momentum, more physical evidence is being gathered and studied by doctors and scientists.

According to UFO folklore, implants are usually located in the nasal cavity. In some famous cases, such as the alleged abduction of author Whitley Streiber, brain scans have shown disturbances in an area of the brain close to that part of the body.

Some abductees have reported experiencing nose bleeds, believing that implants were forced into their nostrils so that their brains could be monitored and controlled.

In recent years, however, implants have begun appearing in different parts of the body, sometimes in the back of the neck, behind an ear or in the hands and feet. Hard evidence of purported alien technology has been very hard to come by. On August 19, 1995, Ventura, California surgeon Dr. Roger Leir and his surgical team, along with Houston alien contact investigator and Certified Hypnotherapist Derrel Sims, removed three "implants" from two people, a man and a woman who had experienced what they believed to be UFO related incidents in their life.

Two of the implants were removed from the woman's toes. The third was in the back of the man's hand. All three were attached to nerves where no nerves are known to exist. So far, two additional surgeries have been performed. Three out of four patients turned out to have nearly identical, highly anomalous iron alloy objects involved.

In all cases, ultra hard metallic highly magnetic "cores" were surrounded by an ultra-dense dark gray membrane which couldn't be cut with a brand-new scalpel. The membrane somehow prevented any sign of inflammation or rejection. Dr. Leir noted that: "If the implants can teach us how to prevent tissue rejection, we could revolutionize surgery."

Interestingly, the membranes on these objects turned out to be made of a tough matrix of proteins from skin and blood. This could explain why the body accepted the objects so readily. It might also explain the very common "scoop marks" that abductees often find on their bodies.

The removed tissue could be wrapped around an implant to "fool" the body into believing the object is part of the system. Also not so easily explained is how the implants got into these people's bodies. Even with a powerful magnifying glass, Dr. Leir could find no sign of a scar or other evidence of a point of entry for objects which had come to be placed deep in the victims tissues.

If implants are actually electronic devices of some kind...what is their purpose? The most prevalent explanation for implants is that they are used to tag an individual to make sure they can be found again. Others believe that the implants are bugging devices, used to monitor conversations and actions. Another theory is that the implants are a means of mentally controlling human subjects.

Often, victims of UFO abduction complain of the feeling that their minds are being influenced by aliens. Abductees report a number of experiences that could be induced by the implants: Buzzing, beeping and strange voices, missing time, inexplicable emotions in inappropriate circumstances, loss of self control and telepathic communication. Many report the disturbance of electrical objects in their presence, perhaps a side effect of such implant technologies.

THE PURPOSE OF IMPLANTS

One certain group who refers to themselves as "The Light," stated in an e-mail received by the author that people worldwide have been implanted with devices to allow certain kinds of control by extraterrestrial entities.

"Extraterrestrials are currently living among us as humans to monitor human development and assist mankind. Through metabolism cloning, they have the capability to transform their body into a human form taking several minutes. By choosing a desired path, they discreetly & consciously live under a human guise among people without revealing their identity until the correct time. Before society can accept the alien presence, its culture and organization must be changed, which is why they form an influential global network responsible for waves of UFO and alien phenomenon. These part alien/part-human individuals or hybrid-aliens are called 'Guardians.' The Guardians have been selectively breed with humans over the millenniums in order to produce spiritually evolved beings.

"Alien races have visited the earth for thousands of years for different purposes, but the explanation behind the majority of abductions is that alien beings based on earth are implementing a program to implant selected individuals with technically advanced information to condition, educate, and improve humanity. Across the globe and after an examination period, these people were chosen because of specific traits these beings were comfortable with. This microscopic implant, which lies dormant, is inserted into the brain through a condensed light source or manually using surgical instruments.

"The implant contains the foundation for understanding basic extraterrestrial knowledge, principles, and concepts. Very simple examples include: cures for diseases, undiscovered power sources, formulas for food processing and growing, applications of light, utilization of crystals, etc. The power of advanced knowledge will become second nature without ever affecting the implantees personality and memory. The process of learning has been condensed in a microscopic implant: all the chosen will have a sudden interest in an area that they never had previously as if an extraterrestrial course has been studied. This knowledge will be permanent, even if the implant is surgically removed. There are parts of the human brain that naturally becomes a 'biological storage area' for the information stored in the implants.

"A guide is free to scan any field of interest he or she desires. After implantation, these people are called 'Implantees.' After the implant is unlocked, these individuals are called 'Guides.' The Formation is the global event that will simultaneously notify and gather the selected implantees and activate or unlock the implants. The crucial conditioning period after The Formation is called 'The Convergence.'

"The implant also acts as a tracking device in order for the movements of each implantee to be occasionally monitored by a Guardian in close proximity. Through this means, each person will be protected and prevented from an unnatural death. Prior to The Formation, each implantee, regardless of what he or she is doing, will be confronted and informed in detail by a Guardian either verbally or telepathically of what is about to take place. Simultaneously across the world in different countries, all implantees will be transported by means of small crafts to larger crafts situated above the earth. Here the implantee is free to mingle and converse with others across the globe that has been selected, which may or may not include past acquaintances.

"Demonstrations will be given, there will be freedom to interact with hybrid-aliens, and virtually all questions will be answered. Sometime during this period, the implant will be activated or 'unlocked' via a harmless fine-tuning light directed at each person's head, leaving a small red mark for several days. The Convergence has now commenced...the great transformation and advancement these extraterrestrials have been guiding humanity toward. The Guides are now ready to introduce revolutionary and innovative ideas to mankind. For the first time in history, there will be a direct relationship between alien knowledge and society."

CONTACTEES – OR ALIEN MIND CONTROL VICTIMS?

The UFO phenomenon is complex and offers no easy answers. On one side UFOs appear to be physical, constructed machines, flown by creatures who claim to be from other planets. On the other side is the unphysical nature of the phenomena, with

UFOs and the strange beings associated with them manifesting like ghosts. People who are unlucky enough to get caught up in the confusing world of UFOs and their occupants are often subjected to weird forms of possession, behavioral changes and mind control. Victims of UFO abduction usually report periods of "missing time" which is almost certainly achieved with some kind of mental manipulation of the abductee.

The late John Keel speculated that the contactee syndrome is a fundamental reprogramming process. No matter what frame of reference is being used, the experience usually begins with either the sudden flash of light or a sound - a humming, buzzing or beeping. The subject's attention is riveted to a pulsing, flickering light of dazzling intensity. He finds he is unable to move a muscle and is rooted to the spot.

Next the flickering light goes through a series of color changes and a seemingly physical object begins to take form. The light diminishes revealing a UFO, or an entity of some sort. What is really happening is that the percipient is first entranced by the flickering light. From the moment he feels paralyzed, he loses touch with reality and begins to hallucinate. The light remains a light, but the contactees mind is hypnotized to see a spaceship and/or a strange alien creature.

Keel writes in his book, **The Mothman Prophecies**, that he was concerned with the falsified memories of the contactees. "I wondered what happened to the bodies of these people while their minds were taking trips in flying saucers. Trips that often lasted for hours, even for days."

A young college professor in New York State was haunted by the same question in 1967. After investigating a UFO-related poltergeist case, he suffered possession and was led to believe that he had committed a daring jewel robbery while he was in a trance or possessed state. He abandoned Ufology and nearly suffered a total nervous breakdown in the aftermath.

Are contactees and abduction victims being used by exterior intelligence's to carry out crimes, even murder? The answer is a disturbing yes. If you review the history of political assassinations you will find that many were performed by so-called religious fanatics who were obeying the "voice of God," or were in an obvious state of possession when they committed their crime. Assassins such as Sirhan Sirhan, who murdered Robert Kennedy, had a strange fascination with the occult and hypnosis. It is not unusual for them to say that they have no recollection of committing the crime...a telltale indication of mind control.

In contactee parlance, persons who perform involuntary acts are said to be "used." A contactee may feel a sudden impulse to go for a pointless late-night walk or drive. During that drive he encounters, he thinks, the space people and is abducted. Actually his body goes on to, say, Point A where he picks up a letter or object left there by another contactee. He carries the letter or object to Point B and deposits it. Later he has no memories of these actions.

ALIEN ABDUCTIONS OR MILITARY EXPERIMENTS?

According to Helmut Lammer Ph.D., UFO abductions are generally a very complex phenomena. For skeptics, journalists and the public, it is difficult to believe that abductions by alien beings have their basis in physical reality. However, well respected researchers have shown that the core of the UFO abduction phenomenon cannot be explained psychologically as hallucinations or mass delusions. Recently, some UFO abductees have reported that they have also been kidnapped by military intelligence personnel and taken to hospitals and/or military facilities, some of which are described as being underground.

Very few books on the subject of UFO abductions have mentioned these experiences. Especially disconcerting is the fact that abductees recall seeing military intelligence personnel together with alien beings, working side by side in these secret facilities. Researchers in the field of mind control suggest that these cases are evidence that the whole UFO abduction phenomenon is staged by the intelligence community as a cover for their illegal experiments. Could the whole abduction scenario be a carefully manipulated hypnotic cover for experimentation by government or military intelligence services?

The alleged military involvement in the abduction phenomenon could be evidence that the military uses abductees for mind control experiments as test-targets for microwave weapons. Moreover, the military could be monitoring and even kidnapping abductees for information gathering purposes during, before and after a UFO abduction.

Lammer's research suggests that abductees are often harassed by dark, unmarked helicopters that fly around their houses. The mysterious helicopter activity goes back to the late sixties and early seventies, when they showed an apparent interest in animal mutilations, but not in alleged UFO abductees. However, UFO researcher Raymond E. Fowler reported some helicopter activity in connection with UFO witnesses during the seventies.

Many abductees report interaction with military intelligence personnel after the helicopters begin to appear. Debbie Jordan reports, for instance, in a side note of her book Abducted!, while she was with a friend, she was kidnapped, drugged and taken to a kind of military hospital where she was examined by a medical doctor. This doctor told her he was going to remove a "bug" from her ear and proceeded to take out an implant that resembled a BB.

The abduction experiences of Leah Haley and Katharina Wilson also includes military-type encounters. Some of Wilson's experiences are reminiscent of reported mind control experiments. For example, she writes of a flashback from her childhood where she remembers being forced into what appeared to be a Skinner Box that may have been used for behavior modification purposes. In some military abduction cases military doctors searched for implants and sometimes even implanted the abductee with what appeared to be a man-made implant.

The technology does exist for small, radio frequency electronic implants. More than three million animals worldwide have been successfully implanted with a transponder manufactured by Destron-Fearing. The transponder is a passive radio frequency identification tag, designed to work in conjunction with a compatible radio-frequency ID reading system.

The transponder is activated by a low-frequency radio signal. It then transmits the ID code to the reading system. The smallest transponder is about the size of an uncooked grain of rice. The transponder's tiny electronic circuit is energized by the low-power radio beam sent by a compatible reading device.

A similar bio-chip for humans was patented in 1989 by Dr. Daniel Man. The homing device, which can be implanted under the skin, was originally developed to locate missing children. This device is slightly larger than the

Destron implant and a small surgical incision must be made for it to be implanted. Dr. Man claims that the best location for his implant may be behind the ear.

It is possible that some of the information received from abductees may be cover stories, induced by hypno-programming techniques of military psychiatrists. It is also possible that the military uses rubber alien masks and special effects during a supposed alien abduction. Katharina Wilson reported flashbacks where she remembered holding a rubber mask of an alien head in her hands. Facts such as these lead some mind control researchers to believe that all alien abductees are actually mind control and/or genetic experiments staged by a secret group within the government of the United States.

In a declassified memo dated February 17, 1994, former Naval Intelligence Commander Scott Jones, Ph.D. wrote to White House Presidential Science Advisor John Gibbons: "Whatever Roswell turns out to be, it is only the opening round. I urge you to take another look at the *UFO Matrix of Belief* that I provided you last year. My mention of mind-control technology at the February 4 meeting was quite deliberate. Please be careful about this. There are reasons to believe that some governmental group has interwoven research about this [mind-control] technology with alleged UFO phenomena. If that is correct, you can expect to run into early resistance when inquiring about UFOs, not because of the UFO subject, but because that has been used to cloak research and applications of mind-control activity."

Write for your FREE Catalog of interesting books, fascinating videos and other incredible items of interest.

Send your name and mailing address to:

Global Communications
P.O. Box 753
New Brunswick, NJ 08903

Email: mrufo8@hotmail.com

www.conspiracyjournal.com

Visit Mr. UFOs Secret Files on YouTube
https://www.youtube.com/user/MRUFO1100

ALL TITLES AVAILABLE ON AMAZON.COM — PRINT AND KINDLE EDITIONS.

NORDIC LOOKING ALIENS GIVE HITLER PLANS FOR A TIME TRAVEL DEVICE!

THIS IS BY FAR THE MOST SHOCKING AND POTENTIALLY TROUBLING BOOK WE HAVE EVER PUBLISHED.
IT COULD VERY WELL CHANGE THE FUTURE— AND THE TRUTH IS—IT MIGHT HAVE ALREADY!

Here is disturbing evidence that Hitler had a top secret brigade of Nazi engineers working in deep underground laboratories – in conjunction with off world interstellar cosmonauts – to establish space flight and time travel, years before the start of America's rocketry program in which the U.S. sought the help of thousands of Nazi war criminals bought into this country under the auspicies of the tight lipped Project Paperclip. Information recently obtained by the authors indicates that the UFO

that crashed outside Roswell might have been part of this Nazi space/time travel program cleverly covered up by our military in order to look like the arrival of an out of control interplanetary vehicle. The top brass was ultimately looking to cover their tracks which showed that they were inappropriately working in tandem with war criminals, whom they had excused of all evil misdeeds, eventually giving them citizenship. This "wonder weapon" and time travel device was named Die Glocke or "The Bell," and it is probably being seen and flown to this day; some even manned by Aryan- looking occupants (possibly Ets).

Devices like "The Bell" may have been used to bend both space and time and give the Nazis the unthinkable power to explore the past freely and even to CONTROL THE FUTURE. Are we plummeting headlong toward a world under fascist domination – a nightmare in which sadistic, jackbooted thugs are waiting for us to "catch up" in time with our own predestined subjugation to open worldwide rule by the Nazis, possibly hiding out on the surface of the moon or at "secret cities" at the Poles? Do they lie in wait for us as the clock on our freedom runs down?

The shocking facts can be read in **NAZI UFO TIME TRAVELERS** / Just $20 + $5 S/H

— **WANT TO READ MORE?** —

☐ **THE OMEGA FILES: SECRET NAZI UFO BASES REVEALED!**

Did Hitler's henchmen escape from Germany and set up secret bases at the South Pole and deep in the Amazon? Are they operating from these top secret quarters to establish a Fourth Reich and take over the world? – $21.95

☐ **UFOS NAZI SECRET WEAPONS**

Banned in 22 countries the author was imprisoned for over 20 years because he spoke out on this controversial topic. Did the SS have its own arsenal of super secret weapons which they planned to unleash? Here are pages of drawings showing these devices along with German plans of operation. – $24.00

☐ **THE SECRET SPACE PROGRAM**

Do we already have bases on the Moon? Who is responsible? Tesla? Nazis? Secret Societies? NWO? Something pretty damn strange is happening under our very eyes! – $24.00

FREE AUDIO CD OF THE MYSTERIOUS INTELLIGENCE OPERATIVE COMMANDER X TALKING ON THE NAZI UFO SPACE PROGRAM WHEN ORDERING TWO OR MORE TITLES FROM THIS AD. Special – All 4 books this advt $79.95 + $8 S/H

TIMOTHY G BECKLEY, BOX 753, NEW BRUNSWICK, NJ 08903

BERNIE SANDERS IS RIGHT ABOUT WALL STREET

FIND OUT WHY WHEN YOU READ WHAT SOME ARE CALLING THE MOST DANGEROUS BOOK IN AMERICA.
Breaks All The Rules! – Goes Against All The Systems!

In fact, the Vermont Senator has only grazed the tip of the iceberg when it comes to deceit and fraud in the banking and financial sectors. They are not just sucking your retirement fund dry. The truth is they are manipulating the politicians who take money from them and have secretly been financing our global conflicts since WORLD WAR ONE. They have become the richest individuals in the world off our blood, sweat and fears.

This hefty volume exposes a world of treachery, answering the questions: Who are the masterminds behind global domination? Who actually manages the flow of paper money and controls commerce and the banking system? Who really profits from war?

☐ **Order WALL STREET BANKSTERS – 334 pages. Large Format. $22.00 + $5 S/H**

AND IT DOESN'T STOP THERE!
☐ **FIGHTING THE FEDERAL RESERVE**

Here is the story of Congressman Louis T. McFadden the man who took on the Fed and was nearly assassinated when he boldly insisted that WW I, the Great Depression and World War II were events which were not desired by the American people, were not planned by the American people, and were not voluntarily entered into. But all of these events were instead the result of the planning of men who have no addresses, no fixed homes, and no substantial loyalties — save only to their own criminal interests.

Over 600 pages. $24.00 + $5 S/H

☐ **SPECIAL – BOTH BOOKS $34.00 + $6 S/H**
TIMOTHY G BECKLEY, BOX 753, NEW BRUNSWICK, NJ 08903

Radionics Boxes are custom made and may vary slightly from illustration.

FIRST TIME AVAILABLE CUSTOM MADE— AUTHENTIC MIND MACHINE THE RADIONICS BOX

Many have asked for this controversial box which it is said can be used multiple times to help manifest your desires in an almost "magical" way. However, the Radionics Box is based upon a strong foundation, whether you want to dramatically improve your finances, health, or relationships.

By setting your goal, and tuning your mind-body-environment relationship with the 9-knobs, stunning things can manifest. *VIRTUALLY WHATEVER YOU CHOOSE.* Thus, it must be used wisely. Some call this advanced "magic" or "techno-shamanism."

☐ *ONLY $250.00 FOR YOUR PERSONAL RADIONICS MACHINE AND WORKBOOK*

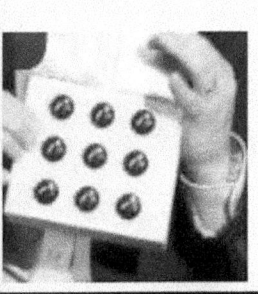

If you wish, our technician will customize the box for you! Along with your order, send us details of your innermost desire. This will ensure your box is designed properly for **you**. Our *MIND MACHINE* study guide will be included. Send payment of $250 to;

TIMOTHY G. BECKLEY BOX 753, NEW BRUNSWICK, NJ 08903

Note: Allow time for customizing. Since this is an experimental product, we **CANNOT** offer refunds or accept returns. PayPal and all other payment forms accepted.
Send email mrufo8@hotmail.com for PayPal requests.

www.ingramcontent.com/pod-product-compliance
Lightning Source LLC
Chambersburg PA
CBHW081917170426
43200CB00014B/2753